HIGH-RISE HARRY

A biography

HIGH-RISE HARRY

A biography

"I always say that you should
be the tallest tree in the forest,
not the only tree in the desert."

Harry Triguboff

MEG O'NEILL'S PATH TO WOODSIDE
JESSICA SEPEL'S VITAMIN EMPIRE

ISSUE No 10

KELLY RYAN ON NETBALL AUSTRALIA
PETER FOX ON GREENING LINFOX

Forbes AUSTRALIA

IRREPRESSIBLE
HARRY

PROPERTY MOGUL **HARRY TRIGUBOFF** SHARES HIS EXTRAORDINARY 91-YEAR JOURNEY TO BECOMING AUSTRALIA'S THIRD RICHEST PERSON

APRIL/MAY 2024

HIGH-RISE HARRY

A biography

HARRY TRIGUBOFF

First published in 2024
High Rise Harry
Harry Triguboff

Copyright © 2024 Harry Triguboff

Meriton
Level 11, 528 Kent Street
Sydney NSW 2000, Australia
Copyright © 2024 in images.
Front cover image: Supplied by Meriton.
Back cover image: CGI of Iconica, Surfers Paradise.
Other images: Forbes photography by Mick Bruzzese. All other internal images belong to the publisher or have been printed under licence or with permission of the copyright holder. If you believe your copyright has been infringed, please contact the publisher above

Written by: Cindy Martin
Edited and designed by: Claire McGregor
Hardback Limited Edition

Paperback Edition:
ISBN: 9781760797881
New Holland Publishers
1/178 Fox Valley Road, Wahroonga NSW 2076, Australia

The moral rights of the author have been asserted.
All rights reserved. No part of this publication may be reproduced, distributed, or transmitted in any form or by any means, including photocopying, recording, or other electronic or mechanical means, without the prior written permission of the publisher, except as permitted under the Copyright Act 1968.

A record of this book is held at the National Library of Australia.

Disclaimer
The conversations in the book all come from the author's and subject's recollections, though they are not written to represent word-for-word transcripts. Some names and characteristics have been changed, some events have been compressed, and some dialogue has been re-created.

CONTENTS

Introduction		1
Prologue		5
PART 1	**THE EARLY YEARS**	**13**
1	Life in China	15
2	Calling Australia Home	32
3	The Business Begins	45
4	Doing It His Way	57
5	Union Troubles	67
6	Fight or Flight	85
7	The Early Years in Queensland	100
8	Family Arrive from Russia	114
PART 2	**THE START OF A NEW MILLENNIUM**	**121**
9	World Tower	123
10	The Gold Coast and Brisbane	140
PART 3	**THE MERITON FAMILY**	**161**
11	The Meriton Women	163
12	The Family	192
13	The Directors	212
14	The Next Generations	224
15	The Archi-Construct Family	236
16	A Jewish Community	252
PART 4	**HARRY, THE MAN**	**263**
17	How the Mind Ticks	265
18	Downtime	276
19	Harry at His Best	310
Epilogue		320
Cindy Martin		324

INTRODUCTION

By Harry Triguboff

For those of you who know me, it will be of no surprise to read that I have a pretty basic rule of engagement. If I say no, you should know better than to ask me a second time. My family, however, did not seem to understand this. They have badgered me for years to have the story of my life written. After a couple of false starts, I eventually agreed to go down this road for the third and final time. This is my life, *High-Rise Harry*.

I am often asked how I succeeded. Short answer – I bucked the trend. When Australians wanted a house on a quarter-acre block, I built apartments. Then I set about changing the perception of apartment living. That was not with the hardcore cottage traditionalists but with those who never thought home ownership could apply to them. There were two markets that had been overlooked: those who couldn't afford a cottage, and one-half of the population – women. They were a large, untapped market with a common need. That was to have a roof over their heads – a place they never thought they could call their own.

With those people in mind, I built an affordable product that was value for money, and I gave them vendor finance to pay for it. In the 1960s, the banks wouldn't lend to women, even if they could prove they could service the loan. The banks were ignorant. I remember out of all my many loans to women, at most one or two defaulted. Not a track record of which any of the banks could boast! When those buyers sold, they made a profit like no amount of money they had seen in their lives. I did that for the women and for those who simply needed a leg up.

From those humble beginnings, I have been hailed as one of the greatest entrepreneurs Australia has seen. I achieved that with an unwavering self-belief that I could make apartment living the preferred housing option for the future.

I never doubted myself for a second, so when I made decisions, I believed them always to be the right ones. I had commitment, resilience, perseverance, and passion. I was stubborn and fearless. Did I mention the healthy ego I have? All those characteristics I still have today, and I will still do what any good entrepreneur can always do – find a hole and fill it.

There are, of course, other highly successful Australian entrepreneurs filling different holes. Gina Rinehart is clearly very successful. She has, as one of the biggest mining magnates ever, stuck to what she knows and has filled a need for iron ore around the world, particularly in China.

If people ask me if entrepreneurs can still be successful today, I tell them that of course they can. They must, however, choose an industry with a solid future.

I first arrived in Australia with £25,000, and my wife at the time was surprised we weren't using the money to buy a house. We rented a small apartment, and I immediately started looking for investments and a job for myself. I bought a taxi and a milk run. I didn't drive the taxi or run the milk. I left that to others while I worked in a job that paid me better money.

I came up with new ideas for both investments and I made good money at the time, but neither offered long-term security. Better refrigeration ensured a longer shelf life for the milk, so daily milk runs became obsolete. I tried to expand into shopping centres with flavoured milk in vending machines and, while that boomed for a while, it didn't take the centres long to figure out they could cut out the middleman. Those short-term investments still gave me enough profit to go after something bigger – something with a far greater future.

You can make money in any industry, but it must be one that is succeeding and that has longevity. You don't have to reinvent the wheel. There are many spokes to a wheel. Take one that is already there and make it your own. It's important to know when to get your money out. As soon as you see a decline in profit, get out. Find something else.

I was able to build my first block of apartments with my friend

Introduction

Tommy Gluck. There is more to that story later! The build was successful, the partnership was not. Although Tommy and I remained good friends until his death, I knew the buck had to stop with me. I had to be the boss. I didn't want someone else weighing in on my decisions and I didn't want to waste time listening to their arguments. They were superfluous when I had already made up my mind.

I have worked every day of my life, and the more successful I became, the harder I had to work. The harder I had to work, the more I enjoyed it. My business was already huge when I reached retirement age in 1993. Thirty years later it is a massive empire. I am still at the helm because I never put limits on myself as to how far I can go.

True entrepreneurs have little time to waste. With every conversation, I start it and I finish it. The first words are usually, "So what's happening?" The last words are usually, "Why are you still here?" People find it hard to keep up with me, so they never know when to leave. They are sitting at the boardroom table in my office with 10 other people, each with their own issues to be resolved. Some are an easy fix, others not so much. Between us, we collaborate and make decisions. The final decision will always be mine. We are done in 15 minutes. No agendas, no minutes, no procrastination. Decision made, we move on.

Good entrepreneurs fit as much into their day as possible, and they know when to shut a conversation down. I don't always do it with grace. I do not have time for the insecure ones who come looking for a pat on the back. I am not that man; go and be reassured somewhere else.

Being so invested in the business sets a good example for my team. I am, except for that touch of insecurity from a small number of people in the business, surrounded by very clever and capable people. They are the best of the best. I have always approached recruiting with an open mind. I place a lot of value on those who are recommended to me. For certain positions, having scholastic capabilities is important; for others, it doesn't matter. Skills matter. I also consider how they will get on with the rest of the team. If you are joining my family, you need to fit in. Having a degree is not enough. I have people who have been working at

Meriton for decades, so wanting longevity is important to me. A stable career is very important. I believe in what I do. My people believe in what I do, and we succeed together.

I don't like change. One of the hardest things is when people leave. If they want to leave, I don't try to stop them, no matter where they rank in the company. I want them out as soon as possible. It's no good for morale and others start to take their eye off the ball because the one leaving is a distraction. The only way to get people back on track is to remove the problem.

Later in the book you'll read about generations of contractors and employees who have worked with me since my business started. I have used the same sub-contractors, the same lawyers and accountants for decades. They become partners. They become dependent on you and they know how to work with you. Again, longevity with suppliers outside the business is crucial to success.

A good entrepreneur will never waste time worrying about the competition. Many people have tried to copy me over the years and many of those people are now bust. I am so far ahead of the game I don't view anyone as competition. I am the best at what I do and that is all that matters to me. I will always be the tallest tree in the forest. If I think anything at all about others oiling a spoke on my wheel, I am thankful they are contributing to help solve the housing crisis and not leaving it all up to me.

There will always be entrepreneurs disrupting industry. The future is dynamic and full of opportunities. Entrepreneurs will make money like we have never seen before while, like me, making a positive impact on society. It is the very best of both worlds.

As for my book, it's in a world of its own where verticality is victorious.

Happy reading,

Harry

PROLOGUE

The building is dazzling – a towering, majestic icon of architectural modernity. The stunning, expansive glass panes and steel reflect two men as they walk side by side through the magnificent foyer. One with his hands clasped behind his back and the other with his hands by his sides; their gaits are strong. The men, deep in conversation, are of a similar height. One gently squeezes the shoulder of the other and they break into peals of laughter. Good friends. Proud Australians. Two of the most powerful men in the country. One, John Winston Howard, the 25th Prime Minister of Australia, and the other, billionaire property developer and hotelier Harry Oscar Triguboff, the founder and managing director of the Meriton empire.

The two had come together to celebrate the reinvented 'Great Australian Dream'. That was not the freestanding cottage in suburbia on a quarter-acre block with a Hills Hoist and a barbeque. Harry turned all that on its head. His way became the new domestic ideal: oversized inner-city apartments, close to transport, with expansive views and open spaces, and with supermarkets, restaurants and childcare centres on the doorstep. No maintenance, no commuting. Every convenience to simplify life.

This night was just one in a string of similar occasions. The list is long and distinguished of those who have opened buildings for Harry during his 60-year reign as the father of urbanisation. While others have attempted to follow in his footsteps, copy what he has done, Harry will always be recognised as the trailblazer for apartment living.

A former chief information officer at NASA, Linda Cureton, wrote a paper on the word 'trailblazer', defining it this way: "A pioneer or someone who is considered first in their area of expertise. As leaders,

Image from the cover of Good Weekend *magazine, 2014.*

Prologue

they point the way, take the risks, and change the environment. They have a vision for a different future, a faith that turns dreams into reality, and a determination that cuts through barriers and obstacles."

She went on to say they are "known for being innovators – those people who do things that have never been done, create things that never existed, or perform in ways unimaginable".

Linda, by her description, had unwittingly described Harry to a 'T'. And NASA would know. Who could ever accuse NASA of failing to trailblaze?

"I like her definition, but what I do isn't rocket science!" Harry laughs. "But of course, we are on the same page when it comes to verticality."

Even the media bestowed on Harry the moniker 'High-Rise Harry'. He delivers vertical housing at its best.

Fast track to 2023 and it was a year of celebration. Harry had turned 90, Meriton had celebrated its 60th anniversary, and major developments had opened in Sydney, on the Gold Coast, in Melbourne and in Canberra. It was also the year that Harry finally agreed to a book about his extraordinary life.

The official opening of Harry's first hotel in Melbourne in September 2023 is where we begin …

As the landing gear smoothly ascends into the undercarriage of the private jet, Harry relaxes into the deep, comfortable leather seat. He is still looking fresh and impeccable in one of the nine new suits he recently had tailored. He is content. Happy, even. It has been a good day, albeit a long one, and he is pleased to be heading home.

The day had started as it always does, with exercise. Today, Harry chose to swim rather than walk. There would be a lot of walking and standing later in the day, so he hit the pool and did his usual 20 laps. After he showered and dressed, he discussed his day over breakfast with his wife, Rhonda, then he made multiple calls to the office. When it was time to leave, he called out to his driver, Pablo, that he was ready to head off. A kiss goodbye for Rhonda, a pat for pooch Susie, and he was out the door. He would visit at least two of his projects under construction on his way into the office.

After the site visits, Harry arrived at Meriton Tower at around 11am. His offices occupy three levels of the Kent Street building. Meriton's head office is on the lower levels of the tower and Harry's personal office overlooks busy George Street and the new light rail. The building, in the Chinatown southern end of Sydney's central business district, is Harry's favourite area in the city. The hustle and bustle remind him of his early years in China.

Harry's first port of call when he headed upstairs was not to his own office. He headed straight for Kim Jorgensen's office. Kim, who has been working for Harry for 35 years, is commander of the most important daily information – the sales report. She is always in the position to give Harry an up-to-the-minute account on the most recent sales. How many, how much. With this information, a sales meeting at noon helped Harry decide on any changes that needed to be made to price or purpose.

There had been no lunch out today. Harry loves his lunches with the doyens of business, politics and the media. It helps keep his finger on the pulse, but there was no time today. A quick sandwich with his head of town planning of 20 years, Walter Gordon, before there was a revolving door of heads of departments coming in and out of his office for the next hour.

Harry had a busy afternoon and evening ahead, and Pablo was waiting outside his office to take him to the airport. Other than Rhonda, Harry didn't know who else would be in the jet with him. He had left the details to Loreto Escobar, his executive assistant of 20 years, to work out. His wife, his daughters, his grandchildren, and his four directors were all joining him on this trip.

At the last minute, Harry decided he wanted to stop off in Canberra on the way. Loreto was used to that and efficiently made the changes to

Prologue

his schedule. He wanted to check in on the progress of his first hotel in the nation's capital that had opened the previous week.

This hotel, and the opening of another one in Liverpool as part of a $400 million hotel expansion, sees him as not only the largest apartment developer in the country, but the biggest hotelier in the nation as well. He has built nearly 80,000 apartments since Meriton started 60 years ago, the majority in Sydney and the rest on the Gold Coast and in Brisbane. In 2023, a 57-storey, 298-suite Melbourne hotel was added to the hospitality magnate's Meriton Suites chain, taking the number of hotels to 23.

This official opening evening of the Melbourne hotel coincided with visitors arriving from across Australia for the Australian Football League (AFL) Grand Final. The new Meriton Suites, in King Street, was almost at capacity and the opening was a huge success. Harry and his family, following the formalities and after-party, headed back to the airport to catch their ride home to Sydney.

Harry has never felt better. A gruelling schedule that would be tough for a man half his age is taken in his stride. He is robust in mind and body. He still feels like a young man. This energetic, strong and dynamic figure sits in the plane surrounded by the people he cares for most. He listens to the banter within the confines of the cabin. The familiar voices of his wife, his daughters, his grandchildren and his directors help him to relax. He loves them all, blood or otherwise; they are his family and the future of his empire. If succession were a picture, this snapshot, and the people in it, is exactly what it would look like.

As they begin their descent into Sydney an hour later, the chatter has ceased and the cabin is quiet. Harry looks out the window. Below him, millions of lights sparkle in the dark of night. The warning beacons flashing atop the tallest buildings, many are his. There are apartment buildings as far as the eye can see and many are his. A million lightbulbs, maybe more, are his. His future, like the lights below, has never been brighter. Harry feels invigorated and invincible. This next decade will be his best yet. The start has already been one of much celebration.

Aside from his 90th birthday bash at the Sydney Town Hall and Meriton celebrating its 60th anniversary, Harry also graced the front cover of the *Australian Financial Review* 'Rich List' in 2023, itself celebrating its 40th anniversary. He has featured on the list every year since its inception.

Meriton, after 60 years, is not only the most recognised apartment brand in Australia, but the Meriton Suites brand is also the preferred choice for travellers from all corners of the globe. There is nobody anywhere in the world like Harry. He is a man of defiance, courage and resilience.

For 60 years he has unwaveringly fought the system. His greatest nemesis – red tape – has tried its best to tie him in knots, but failed. The Meriton brand is everywhere, and without Harry's contribution to the apartment market, the ongoing housing crisis would be almost 80,000 times worse off.

Now, as he leans on his left arm and pulls himself closer to the jet's window, nobody really knows what he's thinking. Is he calculating what he could do with all the black areas with no bulbs, or is he simply enjoying the view?

As the plane touches down in Sydney and taxis along the runway, Harry sits poised, ready to unclip his seatbelt. He will stand as soon as the pilot says it's safe. He catches one of his young family members yawning after the long day and he smiles. As he navigates the steps down from the jet to the tarmac with ease, Pablo is waiting to take him home. He and Rhonda take a moment to say goodnight to everyone and then they slip into the car.

For a fleeting moment Harry allows his head to rest against the headrest of his luxury Mercedes-Maybach. Within seconds he is upright again, reaching for his phone. He wants to check in with Kim Jorgensen for a sales update because he hasn't spoken to her since he left the office. As he looks at his watch, he puts the phone back down. It's late. Kim would have to be up early in the morning to travel to work from her home on the Central Coast, 100 kilometres from the office. He decides it can wait.

As they start the drive along the Eastern Distributor route to the eastern suburbs exit that will take them home, Harry's eyes are naturally drawn to his left. Meriton buildings line the gateway to the city. Harry, still not tired, thinks about the time he almost made the decision to head to New York or London in search of his big break. For so many reasons now, he is happy he ditched that idea. This is his town, and he has his stamp all over it. He would never have been as successful anywhere else in the world.

As he rests his head back again, he gently places his hand over Rhonda's hand and allows his mind to wander. Right back to the very beginning.

Moshe, Joe & Harry, 1936.

PART 1

THE EARLY YEARS

Harry with his parents, Frida & Moshe, outside their Tientsin home.

ONE

LIFE IN CHINA

Karik Oskar Triguboff was born in China on the third of the third, 1933. His proud, traditional Russian parents gave him that name at birth. Three, for obvious reasons, would be his favourite number throughout life. In fact, it was third time lucky when he chose his own name in Tientsin (renamed Tianjin from 1958) before coming to Australia to attend his senior years of school.

When little Karik Triguboff started junior school at the Jewish school in China, he was given a more traditional Jewish name to help him fit in. He would be known as Asher Oskar Triguboff for nearly the next 10 years. Before the teenage Asher was sent to Australia to attend senior school, he decided, like many others, to anglicise his name because a new world required a new name for his new life. 'Harry Oscar Triguboff' became the keeper.

Harry's great lifelong friend, who also migrated to Australia around the same time, was Pinchas Levy. He is better known as Westfield co-founder Sir Frank Lowy. The other co-founder of Westfield, the late Samuel John Chapman Huxham, was better known as John Saunders. Name changes were a given. Harry's brother Joseph (Joe) changed his surname to Travers, but Harry never considered the anglicisation of his surname. He was proud to be a Triguboff and he liked the name.

Harry arrived in Australia in 1948, a month before his 15th birthday.

He had already experienced a life of change and uncertainty, and he was so excited about his new adventure that he felt no guilt about leaving his parents behind.

"I had my older brother, Joe, with me, so I never felt alone," Harry says.

"At the time we left, we thought it was only going to be a matter of time before our parents joined us. I could hardly contain my excitement about starting a new life in a wonderful new country."

What Harry didn't know at the time was that his parents would never be allowed to come to Australia.

The school Harry's parents chose for him was The Scots College in Bellevue Hill in Sydney's eastern suburbs. There was a large Jewish community in and around the area. Harry remembers how proud he was wearing his school uniform for the first time.

The school had only recently re-opened after the Second World War and the students were determined to excel and make their fallen fathers proud. Harry seemed to be the only student who wasn't sports obsessed. In fact, The Scots College used to win many of the Great Public Schools (GPS) sports. The year Harry started, Scots won the tennis, rugby, cricket and swimming.

The only other school to get a look in was Sydney Boys High School. It won the GPS Head of the River for rowing that year. The Scots College lived by its motto, *Utinam patribus nostris digni simus*, 'May we be worthy of our forefathers'. They were fathers who gave their lives to protect Australia. Harry would one day realise that motto would also apply to his father, who was not lost at war but lost through a miscarriage of justice.

While the boys at Scots excelled in sports, in China Harry's education had been a lot more traditional.

"My mother wanted me to know and understand my Russian heritage," he says. "She forced me to read and memorise the great Russian writers, Tolstoy and Pushkin. She also made me play the piano. I loathed both.

"Even at a young age, I was excited over what lay ahead in the new world. I wasn't interested in the old country.

"There are many jokes about Siberia, but it's very true that you don't mess with anyone from Siberia, so I always did as I was told." He laughs.

Harry's mother, Frida, did indeed hail from Siberia, the coldest, bleakest, most desolate 13 million square kilometres of land in the world. The inhabitants needed to be sturdy, resilient and tough. Frida was no exception.

"Tradition is far more important to me today than it was back then," Harry says. "I think now that it is very good to know where you come from, and I am pleased my mother taught me that."

It is Harry's history that helps us understand what drives him today.

"In 1916 my father, Moshe, fled Russia to avoid conscription into the Tsar's army," he says.

"He was sent to the Russian settlements in China and that's where he met my mother. Neither my mother's family nor my father's family had any money, but both were from traditional Russian families, so the match was considered a good one.

"My mother joined my father in the main Russian colony of Harbin in China. They married and, when my brother was born in 1926, the family relocated to Dairen (now Dalian), a port city in northern China, where there were better trading opportunities for my father.

"My father was still struggling to make ends meet, so he moved the family to Tientsin, which was the maritime gateway to Beijing. I was just a year old when we moved."

Moshe, with more lucrative opportunities, set up trading in all kinds of textiles, including, but not limited to, furs, wool, cloth and leather. He would trade in almost anything he could get his hands on.

The Triguboffs were a respected Jewish family with strong values, but they weren't recognised socially. Regardless of Moshe's hard work and efforts, they were still poor. Although traditional, they were not overly religious, but Moshe still wanted Harry and Joe to go to the Jewish school. That worked out well as it was the cheapest. It was at that time that Moshe and Frida changed Harry's name from Karik to Asher – a more traditional Jewish name.

Harry never realised his family was poor. He enjoyed school and, while the family spoke Russian at home, his classes were in English, so he learned English at a young age, picked it up quickly, and spoke it fluently.

Moshe, until the start of the Second World War, struggled to pay the rent for their small two-bedroom flat. Surprisingly, Harry still had a nanny, a widow. She looked after him in return for food, board and the little bit of money the Triguboffs could spare. She shared a small room with Harry and Joe and later stayed on as a companion to Frida as they were good friends. When Moshe and Frida later moved to Israel, she went too and lived with them until the day she died. Her name was Anna Parfiryevna Kolovos. Harry remembers her fondly. In fact, to this day when he visits Israel, he not only visits the graves of his parents but Anna's as well.

Harry was not oblivious to the war raging across the world, but he was shielded from the worst of it.

"China was a world away from the atrocities happening to the Jews in Europe," he says. "There were the occasional snippets about the Nazi concentration camps, but the Russian-Jews were relatively safe in China. There definitely was not the same hatred."

When Harry was done with his day at school, had practised the piano and completed his Russian studies with his mother, he liked to head down to the Tientsin port and watch the Chinese labourers loading sacks of grain onto barges.

"I would watch the poorest of the poor, in their filthy rags, slash the grain bags as they were being carried to the barges," Harry says.

"Stealing the grain was the only way they could feed their families. I felt sorry for them and perceived myself as privileged and my family as rich, although we had very little money ourselves."

After the bombing of Pearl Harbor in 1941, the Japanese occupied Tientsin and life totally changed again for the Triguboffs. As luck would have it, the Japanese didn't care about the Russian-Jews.

"The Japanese had no interest in us," Harry says. "They were preoccupied with the war against Chinese Nationalists. My family, along with others from our Russian community, were left to take over the trade moving through the port.

"My family's financial position changed overnight. My father became the owner of a chain of shops, and that was only the start of his growth."

Moshe still had far greater ambitions. China didn't have much industry at the time and used to import their textiles from Japan. The big stores in town were owned by the British – Hall & Haltz Co. and Whiteaway Laidlaw & Co. Ltd.

"When the war started, the Japanese threw the British into camps and they locked up the shops and took the goods. There was nobody to sell them, so my father went to the Japanese and said he could buy all the goods from them. They laughed at him and asked how he would be able to pay for them. As it turned out, my father had the last laugh."

In Tientsin, many Jews were money lenders, so Moshe went to see them and asked for the money he needed to pay the Japanese for the goods. They wanted to give Moshe the money, but they didn't have as much as he needed, though they had some.

"I remember I went with my father, and he sat and negotiated with them all day," Harry says.

"They eventually gave him as much money as they had, but it still wasn't enough. My father went to the Japanese and told them he only had 10 per cent. He told them to give him 10 per cent of the goods and he would then gradually pay them for the rest. They had few options, so they agreed."

At the time, no goods were arriving in China. Moshe was the only one with goods so he could charge whatever he liked. He had the monopoly and in no time had paid off the other 90 per cent. That is how his growth really started, but Moshe still saw greater opportunities.

"My father told the Japanese they needed to let him sell from their factories. The Japanese big shots wanted to meet him, so they told him he needed to go to Japan. My father was scared to death to travel because of all the war planes flying around, but he went to meet them. They liked him and were happy to send the goods to him.

"Even when the Japanese were forced to surrender in the war, my father was able to take advantage," Harry says.

China, before the war, had been selling goods to America, but that stopped during the war. Moshe, through his contacts, bought cloth from Japan and many other export goods for next to nothing, including ivory and pig bristles, and he could charge whatever he wanted because supply was short. Moshe became a rich man overnight.

The Triguboffs, with their new-found wealth, were able to buy the house that was previously owned by the local head of the Hong Kong and Shanghai Bank. They also bought a beautiful home a six-hour train ride away in the seaside resort of Beidaihe.

The family would spend their summers there. It was on one of his trips home from the family's beach paradise that Harry would learn a little more about the casualties of the war.

"I was travelling home on the train at the end of one of our summer holidays when curiosity got the better of me and I decided to explore the other carriages," he says.

"Instead of tourists, I found every carriage was filled with boxes. Boxes carrying the ashes of Japanese soldiers.

"It was my first glimpse of the massive casualties of war. I was overwhelmed by the number of boxes. I was sorry to have left my carriage, and the Japanese soldiers escorting the ashes weren't happy about me snooping around either. I can still see all those boxes as clear as the day I saw them, and that was almost 80 years ago."

When the Japanese did eventually lose the war, life changed yet again. Harry was now used to change and generally went with the flow. When the US Marines arrived in Tientsin from Okinawa, Japan, he watched as the Japanese were loaded into trucks. They were taken to the docks where they were shipped back to Japan. The Japanese were going home, and the Americans were coming in.

Harry had seen a lot for one so young, but he loved watching all the comings and goings down by the port. The Americans were his new fascination, especially as they seemed to be divided into two camps: black Marines and white Marines. They not only represented a brave new world to Harry, but they also brought something special with them – American culture, especially black American culture.

It was a far cry from Harry's traditional Russian-Jewish upbringing, but he liked everything about this culture. He was in his element talking to the Marines. His English by then was impeccable, but there were still a few words being thrown around that he hadn't heard before. That more colourful language became part of his vocabulary, but he still knew better than to use it in front of his parents, or when in other polite company.

When the Marines moved into Tientsin, they were told which bars they could drink in and to which hotels they could take their women.

"They had such a sense of humour," Harry remembers. "They used to joke with me and tell me that when the Chinese women asked why there were black Americans and white Americans, they would tell them their skin had been covered with camouflage from the war and the black wouldn't come off.

"I admired them. After everything they had been through, they still loved life, were at peace with their circumstances, and chose to be happy. They were brave," he says.

What is worthy of note is that the US Marines had arrived in Tientsin from Okinawa, Japan. The island of Okinawa is recognised for having the highest proportion of people over 100 years old in the world. They put their longevity down to embracing an *ikigai*. 'Iki' in Japanese means 'life' and 'gai' describes value or worth.

An *ikigai* gives a person a sense of purpose, a reason for living. It is a convergence of four areas of your life: what you love, what you're good at, what the world needs, and what you can be paid for. Having an *ikigai* makes you happy and is proven to promote longevity, and that is why Okinawans are the longest-living people on the planet.

Harry has his own *ikigai* without even knowing it, and he has longevity to show for it. It would seem the US Marines would also take home some of the teachings of Okinawa, and that is what Harry saw in them – happiness, positivity and bravery. He loved them and they had a huge influence on the young Harry. He wrote to them for decades after the war, and they would respond with the same happy positivity.

At that time, Harry wasn't the only one fascinated with the Americans. Moshe could see a huge new market in exporting to the United States. He was always looking for the edge, the big moment, and he found it. He developed a market selling Chinese pig bristles to major department stores in the US. The bristles were used in hairbrushes. His largest customer was the biggest department store of them all – Macy's.

The Triguboffs, with their new-found wealth, were also able to upgrade their family rickshaw to a new Dodge car.

"I was very excited," Harry says. "That is until I found out that we could only drive it at walking pace because the Chinese still strolled down the crowded streets. It took all the fun out of it, and I decided that no matter how flashy the car might have been, the rickshaw was more practical."

Many years later, when money was no obstacle, Harry was on one of his regular trips to China. He wasn't happy when told he could only rent a car for four hours. He only needed it for two hours. He walked away and decided to hire a rickshaw instead. As far as Harry was concerned, renting a car for longer than he needed was a waste of money.

That's his story, anyhow. Harry would never admit to being sentimental about the old family mainstay, but just maybe he was trying to find an excuse to take a trip down memory lane. Truth be known, he probably ended up tipping the rickshaw driver more than the cost of renting the car for the additional two hours.

Back to Moshe, and he now had all the trimmings of wealth. The Triguboffs were deemed socially acceptable. In fact, they were on the highest rung of the social ladder. Moshe was given the honour of reading the prayers at synagogue on Saturdays and Harry remembers standing next to him.

"I was happy for my father, but I didn't see what all the fuss was about. While a traditional upbringing was important to my parents, it felt dated to me. I felt the world symbolised by the US Marines represented a new freedom, and this is what I was excited about," he says.

Harry, because he was so fluent in English, regularly went to the cinema, where he was particularly taken with the wartime classics – hits that represented glamour, colour, dancing and the fabulous music of the big bands. He loved everything about the cinematic experience.

His favourite movies were those that featured 'the greatest trumpeter in the world' – Harry James & His Big Band. Harry James had swagger. He was suave, charming and sophisticated and played the trumpet to perfection. He floated around the dancefloor with the beautiful leading ladies.

The movies were fun, with comedians and stars like Hollywood greats Lucille Ball and June Allyson. Harry was mesmerised by it all and, after being caught up in that world, he decided to call himself after his Hollywood idol, Harry James.

The Triguboffs first contemplated a move from China in 1946. In a short biography on Moshe, in files from the Department of Immigration in Australia and held in the National Archives, it reads:

> *Triguboff was always respected by the community in which he lived. He helped a considerable amount of people to get on their own feet, when they arrived in Tientsin from Russia, or when they had economic difficulties. He was known as a generous donor towards the religious, educational and social needs of the society in which*

he lived. Also, he was instrumental in organising, financing and building a Jewish centre (club) and Jewish hospital in Tientsin. He donated large sums of money towards the total cost of building a large synagogue and was elected vice-president of the committee for the running of religious affairs of the Jewish community.

Notable also was a large building that Triguboff donated to the Jewish community of Tientsin, which was used as an old-age home, accommodating thirty people who had no relatives to look after them in their old age, and who had previously been living in desolate circumstances in poverty-stricken areas. This home had a large dining hall, and catered for the poor of the community in giving a free lunch to the needy, and it was often that over a hundred meals were served in one day.

Despite this, the competing Chinese business houses didn't care how much good Moshe was doing for the community; they were jealous of how much business he was doing exporting to the US. They suggested to him that unless he limit his trade activities to the US, they would see to it that he would be put out of business.

The biography went on to read:

Triguboff ignored these warnings, and replied that everything that he ever did, or was doing, was always legal and within the framework of the law. He maintained that he was a law-abiding citizen, and that he could trade and compete with them freely, without in any way restricting his commercial activities. He considered China a free country, and had resided there for over 25 years. However, the Chinese merchants would not accept this from a foreigner and threatened to put Triguboff out of business ...

And that is where all the trouble began. This became a huge contributing factor in Moshe and Frida never being able to come to Australia.

The biography also notes:

One day, in 1946, several officers from the Chinese police force came to Triguboff's office in Tientsin. They requested that he produce his books and other office documents for the last six years, and that he also accompany them to police headquarters for questioning. At that time, they were fully aware of the fact that they had nothing on Triguboff but they were under pressure from the wealthy Chinese merchants, and were therefore determined to make out a case against him.

After careful examination of all the documents and papers now in their possession, the police found two documents on which they intended to build their case. One dealt with the confiscation of a small quantity of leather goods – which they interpreted as selling for a cheap price to the 120 Japanese infantry, and the other a certificate from the Municipal Council (puppet government) stating that in accordance with the fourth movement of collecting copper by the Tientsin Council, Triguboff has given a certain quantity of copper as was required by the order and regulation of the Municipal Council.

These two documents were the basis of their charges and accusations. They are dealt with in great detail in the High Court of Ranking (which was the highest judicial authority in China during the Nationalist Government). This judgment found that Triguboff was not guilty of these charges and that the acts were done under duress. They acquitted Triguboff.

That says it all. Moshe was accused of collaborating with the Japanese, but *he was acquitted*. All charges were dismissed. End of story – or so you would think.

It was at that time, with more political unrest in China, that Moshe and Frida made the decision to send Joe and Harry to Australia. The intention was always that they would follow soon after.

By early 1948, however, Australian policy had changed. Australia didn't want rich Jews in the country, particularly if they were facing, or had faced, allegations of collaborating with the Japanese. Regardless of whether all charges had been dismissed, Australia didn't want Jews like the Triguboffs.

"An urgent telegram was sent to say that Joe and I had left Tientsin, and we were on our way to Australia, but we must not be allowed in," Harry says.

The National Archives of Australia contains the following cable, sent on 5 March 1948, a couple of days after Harry's 15th birthday:

> *Joseph and Harry Triguboff reportedly left Tientsin by air within the last three weeks. Please advise urgently whether they have arrived at your port. If these persons have not arrived, please warn all the airlines that they should not be accepted as passengers and that if they come to Australia they may be restricted from landing.*

"It arrived too late," Harry says. "And we, of course, knew nothing about it.

"We were already in and we were safe. My parents' situation, however, was becoming dire, with Communist China closing in on Tientsin.

"Once Joe and I were settled, Shanghai officials asked my brother to send some final documentation for our parents' entry into Australia. Joe thought it a mere formality, but when he had a meeting with the Australian Immigration Department, they told him that our parents could not come to Australia.

"There was no reason given. My parents were desperate. If they stayed in China, they would be sent back to Russia."

Joe wrote ad nauseam to the Immigration Department, reassuring them that Moshe had been cleared of any collaboration. He explained how the situation in China was "too politically strained for me and my brother to return".

In early 1949, Harry received a telegram from a place he had never heard of – Ramat Gan.

"I asked the postal officials and they hadn't heard of it either," Harry says. "I read the telegram and was able to work out that Ramat Gan was a suburb of Tel Aviv.

"My parents couldn't come to Australia, so they went to the only other place to which they could turn – Israel. That was the first time I knew they were out of China."

Harry's parents were safe, but they were still on the other side of the world, and they had travelled thousands of miles in the wrong direction from Sydney, Australia. The chasm between Harry and his parents was only getting wider and he feared he would never see them again.

The official who had tried to stop the brothers from entering Australia was one Osmond Fuhrman. He was the Australian Consulate-General in Shanghai from 1947–48.

Fuhrman did little to hide his antisemitism. Call it spite or disdain, but he included information in his cable to the authorities that the boys were bringing millions of pounds into Australia. Joe and Harry had only brought £8,000 into the country. The Immigration Department, as there was no collaboration and no millions, decided there was nothing untoward about the boys' entry into Australia and had no choice but to back off. They could, however, keep the family apart by refusing Moshe and Frida entry.

"They believed that if they refused entry to my mother and father, it would force Joe and I to leave Australia voluntarily so we could be reunited with our parents," Harry says.

"Joe and I decided to stick it out, believing our parents would one day be allowed into Australia. Joe continued to plead our parents' case, so it became a waiting game, a very long waiting game."

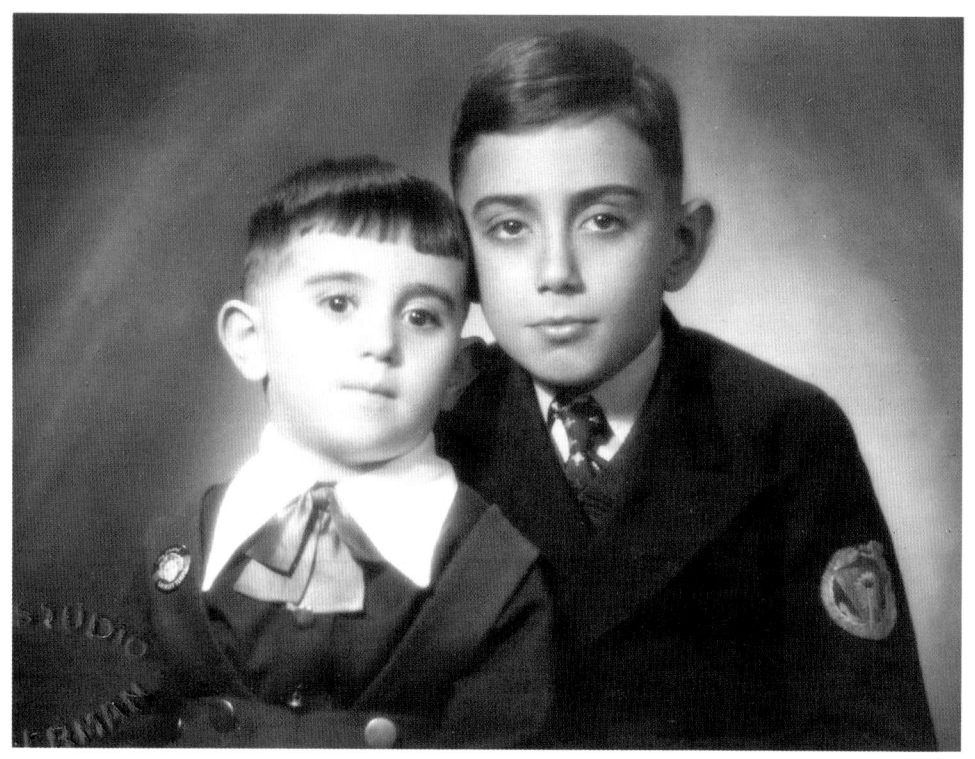

Harry with older brother Joe.

Harry and his nanny in front seat of rickshaw, Joe and Frida at the rear, China.

Joe, Frida & Harry at the beach on holiday in Beidaihe.

Harry and Joe with friends at the beach, 1935.

Harry with his mother, Frida, 1936.

Tientsin Jewish School, 1935.

Harry & Joe sailing.

Harry & Joe on horseback.

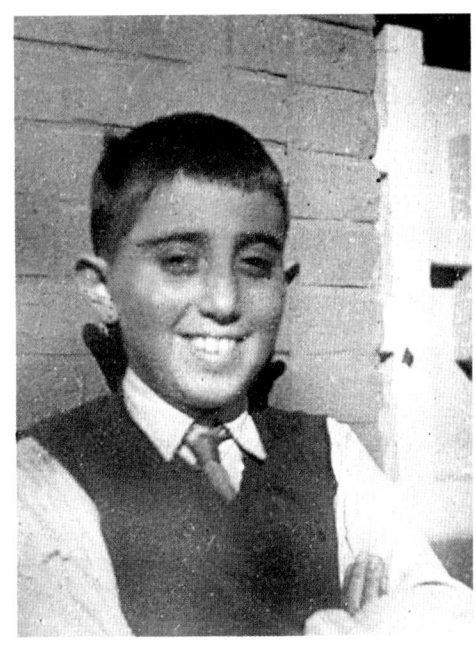

Harry at school in China.

TWO

CALLING AUSTRALIA HOME

When Harry and Joe arrived in Sydney in 1948, both were excited. Joe was heading to Sydney University to study law, and Harry, as we already know, was going to do his final senior school years at The Scots College in Sydney's Bellevue Hill.

First, the brothers needed to find a place to live. They stayed with a Jewish community leader their first night, and then they went in search of a hotel room until they could find a more permanent home.

"It was love at first sight," Harry says. "My first view was looking over Bondi Beach and all the bronzed bodies, the blue sea, crashing waves and red roofs. It was beautiful. Unlike China, there was no concrete to be seen and there was no pedestrian congestion. People moved around freely.

"When we inquired about finding a hotel room, we quickly learned that in Australia that was a room above a pub. It was a small room, nothing special, but it was very cool living above a pub," he says with a cheeky grin.

Joe didn't think so. He thought it inappropriate and was sure Harry's headmaster would feel the same way. He quickly found a house for them to rent in Vaucluse.

Harry tried to fit in at school. He was so strong in maths that the principal, Alexander Knox Anderson, put him up half a year. Harry thought that was terrific and was very proud, but he still felt somewhat displaced because he was attending a predominantly Christian school. He wasn't the only Jewish student, but there was only a handful, so he was required to attend divinity classes. Not only did he attend, but he excelled. He topped his class and won an award. He was not, however, able to accept it because he was Jewish!

Harry befriended one of the Jewish boys, but eventually also made friends with the Christian boys, even some of the boys from 'the bush'. He experienced no antisemitism and found the students and parents inclusive when they found out he was on the other side of the world to his parents.

By the time Harry finished at Scots, he did fit in. The school was progressive for its day and wasn't bound by background, colour or religion. It was focused on excelling and representing the school, whether that be academically or in sports. There was more admiration among students of each other than prejudice.

Harry and Joe, outside of school, were part of the Jewish community and had been since the day they arrived in Australia, but they were not observant Jews. They would attend the Central Synagogue in Sydney for high holidays, but that was about it.

Joe, when he finished his law degree, got a job with Abe Landa, a well-known and respected Jewish lawyer. It was around that time that he changed his surname from Triguboff to Travers. He had been totally swept up by all things Australian and wanted a name to match.

Harry, when he finished school in 1950, was surprised that his parents wanted him to join them in Israel. He thought, all the delays aside, that his parents were still coming to live in Australia. Joe had already decided he wasn't going to Israel because he wanted to stay in Australia. He had a good job he loved, and he was still working tirelessly on getting his parents into the country. Harry headed to Israel.

Israel at the time was nothing like Australia. It was poor and depressing. People were flocking in from Iran and Iraq, forced to leave their countries. The good news was that much of Moshe's fortune was intact and he was allowed to transfer the monies to Israel.

"With the money, my father bought a blanket factory in Tel Aviv and, much better than being a trader, he became an industrialist," Harry says. "The business was called TriguSin. 'Trigu', an abbreviation of our surname, and 'Sin', the Russian word for son. Triguboff and Son. Although I was thrilled to see my parents again, I could now see my future had been mapped out for me in my absence. I wasn't sure I liked it."

Within months of Harry's arrival in Israel, his parents decided to send him to the Leeds Institute of Textiles at the University of Leeds in England. They wanted him to learn everything about textiles so he could assist his father in running the factory. Harry wasn't keen. He was still hoping the whole family could eventually go back to Australia and settle there, like Joe.

In May 1952, Joe's boss, Abe Landa, went to Tel Aviv. By way of introduction, he made an appointment to meet with the ambassador at the Australian Embassy.

During his meeting, Landa carefully brought the name Triguboff into the conversation. He told the ambassador that Joe, the older of the two sons, worked for him at his firm in Sydney. They discussed the fact that Moshe was no longer a trader and that he was now an industrialist in Israel.

"Landa told the ambassador that my parents were still hoping to settle in Australia," Harry says. "He told the ambassador that my brother worked for him in Australia, and that my father was devoted to his family and wanted to see them back together. Landa said he was looking forward to welcoming my parents to Australia. He left no question of if, but when."

The recommendation for the Triguboffs, regardless of the high praise and endorsement by Landa, fell on deaf ears. Unbelievably, Landa had delivered his recommendation to the same diplomat from Shanghai that had sent the telegram to the Immigration Department in Australia to stop Joe and Harry being allowed into the country – Osmond Fuhrman.

Fuhrman, after the conversation with Landa, cabled the Immigration Department to check the files.

"The files couldn't be found," Harry says.

"We now know that Fuhrman persisted because he couldn't remember the details off the top of his head, but he knew there was some reason he wanted to keep the Triguboffs out of Australia. Surprisingly, his recollection of what happened with us didn't immediately come to mind.

"The files were eventually located, and Fuhrman's memory was jogged, resulting in him vehemently rejecting Landa's request. With his memories now forefront of mind, he was again seething that we had slipped quietly into Australia. My parents were blacklisted, and he warned Australian authorities again to keep them out."

Harry, although he didn't know it at the time, says this explains why he was harassed by immigration authorities for the next few years every time he tried to travel.

"I was studying in England and returning to Israel to spend time with my parents," Harry says. "I remember on one trip back to Israel I made a stopover in Paris. I was surprised to be met on arrival and taken by an official car to my connecting flight.

"The captain had to sign a declaration that he had taken responsibility for me. It was all very strange."

Harry continued to be hounded and believes he was a victim of persecution by the Australian authorities. His dislike of bureaucracy and associated red tape, which has been a constant throughout his life, remains to this day.

Harry wasn't really taken with Leeds. He didn't think much of the curriculum, and he felt that the institute was somewhat antiquated. However, unlike Scots College, the Institute of Textiles was full of Jewish students. Harry's great friend there was a Jewish student called Menachem. He was a Holocaust survivor.

"I'm not one to show great emotion, but nor am I made of stone," Harry says. "Menachem's story was not one about the Holocaust horrors, but one of hope.

"Menachem's father had disappeared during the war. Menachem waited as each new refugee ship came into Israel, hoping by chance his father might be on one of the ships.

"Just when he was losing hope, incredibly, his father walked down the gangplank.

"I still get goosebumps talking about it. Against all odds, Menachem and his father were reunited. I was so proud of my friend for continuing his search.

"Menachem, with his dogged determination, would have fitted in well at Scots College."

Generally, Harry was a man of practicality. He was a problem-solver so found his very technical lessons at the institute boring. He did, however, have fun outside the classroom. Although Menachem was very religious, Harry would use all his charm to convince him to go to the university dance hall.

Harry had started dating a girl whose father owned a fish and chip shop, and he liked to impress her. He used to spend his money on renting a car when he took her to the dances, but he still liked having Menachem as his wingman.

It was a bit of harmless romance. Harry had no serious entanglements because he knew he was destined to return to Israel and work in the family business. He didn't want complications.

Harry, after completing his studies at the textile institute, finally returned to Israel, but there was trouble between father and son from the onset. The 20-year-old Harry had been looking after himself for years, but his father was intent on treating him like the child he was when he'd left.

"My father didn't appreciate how independent I had been during our time apart," Harry says. "I used to do a lot with Joe in Australia, but I also did a lot on my own, which included swimming in the rough surf at Bondi Beach. When I returned to Israel my father would panic about me swimming in the far calmer waters of the Mediterranean.

"He would insist on taking me to the beach. He was scared of the waves and thought I might drown. He still thought I was a little boy," Harry says, mildly irritated by the memory.

"I wasn't loving Israel at all at that time, unlike today. I didn't care that it was a poor country, but I wasn't expecting such intellectual snobbery. I did have a car though and that was considered a great luxury.

"There was rationing at the time so I would drive in my Jeep to the Arab villages to buy fresh food, avoiding the Israeli police at every turn. Interestingly, my father seemed unfazed by that. He still thought body surfing was far more dangerous!"

One of the first things Harry noticed was that his parents hadn't created a home for themselves. It was a house with little furnishings and no personality. It could have been anyone's house. There was nothing familiar about it. Moshe and Frida had never intended for it to be their forever home, so they were ready to move at a moment's notice. They still expected to go to Australia. Israel was a temporary solution and they lived accordingly.

With that in mind, Harry wrangled his way out of serving in the Israeli Army.

"I never went into the army. My friend Menachem was called up, but he didn't go to war. They sent him on a job supervising the supply of uniforms because he had a degree in textile engineering. I didn't want the same desk job. If I had to go into the army, I wanted to fight.

"As it turned out, I never had to go into the army. I was needed at the factory to continue the supply of blankets to the army and that was a priority," he says.

While Harry made a lot of positive changes to the business, Moshe didn't appreciate his efforts, and Harry didn't enjoy working for his father at all. Harry thought him old and not up with the times. Moshe was by now in his late 50s.

In 1953, Joe moved back to Israel. There was no real explanation given. Harry thought it was as simple as him missing the family. Joe started to boss Harry around, which was made worse by the fact that Joe had brought his wife, Ruth, from Australia, and Harry says she caused trouble between the brothers. Moshe also made Joe the financial controller, even though he wasn't nearly as good with figures as Harry. Harry was furious! Figures were his big thing.

Harry fought with Joe and his father all the time. It was exhausting for all of them. Moshe decided to separate the boys and helped Harry set up a carpet factory to run separately from the blanket business.

"I now had my own business. *My* business," Harry recounts. "I was no longer under my father's control, or that of my brother. I turned the business around and it was a huge success. I never had any doubt it would be," he adds, with a touch of arrogance.

It proved Harry could run a business more efficiently than his father and brother put together. That business still exists today under the ownership of Carmel Carpets.

Although Harry had control of his business life, when it came time to marry, of course Harry's parents thought they should decide when that was to be, and to whom.

There were more arguments. Harry introduced his parents to a beautiful girl called Sylvia. Harry's mother was shocked that she was a darker-skinned Jew from Iraq. This meant that she was a Sephardic Jew, people who are from Africa and the Middle East. The Triguboffs are

Ashkenazi Jews. The European Jews were thought to be more elite at the time. The Sephardic Jews were seen as lower class, and Harry's mother wasn't happy about his choice.

Harry liked Sylvia very much, but he wasn't in love with her. To stop the constant arguments and badgering from his parents, he stopped seeing her.

Not long afterwards, Harry met a spirited Ashkenazi Jew whom he was proud to take home to meet his family. Her name was Hana, and he had picked her up in his Jeep while she was hitchhiking. She was a military nurse and had been headed to her post at the time.

Frida approved, even though Hana's parents were poor. Hana's father, once prosperous, was from Vienna, but in Israel he earned a living as a port administrator. Harry and Hana married in 1959 at Moshe's expense. In those days it was unusual for the groom's family to foot the bill. Harry didn't care.

The more people that came into the Triguboff family, the worse the tension became. Neither Harry nor Joe felt happy. Harry wanted to go back to Australia, and he thought Joe would follow.

"Joe never fitted in, in Israel," Harry says. "He couldn't speak Hebrew, and he was sick of trying to save the blanket business. He was a better lawyer, and his Australian-born wife was missing home."

Even though Harry had gone to school in Australia, there were issues with his visa to return. It was to be another waiting game. He went to London to arrange the visa, but he really wanted to go to South Africa for a while before heading back to Australia.

An official told Harry his timing was good because the biggest textile magnate in South Africa was currently in London. Harry went to meet him.

"He asked me if I was just using him to go to South Africa," Harry says. "I told him I would go to South Africa at my own expense. I told him that when he came back to South Africa, he must let me know. So, I went to South Africa and worked as a real estate agent in Johannesburg until he came back."

When Harry did eventually move to a role at the textile factory it was a boring desk job as an accountant. Fortunately, within weeks, he was able to secure his Australian visa, and so returned to Australia with Hana in 1960.

As predicted, Joe followed, and he became a successful lawyer. By then he had a son, Michael, and Ruth was happy to come home.

"Joe became a big success here," Harry says proudly. "He had a thriving legal practice and was very happy …"

Harry manages to keep his sibling rivalry in check, but you can just see that he wants to finish with, "… but he wasn't nearly as successful as me."

Harry & Joe with the Schwartz family in Sydney.

Harry in Scots uniform, 1949.

Harry with his parents in Israel.

Moshe outside his TriguSin Textile Works factory in Israel.

Frida, Harry, Moshe, Ruth & Joe.

Harry & Joe as young adults.

Triguboff family in Israel.

The family car, Israel.

Joe & Harry at Trafalgar Square, London.

Harry at Leeds University.

THREE

THE BUSINESS BEGINS

Harry was happy to be back in Australia. It wasn't as developed as some of the other countries he had been to, but he could definitely see potential. Harry's business in Israel had been a great success, but it was his father's money that had bankrolled it, not his. Now he wanted to make it on his own, and he didn't need, or want, his father's money.

In hindsight, that was probably a conversation he should have had with Hana. After the life they'd had in Israel, she wasn't ready to live above a shop in the industrial boondocks of the western suburbs of Sydney. Yet, if that is what it came to, Harry would expect her to do it.

Harry had come back to Australia with £25,000. It was his share of the profits from the carpet business. It was by no means a fortune, but if he found a good job, it was enough for him and Hana to buy a house in a good area and live a comfortable life. Unfortunately for Hana, Harry had other ideas.

When they first arrived, Harry took Hana to his old stomping ground in Sydney's eastern suburbs. It was familiar turf to him, and he knew that Hana would feel comfortable and happy being amidst the Jewish community. Since Harry had last been in Australia, the number of Jewish immigrants had increased by 17,000, with Jews arriving from

Europe and Shanghai. A further 10,000 had arrived by 1961. Thus, between the year Harry was born, in 1933, and the year he became an Australian citizen, in 1961, Australian Jewry had almost trebled in number from 23,000 to 60,000. It made Harry even more furious that his parents were not part of those statistics.

Because much of the Jewish community lived in Sydney's eastern suburbs, Harry rented a flat in Woollahra. It was a nice area, but Hana would have preferred to buy a house and get settled, like Harry's brother and his family had done.

Unfortunately for Hana, Harry had no interest in buying a house because he had no intention of putting all his eggs in the one basket. He wanted quick access to his money in case a great business opportunity came along. Harry was unsure what that opportunity might look like, but he was happy to put some feelers out for work while he figured it out.

"My first job was with a stockbroking company called Parker & Stewart," Harry says. "I liked the boss very much, but I was a bit surprised when he hit me up for a loan. I gave him the money, but I made sure it was against security. Not long after, Parker & Stewart went bankrupt. The company had been on the wrong side of a failed float with a mining company. My job was gone but the money I'd loaned was secure, and now I needed to find myself another job.

"My next role was at the University of NSW working for a professor who had, strangely enough, taught me at the University of Leeds in the UK. He had also migrated to Australia. I was excited about working for him, but it was a very boring job supervising tests for an automated system of washing and combing wool. I was better than that, and I only lasted a few months."

Harry then scored a job with a textiles company, which he thought would be perfect for him.

"I couldn't understand why they only sold to the Australian market," Harry says. "There was a huge export opportunity, but the boss wasn't interested. He was more interested in playing golf than growing his business. He didn't invite my input, but I gave it anyhow. I told him that his wages were too high, his machines were crap, and if he wasn't interested in expanding the business, he should shut the factory down and sell it for land value.

"Not surprisingly, I was shown the door." Harry laughs.

That is when Harry became more serious about looking for investments. At all the jobs he had worked in, the bosses were happy running a mediocre business.

"Mediocrity is hugely overrated," Harry says. "I knew that the only way I could make a difference was to be my own boss and make all the decisions.

"I thought about opening a café, but I felt that would be very long hours for not much return. Hana, unsurprisingly, agreed.

"Then I considered buying a newsagency in Chullora. It meant Hana would have to live over a shop and raise our brood. That did not go down well either."

Hana was wondering where her successful, feisty, ambitious Harry had gone. These little businesses were nothing like the carpet business in Israel, and she kept comparing how they were living to Joe and Ruth.

"She kept yelling at me that Joe wouldn't drag his family to the horrible outer suburbs of Sydney," Harry says. "None of the areas I was considering at the time were the revitalised communities they are today. They were virtual slums."

Now, of course, Harry is building in many of those suburbs himself.

"I just didn't have the money to be more ambitious," Harry says. "Not for one minute did I think that is where we would end up. But I had to start somewhere, and I wanted to be my own boss."

There was another problem. Harry was still struggling to get full Australian citizenship. The Immigration Department baulked yet again but told Harry that if he could get a recommendation letter from the headmaster at Scots College, they would give him a passport.

Fortunately for Harry, Alexander Knox Andersen was the longest-serving headmaster, leading the school for some 24 years. According to his biography on the Scots College website, "He liked to know the boys, learn their names and took an interest in what they did."

Harry would be hard to forget. The young lad with the strong Russian accent and an early life spent in China was like no other student at the school. The young Jewish boy who'd aced divinity probably stood out as well.

"Headmaster Andersen was still there and he remembered me," Harry says, clearly thrilled he had made an impression and was remembered after all that time.

"When he handed me that letter by way of proof, I could finally call Australia home. I was finally granted Australian citizenship in 1961."

That same year, Harry and Hana were expecting their first baby, and Harry decided it was the perfect time to invest his money. He bought a block of four units in Dulwich Hill, in Sydney's Inner West with a third of his money. He used another third to buy a milk run in Chatswood on Sydney's Lower North Shore and with some of the remaining third he bought a taxi licence. Harry had no intention of driving the cab into the late hours of the night any more than he had any intention of dropping milk on doorsteps at the crack of dawn. He found a driver for the cab and he sub-licensed the milk run to Paul Appleby, who would then stay with him for 20 years and become involved in the future construction business.

Whether Harry chooses to admit it, he spent most of his youth watching his father's business grow through expansion and exportation. It was all he really knew – taking a business and making it bigger. The more volume you moved, the greater the profit. Harry proved that – and then some!

While he let the units sit and create income, he concentrated on expanding the milk business. While Paul Appleby did the legwork delivering the milk to the residential community, Harry saw a greater opportunity in the expanding shopping centre at Chatswood. A new Grace Bros. department store opened there, and Harry installed flavoured-milk vending machines in the shopping mall. Initially, it was a huge success, but then the milk suppliers realised they could cut Harry out by going to the mall direct. With profits on the decline, he decided it was time to look for another investment opportunity.

Harry and Hana were still renting but Hana was happy that none of Harry's investments had taken them out of the eastern suburbs.

Then, Harry met Tommy Gluck – a big man with a big personality. Tommy owned a furniture shop in Double Bay and was one of the more colourful characters in the eastern suburbs. He told Harry he should build on the cheap block of land at Roseville that Joe had talked Harry into buying while he was in South Africa. Joe had said it would be a great investment, but it turned out to be worth less than Harry paid for it. Harry agreed with Tommy. If he built on it, he could flip it and make a buck.

The development arm of LJ Hooker was commissioned to build the house for him at Roseville, but they didn't complete it. Harry kicked them out and organised to finish it himself. He asked Paul Appleby, the milk-run guy, to complete the remaining jobs as he also had experience in construction.

Hana came kicking and screaming, but they lived there for a few years until they eventually moved back to the eastern suburbs with their daughters, Orna and Sharon. Harry's eldest daughter, Orna, was born in 1961, and Sharon was born 18 months later, in 1963.

After Roseville, Tommy suggested they have another crack at building together. With some of the money Harry made from the sale of Roseville, they formed a partnership in late 1962 and bought a block of land at Tempe.

―――

Just as Harry was about to start building at Tempe, he decided to hit other problems head on as well. That meant dealing with the issue of his parents' visa himself.

"I was starting to build my confidence as well as flats," Harry says.

"Joe used to write all these letters, and I got sick of it. I decided to contact the Australian Secret Intelligence Service (ASIS), and I left a message hinting that I had some information about a Soviet spy. I went to Canberra and this huge policeman came to meet me because he thought I was going to snitch on the spy. When he realised why I was there he was very good humoured about it.

"I told him our story and he gave me the answer. He told me there was nothing wrong with our parents and he didn't know why they couldn't come to Australia. Officially, he explained how Australia's relationship with Japan had undergone a drastic change. Whatever dealings my father had at the time of the war with Japan, it was no longer important to the security of Australia."

It made no difference.

Harry then wrote to the Minister for Immigration, Alick Downer, father of Alexander Downer (later leader of the Liberal Party from 1994 to 1995), describing his conversation with the ASIS agent. Harry said that for 16 years they had been pleading with the Immigration Department to allow their parents to settle in Australia.

But every avenue was to no avail. Harry received the same response as Joe had for all those years.

Then, on 26 May 1966, Harry's mother, Frida, died suddenly of heart failure, aged 58.

"Joe and I were both devastated, and Joe immediately started writing again," Harry says. "This time it was to the new minister, Hubert Opperman, again through Government Whip WJ Aston, who was mostly our first point of contact for correspondence."

The letter spelt out the agony Harry and Joe had been through for the 17 years they had tried to bring their parents to Australia and that had culminated in the death of their mother. According to records kept by the Immigration Department, and held with the National Archives of Australia, Joe's letter reads as follows:

Dear Mr Aston,

Re: Application for Landing Permit for Moses (Moshe) Triguboff

This morning, I received a telegram from my father in Israel advising that my mother had a sudden heart attack on Thursday, 26th inst., and an hour later passed away. The tragic news deeply shocked my brother and I and most certainly our father, since Mother never had any heart trouble. You are well aware that for some considerable time, seventeen years, I have attempted to arrange the entry of my parents into Australia. Numerous applications and representations were made, but unfortunately, did not meet with success for reasons unknown to me.

My last application was made on the 28th October, 1964, subsequent to the interview we had with The Hon. H. Opperman, The Minister for Immigration in Canberra.

My father will be 68 years of age next month. He has had three heart attacks in the last two years. He and my late mother were happily married for over 41 years, and lived together in harmony, love, devotion, and respect for each other.

My father has no close relations in Israel, or anywhere else in the world who could look after him. My brother and myself are the only ones he has, and we have both settled in Sydney.

Now due to the sudden and tragic loss in the passing away of his partner in life, and in the light that he is restricted and disallowed by the Minister of Immigration to join his only children and grandchildren in Australia – who could take care of him? We are most apprehensive that he is losing his will to live, and, unless something is arranged by us in the immediate future, we dread another tragedy.

In the light of the above, and in the name of British justice, and on humanitarian grounds, dear Mr. Aston, please plead with the Minister of Immigration to reconsider his previous decision, and permit an early entry of my father into Australia.

Sincerely hoping and praying that your submissions and representations will meet with success.

Yours sincerely, Joseph Travers.

"It still didn't work," Harry says. "The response from Opperman to Aston was the same as the rest."

Similar to the many responses already received over 17 years, and dated 26 July 1966, it reads:

Dear Mr Aston

In view of your earnest and repeated efforts in support of Moshe Triguboff's application for admission to Australia, I have once again made a careful assessment of all the available facts.

In doing so, I have given full weight to those special features of the case, particularly the compassionate aspects, which you have so strongly advanced in correspondence and during your personal discussions with me.

Regretfully, I have to inform you that I still cannot feel justified in departing from the decision reached each time the application was reviewed previously, not only by myself, but by several of my predecessors in office.

Because of the interest you have shown and because the compassionate circumstances are acknowledged to be quite strong, I wish to assure you that the decision to withhold approval for Mr Triguboff's entry has not been taken lightly. Indeed, few individual cases have received so much personal attention by Ministers and senior Departmental officers.

Yours sincerely,
Hubert Opperman

Harry and Joe were devastated because there was nothing more they could do.

Harry flew over to see his father after being told he wasn't in good shape.

"I can still see him sitting there in a chair in a house that still was not a home," Harry recalls.

"My parents had always been in limbo, waiting to come to Australia and the house looked like it. My father was unshaven, which is traditional in the Jewish religion after a death in the family. It was very sad.

"I was mourning my mother myself and there was so much sorrow in my father.

"I have very few regrets in my life, but not spending more time with my father during that trip is the biggest of them. I spent more time with my friends, and it was the last time I saw my father."

Harry's father, Moshe, died less than a year later.

After 20 years of fighting, Harry's parents were gone, never having stepped a foot on Australian soil. Moshe dying alone, after being acquitted of any wrongdoing, was too much for Harry, so after he buried his father, he buried his emotions, then buried himself in his work. That was his coping mechanism to deal with the gross unfairness and cruelty of the government's decision to refuse his parents entry into Australia.

Left: Harry holding his first daughter, Orna, 1962.

Middle: Sharon, Harry, Hana & Orna, 1972.

Bottom: Sharon & Orna, 1967.

Orna & Sharon with their cousin Deborah and uncle Joe.

Orna & Sharon with their mother, Hana.

Orna & Sharon.

Orna, Harry & Sharon on holiday.

Harry & sister-in-law Ruth on his boat "Triggy", 1970s.

Orna, Harry & Sharon.

FOUR

DOING IT HIS WAY

In the early 1960s, while letters were still being sent back and forth by government officials in relation to bringing Harry's parents to Australia, Harry was still excited about his partnership with Tommy Gluck to build eight units at 34 Smith Street, Tempe.

Tommy was happy to discuss the project with Harry, and he was always excited and involved when he spoke to Harry about it, but he wasn't too keen to go to the site or know everything about the nuts and bolts of the building process. That suited Harry perfectly.

The site was a large residential block. No demolition was required as the house on it had burned down. It was in a semi-industrial area close to Tempe Tip and Sydney Airport. It wasn't a fabulous residential area, but it was all Harry and Tommy could afford and, as it turned out, the boys had bagged a bargain. They bought the land for £3,400.

"Even though Tommy and I had done the numbers, we had underestimated how much it would cost to build the two-storey walk-up," Harry says. "I still had the bulk of my money tied up in my investments so the only way forward with Tempe was to borrow the money.

"I wasn't going to risk all the money in my investments any more than Tommy was going to risk his furniture business. I still had a family to support, as did he."

Harry had learned a lot about borrowing money from his father. Moshe had known how to sell an opportunity. He had negotiated for hours with the Jewish lenders in Tientsin until they lent him the money he'd needed. Harry had witnessed that, and he was going to put his father's philosophy into practice. He was sure he could convince a bank manager to give them the money, using a few of his father's closing techniques.

"Fortunately, Tommy knew the bank manager at the ANZ bank next door to his furniture shop in Double Bay," Harry says.

"I knew it would be difficult for two young Jewish migrants with no experience to get money to build on spec, but I believed I could convince him.

"We went to see the manager and talked him through our project. The manager said that if we could get the job to roof level, then he would loan us the money to complete it. I still had to raise the cash we needed to get it to roof level, so rather than sell my investments, I used them as security on another smaller loan."

Harry had a lot on the line now, so he was keen to oversee the project himself. Tommy was busy with his furniture business, so it worked out well. Harry had no intention of doing the manual labour, but he knew he could manage those who did. From the very start he knew exactly what he wanted and, as the boss on site, he expected those working for him to do as they were told. Unfortunately, it was not a great start.

The foreman Harry put on the job turned out to be a drunk and the work he was doing was way below par. Harry sacked him and decided to do the job of foreman himself. The first thing he did was put an advertisement in the paper for bricklayers.

The man who answered the ad was a Scottish bloke, Ken McDonald. He ended up working for Harry for 45 years, and his sons still work with Meriton to this day. For 60 years, there has always been a McDonald on site.

"I turned up at the site and immediately I could see something had gone wrong," Ken McDonald remembers of that first day he met Harry.

"The foundations were built, and a few levels of bricks had been laid. There was one labourer on the site and another bloke out the front dressed in business attire from head to toe. He wasn't dressed to get his hands dirty, but he was the one we were there to see.

"As far as I was concerned, the job was small and straightforward. I had taken my best mate, Les Johnson, with me, who was also a brickie. He wasn't one of my mates from Glasgow but an Australian bloke from the bush. I think I gave Harry confidence that we could do the job, so he offered us the work. I asked the labourer who was still on the site if he wanted to work with us as well. He leapt at the chance. Ian King was his name. He was a young Indigenous lad," Ken says.

Ken had a nose for things, just like Harry. After meeting his new boss, he could see that this job could lead to more work. Harry was tough, to the point and expressed himself in 50 shades of colour.

"He was born for construction," Ken says.

Until Ken met Harry, he and Les would get the paper every Wednesday and go through the tenders. They were going job to job, pay cheque to pay cheque, or, in those days, cash to cash. They lived hand to mouth. Neither seemed too perturbed with that way of life.

Ken asked Harry what happened to the previous brickies. He said, "It was too hard for them. They didn't want to do the more elaborate work around the doors and windows, so they pissed off."

Ken saw Harry was angry about it, but he had no issue doing what Harry wanted. Ken thought that if he reassured Harry that it was a simple, straightforward job that could be turned around in a matter of months, it would appease him. He was right. He was born for construction as well.

Ken was still young. He had arrived in Australia about a year before he met Harry. He was from Glasgow and had come in as a Ten Pound Pom. His parents were poor, and he'd had a difficult childhood.

"I left school at 14, and I was determined to make my own way," Ken says.

"Like Harry, I'd seen the American way of life in the movies and that's where I wanted to go. I knew nothing about Australia.

"One day I was at the technical college, learning my bricklaying trade, and about a dozen of my mates were with me when I walked past a window with a poster of land and beaches on it, the sun the main feature.

"I asked my mates where the place was in the poster. They told me it was Australia. I then asked how you got there. One of my friends said we could get there for 10 pounds.

"So, all of us filled out the forms to say we were going to Australia. I didn't tell my parents. I sold my pushbike and everything that was of any value at all. I still couldn't raise the 10 quid. Then my uncle gave it to me because I said I was only going for a couple of years. I was 16 going on 17. I never did go back. My father died but I brought my mother over to Australia with the rest of my family when I could afford it.

"There are members of my clan everywhere in Australia now," he says with a smile.

There was a mutual respect between Harry and Ken almost immediately. Ken was a hard worker, and he was fast and accurate. Harry couldn't have asked for more.

In a matter of months, they had the building to roof level. The ANZ bank manager came back to inspect the work and agreed to loan Harry and Tommy the rest of the money to finish the building.

"You're a builder now," the bank manager told Harry. He was very happy. Both men were very happy.

As luck would have it, while they were finishing the building, big news hit the airways. Flocks of seagulls, which feasted at Tempe Tip, were causing havoc for the ever-expanding Sydney Airport nearby. With new runways and increased aircraft movements, passenger planes were growing in number by the day. The birds posed a real threat as a strike hazard when the planes were landing and taking off.

When the resolution to the problem was to close Tempe Tip, the site was not the only thing that cleaned up. Without the tip, Harry and Tommy's units were now in quite a nice residential area, and it added thousands of pounds to the value of their property.

Within eight months, with the tip gone, the two-storey walk-up block of flats sold for £25,500. As far as percentages go, it was to be one of the biggest profits Harry would ever make.

That was not the only bit of luck Harry would have. His timing was perfect to get into the apartment building game. Migration had pushed up demand, policy appeared to be working in the property developer's favour, and rent control was now a thing of the past. There was no greater time to be in the vertical building game.

The second development Harry and Tommy did was in Gipps Street, Drummoyne. Paul Appleby was still running the milk business, but he was also there on site to lend a hand if Harry needed it.

Harry always refers to Paul Appleby simply as "Appleby". It suits him. So, we'll follow suit. While Harry had Ken laying the bricks, other sub-contractors were letting him down.

"There was a disaster on the second job with the staircase," Harry says. In short, the problem basically meant that people would have to bend their heads down as they climbed the stairs.

"Appleby was a big bloke, and he told the form workers to pull down the form work and redo it. They refused. Appleby thundered down the dodgy staircase, went and got a crowbar out of his truck and ripped the form work down himself." Harry chuckles.

"There is a time for talk and a time for action," Appleby said at the time. "It had to be redone, so I just sped up the process."

Harry certainly approved, and he decided to sell the milk run and bring Appleby into the business of building apartments.

By the time they got to their third project in Botany, Harry knew that partnerships were not going to be his thing. After the first project was so profitable, Tommy wanted to be more invested in the day-to-day. Harry didn't want that. He'd been shouldering all the responsibility, and he liked it that way.

On this third project Harry decided they should work on different sides of the street and that they could share their workers and other costs. But Tommy's team wasn't able to keep up the pace of Harry's team. Even though Tommy was more invested, he still didn't want to hang around on site. Ken McDonald could see where the partnership was headed, so he decided to only work for Harry.

"Harry was always the clever one," Ken says. "He was always on site watching and listening, and he learned the trade. Harry would go to the pub at the end of the week with the lads who worked on site. It was the Friday night ritual.

"I couldn't believe that he still wanted to talk about work at the pub! I wondered why he couldn't just relax, shoot the breeze and tell some stories.

"Then the penny dropped. Talking about work *was* his relaxation. He loved it. It was all new and exciting, and he thought all the lads were equally obsessed. We all got used to it.

"They all listened because, to them, Harry was a good man, a fair man, and all the boys appreciated that they were paid every week without fail. It wasn't the same on all jobs.

"Choosing between Harry and Tommy wasn't a hard decision because Harry was one of us," Ken says.

Harry and Tommy remained friends, but they dissolved their partnership. Harry was determined never to work in a partnership again, well, not until the next time anyhow. A friend Harry knew from Tientsin, Bob Shteinman, asked Harry to buy a site with him in Croydon in Sydney's Inner West. Harry, out of respect for his father, Moshe, who was friends with Bob Shteinman's father, agreed to do it. Harry suggested he should build one block of flats and Bob should build two, but Harry would get the first choice of where on the site he would build.

Bob took so long to decide if he would accept the deal that Harry sold the site to another builder without even discussing it with Bob. Bob was shocked that he did that.

"If he couldn't make up his mind about the basics, I was in for a whole world of pain," Harry says. "I did the right thing, gave him his share of the money, but selling the site was my only option to get rid of him."

There were no partners ever again. From that moment on, Harry never took a risk on anyone else. Now he was the only boss and he believed nothing he did was a risk. He calculated that he could always win in every deal he did. It was the first glimpse of the famous Triguboff ego. He was the lone wolf and there was no stopping him.

The birth of Meriton occurred in 1963, the name coming from the street in which Harry completed his first building on his own – 18 apartments on Meriton Street, Gladesville.

Harry revisiting his first ever building with former Australian Prime Minister John Howard, 34–36 Smith Street, Tempe.

Elizabeth Court, 20 Meriton Street, Gladesville. Built by Harry, this '60s apartment block was the inspiration for the company name, Meriton.

HARRY OSCAR TRIGUBOFF,
Chairman and Managing Director.

Mr. Harry Oscar Triguboff is the Chairman and Managing Director of Meriton Properties Ltd. To really find out about him, and the sort of person he is, it's much easier to go and see his fellow directors, his staff and friends. It's not that he's shy exactly, but with so much to be done, it's hard for him to find the time to sit, and talk about himself.

He is of course, readily available to answer questions.... from anyone. Most of them concerning his background have already been answered, in the press and by his colleagues.

Born in China, of Russian parents, his path has been, briefly, from China to Australia--where he went to school; to England--where he obtained a degree in textile chemistry from Leeds University, and become an ardent supporter of the famous Leeds United Soccer Club; to Israel and South Africa and back to Australia. All by the time he was 26.

In both Israel and South Africa he had gained experience in the textile industry. In South Africa he had been the secretary of one of the country's largest mills--the Consolidated Textile Mills.

various jobs, including a milk run; the taxi business; as a technical officer at the University of New South Wales; in the costs account section of Davies Coop, and selling real estate for Vale and Company.

As he says himself: he was no salesman of any note. "I could see the bargains, but I couldn't sell them."

Buying the bargains, developing them and finding the right salesman to sell them was more his line. So in 1963, with $6,000 capital, the now memorable site at Smith Street, Tempe--opposite the tip--was purchased, and a two-storey block of flats built.

The Harry Triguboff company of real estate developers was well under way. Throughout the rest of the sixties it grew from strength to strength, with profits dazzling onlookers by jumping from $15,000 in 1966, to $19,000 in 1967; $49,000 in 1968 and $109,000 in 1969. In 1970 Meriton Properties Limited was formed, and its first year is revealed in detail in (... Meriton's First Year...)

Now he's 37, lives with his wife and 2 children at Bellevue Hill. And while he has something of the mysticism of the East in the aura about him, he also holds a multitude of contrasts.

While words such as dynamic and inspiring are used in describing him by people who know him best, a stranger may find him, at first, almost withdrawn with eyes wary like those of a child waiting and anticipating grown ups next movement.

Before too long, he makes a decision about you, and if it's good, the eyes brighten and hold a special warmth.

For all his dynamite, there is the easy, carefree Triguboff. A working day is from nine to five. Hours are spent relaxing at his billiards table at home. He is devoted to his family.

For a self confessing "money mechanist", Harry Triguboff seems to have his values straight - and as most people would want them.

If he had a family motto it would no doubt be: "self reliance is our strength."

In one short decade, Harry Triguboff has proved the worth of self reliance and adaptability.

FIVE

UNION TROUBLES

The unions were almost the ruination of Harry. In 1968, when Harry was getting into the swing of building multiple projects in the outer suburbs of Sydney, a bloke called Jack Mundey was elected secretary of the Builders Labourers Federation (BLF). The BLF wasn't the only union, but certainly the one that caused the most grief for Meriton in the 1970s and '80s.

"In the beginning the bastards didn't give a damn about us," Harry says with a dismissive wave of his hand.

"I met Mundey in the early days, but he had little interest in us while we were sticking to our knitting with small blocks in the suburbs.

"It was a whole different ballgame when he saw us encroaching on 'his turf' in and around the city. That was the arrogance of the BLF back then; they thought they owned the inner city.

"The war was on!"

Once Mundey had set up shop, he turned the BLF into a bit of a conundrum. It was no longer just about the tough guy promising his union members better wages, safer sites and better working conditions. He also preached that, 'progressive unions like ours have a very useful role to play in the citizens' interest, and we intend to play it'.

On the one hand you had the union organisers threatening to brutally kill development bosses in their beds, and on the other, you had Mundey holding court with socialites and celebrities in upmarket suburbs, addressing their concerns about green space, old buildings and even older suburbs. The tough union boss who turned a blind eye to the threats from his organisers on the ground would sit, teacup in hand, pinkie pointed upward, celebrating the success of his 'green bans' with Sydney's society.

The green bans were initiated by Mundey to protect and preserve older-style buildings and green spaces from high-rise development. He was welcomed into the fold by both the working class and society. Therein lies the conundrum.

"Mundey was the first greenie I ever met," Harry says. "We used to have arguments; there was a lot of yelling about whether Mundey's job was ensuring work for the building industry or taking it away by slapping a green ban on everything."

During Mundey's tenure with the BLF, there were 43 green bans imposed in New South Wales alone – far more than in any other state.

Meanwhile, in February 1973, Harry had agreed to buy a group of collective properties at 85–91 Cook Rd, Centennial Park, for $354,000. It was a substantial amount of money back then. Meriton agreed to pay a 10 per cent deposit, with the remainder to be paid within six months. During that period, Meriton would seek approval from the City of Sydney Council to build 48 units consisting of 36 two-bedroom units and 12 one-bedroom units. The contract further provided that if the approval wasn't forthcoming within five months of the date of the contract, Meriton was entitled to rescind. The contract was signed, and council gave its approval within the stipulated time.

Mundey was the greenies' saviour of sorts, and that included the famous author Patrick White, who lived at Centennial Park. When White got wind of Harry's plans for his recently acquired site, he went to see Mundey. All hell broke loose.

Mundey had already been instrumental in saving the oldest suburbs from developers, including areas like The Rocks and Woolloomooloo. Once an area or a site was protected by a green ban, developers couldn't touch it. White wanted Centennial Park left untouched, and he went out with Mundey to drum up support against Harry's site. It worked.

It was devastating for Harry when his Centennial Park site became a casualty of the green bans. The fact that Mundey claimed he had saved Sydney's soul was of little comfort to Harry, who had done so well in the booming Sydney property market until then, but watched as the market spectacularly crashed in 1974.

"It was a very bad time for me, as it was for anyone in the property industry at that time," Harry says.

"Developers were going bust everywhere, including two of the biggest at the time, Mainline Corporation and Home Units Australia. All I cared about was keeping Meriton afloat.

"We had the approval from the council to start work at the Centennial Park site, but it meant nothing once a green ban was slapped on it," he says.

It was a critical time for Harry financially. He couldn't afford to sit on a large, worthless site. He only had one option and that was to try to get out of completing the sale.

The owner, Malcolm McLaurin, of McLaurin & Tait, could see it coming when Harry wanted to pull out of the contract.

"I wasn't going to let that happen," McLaurin says. "I had a signed contract, and there was no provision made in the contract for a green ban being placed on the land." McLaurin says he could see it from Harry's perspective, but he was going to go broke himself if Harry didn't hold up his end of the contract, so he was ready to fight. So was Harry.

It was to become one of Harry's biggest ever court battles: *Meriton Apartments Pty Ltd vs McLaurin & Tait (Developments) Pty Ltd.*

The battle lasted for years, going from one court to the other and back again. Harry dragged it out for as long as he could, allowing him time to get his business back in good shape. Eventually, the High Court rejected Harry's claim because the only condition in the contract was that they receive approval to build from council. That was the only risk contemplated, and that clause was met, so Meriton couldn't back out simply because a green ban was placed on the land. Harry knew he would have to pay, but at least when the time came, he was in a position to do so.

Both men had held their ground but while McLaurin won on paper, Harry had bought himself years until he was in the position to pay the original contract. For Harry, it was still a win.

Although the green ban had been devastating for Harry, he could see what Jack Mundey was doing. Harry wasn't ignorant to the plight of preserving Sydney's history. In fact, he went on to restore and incorporate the heritage features of many of the buildings he bought years later. Harry's daughter, Orna, even published a book detailing the painstaking processes Meriton undertook to preserve the history of buildings while incorporating modern architectural elements.

"There had to be compromise," Harry says. "Australia needed more housing, especially for the migrants coming into the country."

Indeed, despite the ensuing property crash, the demand for housing was immense, with a record intake of 683,000 migrants into Australia between 1968 and 1972.

"The city then was being suffocated by a blanket of green bans, and building in the city was being all but quashed. It wasn't sustainable," Harry says.

"We did our part. We incorporated and restored the heritage elements of buildings we bought. I was proud of what we did, and it was very satisfying to see the old and new integrated so beautifully."

Harry was back in the black, but other developers were still going bust. He couldn't resist the temptation to swoop in and pick up the remains of their sites for bottom-dollar prices. He was confident that the green bans would eventually be lifted. He was thinking like his father.

As soon as the union organisers realised Meriton worked differently to other developers, and that Harry wasn't going to be accountable to them, it was on.

Mundey didn't get much of a run. There was hardly any new

development happening anywhere around Sydney, and by 1975, the developers had had enough of him. With green bans on everything, their industry was all but dead. The builders started flooding the Melbourne-based BLF national office – led by Norm Gallagher – with money, hoping it would push Mundey out. It did the job. The NSW State Government stepped in and de-registered the NSW branch of the BLF. Mundey found himself back on the tools as a labourer.

"Be careful what you wish for because we went from the frying pan into the fire!" Harry says.

While there were no longer the green bans to disrupt plans, the national BLF was even more aggressive than the NSW branch and expected to be able to dictate which trades and workers could be hired and fired. The mere arrogance of it made Harry want to fight them even more. He wasn't going to let the BLF tell him how to run his sites or his business. Harry was the boss, end of story!

By then, Paul Appleby had moved up the ranks and was Meriton construction manager and head of industrial relations. He wasn't expecting collaboration from the unions, but he wasn't expecting sabotage either.

"They'd already sent so many other developers to the wall, so we decided our best plan of attack was to keep the unions off our sites," Appleby says.

"The unions were constantly trying to get on site to make the workers feel disenchanted with their working conditions. I overheard one of our blokes say to them one day when they snuck on site that he was, 'happy as a pig in shit' and 'didn't want to change a thing'.

"We had the workers on our side, which was a huge thing," he says.

There was comfort in working for Meriton. The workers were generally happy, they could sleep at night knowing they could support their families, and they had no intention of letting the unions cause job instability. Having witnessed the unions behaving badly on Meriton sites, the workers weren't interested in joining the unions themselves. They were getting paid every week and that wasn't always the case elsewhere. They liked the fact Harry got off his butt and came to the sites, and even in the toughest of times and circumstances he would crack a few jokes and give them confidence that everything was going to be okay.

The workers just had to keep up a high level of workmanship and they would be carried from one project to the next. They didn't need the unions; they were secure in their own Meriton bubble.

It was a big deal to Harry. He felt he had a responsibility to all his workers and their families to keep food on the table. He knew they were depending on him, and he had genuine concern for them.

"Harry treated us all like family," Ken McDonald says. "He came to engagements, weddings and christenings. He wanted to be a part of our lives, know our families. That affection for all his staff was why they stood behind Meriton during the worst time with the unions.

"He had our backs, and we had his. It was an unusual and unique relationship to have a boss in Harry's position care so much. It's why we survived.

"I don't know of a time when there hasn't been a McDonald working at Meriton and he knew most of them before they got there. He puts his people first," Ken says.

Harry made sure he headed out to the sites nearly every day – something he still does to this day. Obviously, he had a broader business to run and couldn't be around all day, so he left the day-to-day running of the sites to Ken McDonald and Paul Appleby. They couldn't always be on all the sites at the same time either, so they arranged with the foreman on each site to let them know if the unions came around.

It infuriated the unions that Harry had none of their members on site because they had no control when they couldn't get their members in. There were pickets every day at Harry's sites; they did whatever they could to stop work. They wanted to show Harry who was boss and thought that if they disrupted work on his sites, it would force him to let them in to control the workers. But Harry's workers didn't need the unions to control their every movement.

The unions didn't know Harry at all. Because of their frustration, their tactics became worse and worse, and the threat of violence was a daily occurrence. They were pissing Harry off! He never considered giving in, and he always stood up to them.

Until 1978, Harry had never considered having an in-house architect. He always used outside drafting companies. With the number of projects increasing every day, he decided it was time to bring an architect on board. He gave the job to a young, fairly green Jewish architect called Peter Spira.

Peter was a junior architect for a company in Milsons Point, but they were starting to run out of work, so he was casually looking around for another job. He looked in the paper and saw the role advertised at Meriton. Not only the role but the salary as well.

"I was earning $20,000 a year as a junior partner, which was the industry norm at the time, and this role was offering $50,000 a year. It was huge money in those days," Peter says.

"The advertisement requested you apply in writing. I didn't have a resume, but I said to my wife, Suzie, that I was going to send a letter detailing my experience.

"I expected to hear nothing further, but I was called in for an interview."

Peter thought it was going to be a waste of time because there were so many architects looking for work who had a lot more experience than him. He arrived at the office and saw two other architects waiting to be interviewed. He went through the process, saw the construction manager, and showed him the drawings of what he'd been working on (all architectural plans were hand-drawn at the time).

"As I was showing him my portfolio, this guy walks in behind me. I was surprised to see he had bare feet. He looked over my shoulder and asked what the drawings were," Peter says.

"I told him they were designs from my current company, and he said, 'One-bedders are no good, you schmuck.' I said to him that I was no schmuck, and this is what the client wanted."

Peter was surprised when he asked who that 'rude man' was, and he was told it was the boss, Harry Triguboff. Peter, after his interview, was sure that he wouldn't be considered for the role. He was therefore surprised when it was offered to him. He was excited about the opportunity, but he would also more than double his salary overnight. Peter was told that Harry liked the fact he knew what a 'schmuck' was. For those who are none the wiser, *schmuck* is Yiddish for 'stupid prick'.

"What I did should've been more important, but he liked that I was Jewish," Peter says.

"People warned me about his temper, but I had nothing to lose. I was thinking of starting my own practice anyhow."

Peter was set up in an office and he started designing some blocks of units. Ken McDonald went to his office one day to see what he was drawing.

"I looked at his designs and told him to stop," Ken says.

"I told him, 'It looks good, but Harry won't pay the money for it. You need to get used to the Meriton way. Nothing fancy. Our buildings need to be affordable.'"

It didn't take Peter long to get on board with the Meriton way of thinking. He enjoyed working at Meriton immensely and was given responsibilities he'd never had before. He loved that with Harry you got to do a bit of everything. He clearly did it well because he became Harry's second-in-charge for the next 35 years.

Peter remembers being dragged into Meriton's war with the unions at a building site at 204 Victoria Street, Potts Point. It taught him quickly why Meriton was really the only one beating the unions. The property in

Union Troubles

Victoria Street was so controversial, it had the media all over it. It was a black hole for almost a decade while it changed hands constantly from one developer to the next. Juanita Nielsen, publisher of the newspaper *Now*, which campaigned for local causes, disappeared one day from her office, next door at 202 Victoria Street, and was never seen again.

Six years before Harry bought the site, property developer Frank Theeman had wanted to bulldoze a large section of Victoria Street and replace it with an enormous high-rise.

Nielsen didn't like it and constantly called for a green ban in her newspaper. The squatters and unionists blocked Theeman's way, and he responded with violence. He was blamed for the disappearance and suspected murder of Nielsen.

After Theeman gave up on the site, Home Units Australia bought it but went bankrupt while waiting for the green ban to be lifted. It was picked up by a company called Rosemount Investments, partly owned by a prominent businessman at the time, Peter Abeles. He had migrated to Australia at the same time as Harry and became a transportation magnate, managing director of Ansett, and later dabbled in property as well.

Peter (later to become Sir Peter Abeles) engaged in much unsuccessful squabbling with the city council, and Harry bought the property from him. He was surprised when he was told that Rosemount was "shit-scared" of developing next to Nielsen's old business.

"I wasn't worried," Harry says. "I'd heard all the stories and all I knew was that none of it involved me.

"All I was interested in was that the green ban was going to be lifted so I was able to build. My plans had been approved by council, so we were up and running."

All that achieved was to alert the unions of what Harry was doing and, of course, they came sniffing around again. And in force. In an election in the 1980s an alliance of the ALP and anti-developer independents had won back control of the City of Sydney Council.

After Harry started building on the site, the council went to court to try to revoke the approval, or at least cut the size of what he intended to build, as they wanted to preserve the Victoria Street landscape.

Peter Spira remembers one rally after another with protestors and the community carrying placards shouting things like, 'No blonde-brick, high-rise cubes here' and, 'We're not wild about you Harry. Boff off'. They were very vocal about not wanting high-rise apartments in their neighbourhood.

Paul Appleby would address the rallies, and then he and Peter would speak to the media.

The unions kept up the pressure. They included the Federated Engine Drivers' and Firemen's Association (FEDFA) crane drivers and the United Plumbers Union. They started shaking the fence around the Meriton site and they started throwing bricks over the hoarding towards the workers inside.

What struck Peter most was that the workers on site didn't even think about stopping work. They knew who their boss was, and it wasn't the unions. When the unions threw bricks at them, they threw them right back. They didn't care who was watching.

Peter realised then that Harry's model of cultivating his own loyal workers was different to any other property developer. More importantly, he didn't run scared. He would walk past the pickets, head held high, and fight side by side with his workers. He didn't just sit behind his desk and let everyone else do the dirty work – he got involved.

"The workers knew that if they kept Harry going, he would keep them going," Peter says.

"The more the unions threatened blacklisting our trades and workers from other sites, the more the workers didn't care. They didn't need the other sites; Meriton had plenty.

"No-one else had the building model where an army of contractors worked for, and were loyal to, one builder. It was unique."

One of the most dangerous situations the unions put Meriton in, according to Paul Appleby, was when the BLF came to one of their sites in Parramatta.

"They came under the guise that they were worried about the mobile crane we were using because it didn't go to the top of the building," Appleby says.

"They were worried that some materials had to be hauled up the last floor by hand. The bricklayers had gone to scaffold high. It takes a while for the mortar to set and these mongrels, about eight of these gorillas, came on to the job, but I didn't see them arrive.

"They ran up and pushed the bricks off the building. I had plasterers right under them on a hoist. Fortunately, the hoist had mesh, because Harry had insisted on it, and they weren't hurt. They could have been killed, and to this day I cannot understand what they were thinking.

"I saw red and decided it was the last time the unions were ever going to come on to any of our sites," Appleby says.

As payback, the BLF then mounted a picket across the driveway, to stop brick and cement deliveries.

That is about the time Appleby went and ordered a pump-action shotgun. Back then you could have a loaded gun without a licence on private property and, although Appleby had a licence, he still couldn't have a loaded gun in a public place.

"Now we were well and truly back on the radar with the unions, and they even took an interest in our smaller projects," Appleby says.

"We were building some townhouses in Annandale, and the BLF insisted that the site was contaminated with asbestos from the factory that'd just been demolished.

"I was able to prove it'd been removed and had been certified as clean by the authorities.

"Because we'd done everything by the book and made them look like idiots, I knew there was going to be payback, yet again. I was just waiting to see what form that would take."

It wasn't long before Appleby caught the unions kicking down safety barriers on one of his sites.

"What they didn't know was that I was taking photos of them kicking down the barriers. I then took photos of them taking photos of the knocked-down barriers. They wanted to use it as 'evidence' that we didn't have the appropriate safety barriers in place so they could shut us down," Appleby says.

"When they showed their photos to the authorities, I countered and showed my photos to the authorities, and I became even more of a target. Of course, they failed to have us closed down."

Appleby also put a listening device on his phone, and he recorded one of the union bosses threatening him. He told Appleby he was coming to his site with his men at 9am the next morning to "break every bone in my body".

After the conversation, Appleby immediately went to the Balmain Police Station and gave the sergeant on duty an overview of the ongoing issues, and he told him about the conversation in regard to his demise the following day.

He told the sergeant he had a loaded shotgun, and the first man from the unions to step foot on his site, he would shoot in the knees. He explained that his Meriton site was private property, and any response to violence on private property would be considered self-defence.

The next morning, Appleby put the loaded gun in the boot of his Peugeot, and rather than park his car on the street, he drove on to the site and parked it on private property.

According to Appleby, at 9.05am, four cars turned up and about 12 union thugs jumped out brandishing scaffolding spanners; nasty tools with a box-shaped head on one end of a shaft. They could certainly do the job of breaking every bone in your body, as they had promised Appleby.

"The foreman asked me what we were going to do. I told him to start walking backwards to my car. I opened the boot of my Peugeot, pulled out my gun and yelled to them that, 'the first person to walk through the gate will get shot in the knees'," Appleby says.

"The union boss laughed. Nervously.

"Right then, a police paddy wagon turned up and four policemen got out as well as the sergeant I'd spoken to the night before.

"They confronted the men at the gate and told them they should leave quietly otherwise it would end badly for them. They were happy to smash their kneecaps as well! The men hesitated momentarily and left."

The police waited for them to go, and then the sergeant put out his hand and told Appleby that he would no longer need the gun. Appleby handed it over. The unions took Appleby to the NSW Industrial Commission and complained he had threatened them with a gun.

It was pure coincidence that Appleby's wife at the time, Heather, was a judge's associate, and she used to work for the commissioner who was running the court case. He allowed Appleby to play the tape of him being threatened. After hearing the threats, the judge banned the unions from "going to any of Mr Appleby's sites for a month".

Appleby didn't only get involved in the battles on Meriton sites, he also got involved in the union battles of other companies that supplied Meriton. He tells the story of being involved in a battle at the kilns in Horsley Park in Sydney's southwest. The Brick Movers Association and the Transport Workers Union had blockaded the Brickworks Ltd site.

The brick movers were opposed to a plan to replace their smaller trucks with larger trucks. It would diminish the need for truckies. As the stand-off dragged on, building sites across Sydney ran out of bricks. That meant more delays and a very pissed-off boss! But Harry was all about solutions.

Harry and Appleby arranged a convoy of about half-a-dozen trucks to break the blockade. Appleby remembers his ute was right out the front as he edged through the picket line of unionists.

"I had a big bumper bar. I kept bumping them out of the way," Appleby says.

"They kept trying to jump on the ute. There was nowhere to jump on, no running boards. I kept swerving one way to the other, shaking them off like flies. If they got hurt, it was their fault. I returned with two pallets of bricks on the rear tray."

Not long after that, Harry took Appleby off the front line. His contracts manager had died suddenly, so he put Appleby in that position. Ken McDonald took over as construction manager and industrial relations manager.

For years Ken had witnessed the unions doing everything to bring Meriton down. Most of it wasn't legal, especially when they took a contract out on him to have him killed. He says the death threats against him and his family were a daily occurrence.

On meeting Ken, he comes across as a little like Irish actor Liam Neeson – although Ken is Scottish. He has the same smooth, calm tone to his voice as Neeson and he has the whole 'don't screw with me' attitude. He would definitely make those contemplating violence think twice. Even Ken's wife, Jean, says that at no time was she concerned about the death threats they were getting at home because she knew Ken wouldn't let anything happen to them.

"I never felt unsafe," Jean says. "Ken was never going to let anything happen to me or the kids. He was always our protector."

Ken says that Harry didn't even flinch around the unions. They would hurl abuse at him as he walked past the pickets, and he would get right in their faces and share a few choice words with them as well.

"We were sick of the disruption and destruction on our sites. I had fights with them like you wouldn't believe," Ken says.

"Harry had a mind of steel, and he was the gutsiest guy I've ever met. He wasn't fazed by anything. The unions didn't scare him at all. He employed bouncers from Kings Cross to protect his family, and he pushed on."

Ken's biggest challenge was with crane drivers at Museum Towers in Castlereagh Street, where the new Meriton offices were going to be below a residential tower.

"The tower cranes were the responsibility of The Lofty Crane Drivers (Lofties) who sat within the FEDFA," Ken says.

"The tower cranes were their babies, and they did all the dangerous work of carrying materials up high-rise buildings. You could not build higher than 10 levels without the Lofties."

When Harry and Ken decided to hire the Lofties, it was always going to be a risk. The crane was set up, and FEDFA, as was the usual practice, decided which of its members would do the job and which dogmen would work on it. Dogmen are responsible for slinging loads and directing the crane operator when their lift is out of view, either by radio communications, whistles and/or hand signals.

Harry heard, yet again, there was going to be trouble and so, fed up, he called the crane driver into his office and sacked him.

"That was unheard of at the time," Harry says.

"In the heat of the moment I didn't think about what was going to happen next. There was no way to build the tower without a crane.

"On suburban jobs we used mobile cranes mounted on trucks and we could park them outside the building on the street, so we didn't need the Lofties. You couldn't do that in the middle of the city. Tower cranes sit inside the site so there were no issues.

"We stayed away from the unions for a few days while we tried to come up with a solution. Ken saw there was a small vacant block of land behind the Museum Towers' site, so we hired it, for no small price, and put a non-union crane truck from Queensland on the site," he says.

It was of no surprise when the unions retaliated again.

"It was just another day and another threat, but we were well used to that by then," Ken says.

"Harry was such a tough, strong example to the men on site, and every time we had problems the men always stood behind us. It was safety in numbers.

"All the fighting from our men was contained to the unions. There was never any fighting in the Meriton family. They used to fool around pretending to have fisticuffs with each other in mock indignation, but it was all in fun. They were protective of their work home and everyone got on great.

"Nobody had ever taken on the Lofties like that. There was a war going on but, eventually, after outwitting the unions time and time again, Harry agreed to have one Lofty member on site to calm the storm and get back to the business of building. He kept his mobile crane and completed the build in record time."

In 1985 the building unions were a mess in Melbourne. BLF General Secretary Norm Gallagher was in jail. He had accepted cheap home renovations as bribes, but he was released a short time later. Then, in 1986, the federal Labor Government of former union boss Bob Hawke de-registered the BLF, permanently.

Harry had almost singlehandedly dismantled the BLF and, in doing so, did the industry a huge favour. He had shown the union to be home to fools and thugs, but some positives came out of it too. It cemented what is the methodology that remains at Meriton today: prove your ability, move up in the ranks, be loyal and love what you do. Perhaps that's not so much a methodology, but it's what Harry expects. Plenty have met those expectations and remained at Meriton for years – some for the whole life of Meriton. There was never any question of who had the final say. It was the law, according to Harry.

Harry at the office, 1970s.

Meriton building sites, 1970s.

SIX

FIGHT OR FLIGHT

The mid-1970s would prove to be the most challenging years for Harry, both professionally and personally. Harry's parents had died, and he missed, by a whisker, losing the two greatest loves of his life – his business and his daughters. The pain from the deaths of his parents was still raw, and now the rest of his world was being threatened too.

It all came about because Harry hadn't read the fine print on two major contracts. One pertained to the millions he borrowed to fund his expansion, and the other pertained to his marriage. Harry thought both contracts were rock solid, but they both fell apart at around the same time.

First National City Bank of New York would call in their multimillion-dollar loan, and Hana would file for divorce – with most of Harry's assets in her name. She cited infidelity and Harry was shocked that his odd indiscretion gave her legitimate reason to dissolve their marriage. Fine print, Harry.

Harry did what only Harry could do: he bunkered down, planned his attack and fought both wars head on. It was fight or flight, and in neither situation was the latter an option.

Harry was only too aware that First National City Bank of New York could ruin him, but so could Hana. It was tricky that most of Harry's assets were in her name. At the same time, others wondered *why* they were in Hana's name.

"Things were complicated at the time," Harry says. "Along with everything else going on, my life was constantly being threatened by the unions.

"If anything happened to me, I wanted to know the family would be financially secure, especially if there was going to be any kind of argy-bargy with the banks over the distribution of my wealth."

What surprised Harry the most is that Hana wanted to go back to Israel and threatened to take the girls with her.

Hana not only put Harry through the emotional wringer, but she dragged him through the courts until a settlement was reached that was acceptable to her. And a substantial settlement it was. Hana ended up with their beautiful family home in Bellevue Hill, totally unencumbered, and a generous alimony. Part of the deal was that Hana wouldn't take the girls out of Australia.

Harry had hoped that by ensuring Hana's financial independence she would stay in Australia. He believed the girls still needed their mother, but not long after the settlement, Hana lost the house in a failed business venture. She left the girls with Harry and went back to Israel.

"Harry had the weight of the world on his shoulders at that time," Ken McDonald says. "I had nothing but respect. The way his mind worked was extraordinary. It was exhausting keeping up with his thought processes. Getting custody of the girls was a huge win. One down, one to go."

Both Ken McDonald and Paul Appleby tell a similar story of that time. They agree it took Harry a little time to learn to juggle the responsibilities of being a single father while running an empire.

"No matter your seniority at Meriton, everyone chipped in and helped with the girls," Ken says.

"I had four kids, a dedicated wife and extended family I had brought out to Australia from Scotland. I had all the help in the world, so I couldn't imagine raising two early-teenage girls on my own with little family support.

"But the girls were fabulous. They just went with the flow. Even at that young age, they had their dad pegged, well, as much as that is possible. They knew they were top of the pecking order, but they also knew, and understood, that their father was obsessed with his business.

"When Harry started dating, and the women in his life stepped up to help out, it was good for the girls to have a female influence. They spent a lot of time hanging around with us blokes," Ken says with a laugh.

It's interesting to note that neither of the girls remember much about any of Harry's girlfriends being around. They only remember the grouchy country housekeeper and the guys from Meriton.

"They lasted longer than any of the girlfriends," Sharon jokes. "Until Rhonda, of course!"

It was around that time that the notion of Meriton being one big family really took hold.

According to those working at Meriton at the time, the trust was such within the company that there was a commonplace assertion that 'what was Harry's was ours, and vice versa'. Harry and the girls became extended members of many of the Meriton families. They were always included in all events. Harry was always front and centre, having accepted everyone as his extended family. When he fought for Meriton, he fought for his family, all of them. He felt responsible for their livelihoods. They were top of mind when he fought to survive.

When Harry had first started Meriton in 1963, he would build a block of units and sell the entire building to one buyer. The introduction of strata title in 1961 didn't immediately change this. However, he could see the enormous benefits of being able to sell apartments to individual buyers.

Harry, before jumping into this strategy, watched and waited. He let someone else be the guinea pig for the problems that arose following the introduction of new legislation, and when Harry did embrace strata, he never went back.

He kept all the bells and whistles to a minimum in his buildings, allowing people who were never able to buy pre-Meriton to invest in property. For many years, Harry advertised Meriton as offering an 'affordable' option, while filling a need in the market. He became champion to those who never thought they would own their own home, and he was the master of keeping the prices down while still turning a profit.

Harry may have lost some aesthetic impact by keeping the costs low, but he loved that he was providing a home to those who might otherwise never have been able to afford one. He was particularly proud of making it possible for women to embrace apartment living. Single women, no less.

Harry was way before his time in his beliefs that women should be given the same rights as men when it came to owning property. In fact, he thought women should be given the same rights with everything, full stop.

"It was ridiculous," Harry says. "These strong women should need a husband to tell them what to do? What? They can't think for themselves or support themselves? It was a travesty.

"They were shamed for being alone but wanting a place to call home. I advocated for them and made it happen. If the banks wouldn't loan them the money, I would.

"I was very proud of that," he says.

The result of creating this whole new market of affordable housing is that it increased demand.

In 1960, multi-unit dwellings by the private sector represented 30 per cent of total dwellings; this increased to 42 per cent by 1966–67, and then to 51 per cent in 1969–70. With the increase in demand for vertical housing, there was a reduced supply of land for those who still wanted the freestanding house on the quarter-acre block in suburbia. The number of lots registered with the Registrar General of NSW declined from 36,120 in 1964 to 29,485 in 1967.

Harry's brainchild made home ownership possible, not only for the increasing Australian population but also for immigrants pouring into the country. When the biggest property boom of all time was in full swing in the late 1960s, Harry could claim partial responsibility with his spate of high-density developments.

What did irritate Harry was that others jumped on the bandwagon. Securing sites became more competitive, and expansion became more difficult.

In 1969, Harry decided to shake things up. It was time for him to play at the big end of town, so he floated Meriton on the Australian Securities Exchange (ASX). He hoped it would open more doors to access money so he could better fund his expansion.

Harry wanted to keep building at all costs, and that meant he needed money. But the banks were conservative with their lending, the cost of land and property was rising like never before, and what the banks were giving him wasn't helping him grow exponentially. Harry was geared for having numerous buildings on the go at the same time, and he hated that his ambitions were being curbed by the system. He desperately needed access to more funds.

Around the same time as Harry floated Meriton, a company called Industrial Acceptance Corporation (IAC) – known only for the hire purchase of cars – suddenly became the latest source of funds for entrepreneurs. All the big hitters, including Harry, jumped on board.

Alan Bond's Bond Corp, along with other big property companies at the time, including Mainline and Home Units Australia, filled their coffers with the available cash.

"By then, everyone knew where IAC was getting its money," Harry says. "It was coming from a huge bank in the United States called First National City Bank of New York, which later became the more recognisable Citibank. The Americans saw an opportunity with IAC and grabbed it. IAC was the only way to push into the Australian banking system, which at the time prevented foreigners from buying Australian banks.

"As a non-banking institution, they weren't bound by the Reserve Bank regulations so had no limit on their lending capacity," he says.

Despite the government's efforts to curb demand, the need for housing funds was growing. Funds were sought from sources other than banks, notably from the permanent building societies, which increased their housing loans dramatically in this period. In early 1973 there was a flurry of activity in almost every segment of the Sydney property market. Demand for land was intense in both the inner-city and fringe suburbs.

The property boom attracted a stream of new entrants to the development industry. For example, Leighton Holdings, traditionally a civil engineering and construction company, entered the fray. Then, in July 1973, the CSR company acquired 50 per cent of Sydney developer Home Units Australia for $5 million.

April and May 1973 marked the peak of the property boom. A fever, spreading from Sydney through to south-east Queensland, gripped the east coast of Australia. The connections between the Sydney and Queensland markets were very close, with the same agents financing activity in both areas.

The Queensland market was even more speculative than that of Sydney, and it was estimated that 40 per cent of the sales were to overseas buyers from Papua New Guinea, China and Britain.

In November 1973, after three years operating as a public company, Harry decided to privatise Meriton again. The reasons he'd floated his company were null and void and he didn't understand why he should share his profits. In all his meetings with IAC they assured him that "as long as you have the bricks, we can provide the funds". The stock exchange was worthless to him now because he didn't need it to open doors for him. He borrowed a total of $1.2 million – mostly from ANZ – to buy back the outstanding 35 per cent in his company.

"I'd wanted to shake things up by floating the company, and now I wanted to shake things up by buying it back," Harry says.

"I told the shareholders the truth. The market was changing and the profits from 1973 had dropped about 40 per cent. I was giving them a chance to get out.

"I'd managed to accumulate a lot of sites by then, but because of the change in the market, I decided we should retain them long term. Short term, the shareholders wouldn't enjoy any profits.

"The market price for Meriton shares was $2.30 at the time. I offered $3.05 a share. I wanted to make sure I was offering a price too good to refuse.

"They all took it, and everybody made money. I now had full control of my company and its $18 million balance sheet. It was happy days." He smiles.

So, what could possibly go wrong?

Well, they do say bad things come in threes. In 1974 the property market crashed, 'green bans' were introduced on heritage-sensitive land and buildings, and the First National City Bank of New York called in loans for hundreds of millions of dollars. That year, 1974, was Harry's 'annus horribilis'.

Every property company was geared to the rafters and required a large cashflow to maintain profitability. Cashflow came by way of sales. Once money tightened, sales were harder to close. While the number of houses put up for auction increased by 18 per cent in October 1973, the auction clearance rate was only 39 per cent. As money conditions tightened, reserve prices were not often realised. The home-unit market became particularly vulnerable.

In February 1974, the chairman of the Australian Institute of Urban

Studies, Professor Gates, suggested that land prices in Brisbane could fall by as much as 50 per cent in the following six months, which would have a flow-on effect to the Sydney market. This prediction evoked angry responses from developers and others.

"Even in the direst of times, Harry was a genius," Ken McDonald says. "If anyone could dig themselves out of near destruction, it was Harry. And dig he did. He just kept building.

"He was positive that was the right thing to do, but he still had plans in place if it was the wrong move."

As it turned out, it was the right move. With everyone going bust around him, Harry continued to sell. His price point still attracted investors and migrants. If he couldn't sell his apartments, he had been ready to lease them. He still needed cashflow to service his existing loans, but as long as everything continued down the same path, he would be fine. The problem was, every path had its puddle.

While Harry was keeping his head above water, everyone else was defaulting on their loans. All the small and large developers, like Mainline and Home Units Australia, were in trouble. Even Alan Bond was drowning, and it wasn't long before IAC was also in trouble.

The first major collapse was that of Mainline, funded by IAC, which specialised in the development of Sydney office buildings. Then the crisis spread out into the residential market. Two well-known companies, Cambridge Credit and Home Units Australia, hit the wall. IAC had funded both.

Meriton continued to keep the wolves from the door, and Harry was meeting all his financial commitments. Even the most senior banking executives would admit that when it came to figures, Harry was not only clever, he was a genius. He could work out to the last cent exactly how much he could borrow, how much he could afford to pay back over time, and how much he needed to build to make that happen. He could stack all that up in his head, along with stacking up the corresponding number of bricks he needed for each project. Figures were his forte; he left the remaining legalities to his lawyers.

Harry had trusted IAC so much that he'd used their lawyers. He felt like they were a partner of sorts in his expansion.

"I don't think my trust was misplaced," Harry says.

"To be fair, I don't think IAC had even read the fine print. The documents came from the head lender, which was First National City Bank, and every borrower missed the clause that spelt certain ruination – First National could call in its loans *at any time and demand payment in full*. And that is exactly what happened," he says.

Property companies, in particular, fell like flies. Shares in Cambridge Credit plunged overnight in 1974, signalling the most sensational collapse in Australian history. Parkes Development also went into liquidation, spectacularly owing $66 million.

Even though Meriton's balance sheet was more conservative, going from $6 million in 1970 to $18 million in 1973, no amount of affordable housing was going to be able to pay that back in one hit.

The boom had ended in a spectacular collapse that saw the demise of the largest development companies, construction companies and financial institutions. Most were financed by IAC.

The First National City Bank of New York became concerned about the solvency of its Australian partner, IAC. Although First National City Bank didn't become Citibank until 1976, we have taken the liberty of using the shortened version of the bank's name henceforth. It is still the same identity but less long-winded for our reader!

In July 1974, the Americans sent over their global chief executive, Walter Wriston, for a week to work out what was going on. Wriston was horrified to realise that his bank had loaned $70 million to a company in which they only owned a minority stake, and over which they had little control.

Wriston convinced the then Australian chairman of IAC, Bill Edmends, to step aside. A new team, led by an American from Singapore called Richard Kelly, stepped in and, in September 1974, decided to take 'firm' measures, first against Alan Bond. Then they put Harry, who had been lent money by Edmends, on their hitlist.

IAC was insolvent. Not only did Citibank stop lending, but it also demanded immediate payment of its existing loans.

Paul Appleby says that he recalls tense negotiations when bank executives turned up at the Meriton offices to talk to Harry and his chief accountant, Bernard Jacoby. "There was a lot of screaming!"

"The Yanks came to me and told me I was broke. I yelled at them that yesterday they thought I was a genius and they couldn't lend me enough money. Deadpan, they responded: 'The document says you have to pay us on demand. Now we demand you pay. It's that simple!'"

Harry saw their demands as anything but simple, but he was quick to make a key decision, which he says defined his career. He could never have done what he did had he still been a public company answering to shareholders.

"I decided to trade out of my troubles and repay them," Harry says. "I could have extracted the cash I had and handed the business over to them, but I wasn't going to do that. That's what made me different to everyone else.

"Even my friend Tommy Gluck went down that road, took the cash and headed to the US. I could never understand the logic of them wanting to send me broke, so I was going to stay and pay. They didn't even consider I might do that.

"All the others had already gone down like the *Titanic*. I was going to be the survivor."

Harry dealt with the practicalities first. He told Citibank that all his buildings were only half-finished. He reminded them that the property market in Australia was going through the worst crash of all time, and it would be next to impossible to sell half-finished buildings.

"If you think you can complete my buildings and sell them without me, then good luck to you," Harry told them at the time.

Harry then found his own loophole and his own fine print. Paul

Appleby says that what Harry did next was very clever.

"To buy time, Harry had exaggerated a little about where construction on his buildings sat," Appleby says.

"The buildings were nothing like half-finished, but Harry realised there was a loophole in the government ordinances. They said that once certain minor works were performed on a building site, it would be classed as 'substantially commenced'.

"So, Harry sent me out to perform these works. I did minor works including laying a foundation for a garage and erecting a small part of a wall. It only needed to be a couple of metres high to be compliant," he says.

Appleby performed this work on 25 sites in Liverpool, Chatswood and Fairfield.

"I decided I would double down," Harry says. "I turned to ANZ, where I had some of my personal wealth, and borrowed from them to pay to finish the buildings."

Remember, Harry is brilliant with figures and finance. What happened next was totally deliberate on his part. He used all his genius to totally bamboozle Citibank into submission. The greatest financial minds at Citibank couldn't keep up with him.

"Just days before Citibank exercised its lien over Meriton and obtained a court-ordered lien over my properties, I gave ANZ direct mortgages over the same properties," Harry says.

A court-ordered lien is the legal right of a creditor to sell collateral property of a debtor who fails to meet the obligations of a loan contract. Because Harry took out mortgages on the properties through ANZ, he was therefore no longer defaulting on them, making the lien null and void.

"Citibank was stopped dead in its tracks," Harry says. "I told Citibank the properties were no longer covered by the lien they'd obtained, so I opened the sites and started building again.

"Handing the mortgages to ANZ was a bit of trickery. I could have started building again with my own purse, but I was aiming to baffle and confuse Citibank to buy myself time," he says.

Harry was running back and forth between ANZ and Citibank faster than either could follow. (It's okay if you can't keep up either – it's not supposed to be easy to follow!) It was a tactic by Harry that was fully his intention. Meriton was still operating, and Harry was working out a plan of attack to pay back ANZ and Citibank while totally confusing both.

"I set up a 'debt barometer'," Harry says. "It was a large chart like a thermometer. Outstanding debts were at the top, starting at $30 million, with a calendar listing all the days loan repayments were due to ANZ and Citibank.

"Expenses were added from each department, and then as properties settled, they would be recorded against the outgoings. A new barometer would go up each month, and it effectively recorded the debt coming down. It was basic, but more than did the job.

"It showed every day how I came down in my debt," Harry says. "I never wanted to shun my responsibilities to the banks, and that's why I was the only one to survive. I didn't let them send me broke. I continued to come up with new ways to raise finance so I could get rid of the bank debt quicker.

"I could be very convincing. I even talked the gas company into lending me money by promising to install gas heating and cooking in my apartments."

Also, Harry revisited his Plan B. Anything he couldn't sell he rented out to give him cashflow. He swears that saw him through the crisis. By 1976, Harry had paid back much of his debt.

That same year, Citibank sent in a new manager from the US. His name was Glen Moreno, and he had the job of getting things back in order quickly.

"When I knew the boss from the States was coming to see me, I was ready for a fight," Harry says. "But fighting was the last thing on his mind.

"He was talking to me with admiration and respect about what I'd done to meet my obligations to the bank. He then offered to waive my remaining $2 million debt with the bank in recognition of my excellent record of repayment.

"It was the most surprising gift I had ever received and a moment I will never forget.

"I had survived, I had my girls, and I was really back in business."

Even the wizards in corporate finance were shaking their heads. They couldn't work out how Harry had pulled it off.

He had become the poster boy for the popular saying, 'What doesn't kill you, makes you stronger', meaning a person who shows enormous resilience to overcome adversity. That was Harry. He had come out the other side, not only stronger but fiercer too.

With the difficult 1970s behind him, Harry was well and truly back in the game, debt free. He started the new '80s decade by marrying Rhonda, who loved the Gold Coast. That same year, Harry started his development expansion into Queensland by buying his first site on the Gold Coast.

Brochure for O'Brien Towers, Bondi, 1971. *Harry at his desk.*

Advertisement for Kooringa Gardens, Chatswood, 1976.

Harry & Rhonda on their wedding day, 1980.

SEVEN

THE EARLY YEARS IN QUEENSLAND

Until 1980, everything Harry built was in Sydney. He had holidayed on Queensland's Gold Coast for many years with the family but when Harry and Rhonda married in 1980, they both decided they should make the Gold Coast their second home. That being the case, Harry wasn't going to sit there and twiddle his thumbs.

Also, that year, a journalist by the name of Quentin Tod moved to the Gold Coast, where he started writing the business pages of the *Gold Coast Bulletin*, which included the editorial production of the Saturday real estate lift-out. Quentin continues to write for the *Bulletin* and has been friends with Harry for more than 30 years. That, of course, makes him the best person to write about Harry's life in Queensland.

Over to you, Quentin!

The Gold Coast, with a sometimes volatile property market that has brought many a developer undone, has been a favourite for Harry.

The tourism haven has been known for decades for seven-year property cycles, where the market can surge and then tumble, but Harry has never attempted to ride those cycles.

"For me, the cycle is forever upward," he says.

The word 'upward' summarises the veteran developer's various forays in the region. By 2023 the Meriton founder had completed 32 buildings,

The Early Years in Queensland

in all housing more than 3,600 apartments. He had also reached for the sky, in 2022 delivering a 261-metre tower that was the tallest in the state.

In 1956, a decade before Harry's arrival, the Gold Coast's tallest building had been completed and opened by then Queensland Premier Vince Gair. Lennon's Broadbeach Hotel sat virtually in the middle of nowhere – there were few houses within 1.5 kilometres. It sat on land previously mined for mineral sands, and when it opened and its grounds were landscaped, it was seen as an oasis in the desert.

Surfers Paradise soon became a holiday destination for visitors on family road trips, and this spawned a flurry of motel development. At one point there were around 140 motels fronting the Gold Coast Highway, many touting TV and air-conditioning to draw in business. As time went on, the land on which the motels sat was targeted by developers, and by 2023, motel numbers had been decimated.

In the early '60s, the Gold Coast was given a taste of the high life, literally. The first high-rise was built – a 10-floor tower in the heart of Surfers Paradise. Kinkabool remains standing today.

Harry first set foot in what was then an elongated oceanfront town in 1965, the same year that Meter Maids began strolling Surfers Paradise streets and 13 years after bikinis had first appeared on the beach. Harry arrived at a time of beer gardens and beer-belly contests.

Soon, Harry says, he and his family knew only one place to go for a holiday – the Gold Coast.

"We used to go for family holidays when the girls were little. Friends went too, and they stayed at the Chevron Hotel – very expensive. I was saving money to start the business, so we stayed at a cheaper place. We would go to visit our friends at the Chevron and swim there.

"After a few years, with the business going okay, we stayed at the Chevron too," he says.

The Chevron was the place to be and was built on an expansive site fronting the highway in central Surfers Paradise. It included a famous nightspot, the Skyline Cabaret, and a large indoors beer garden in which the décor included blue-carpeted ceilings. The Chevron, later owned by Greek investor Theo Morris, was demolished in the late 1980s, and the site today is home to three towers.

The Gold Coast remained a holiday spot for Harry, one where he could walk on the beach and dine out. The old saying, 'you can't keep a good man down' kicked in at the start of the '80s. After all, a person with a brain that never rests can't help but spot opportunities, even when that person is in relaxation mode.

Harry's good friend Tibor Balog ran the Dainford Group with partners Morven Dan and Michael Hershon. Dainford was a prolific developer which, in the '70s and '80s, built major Surfers towers such as Aquarius and Peninsula.

"Tibor and I were building a lot in Sydney, and we decided that he would go to Surfers and build, and I'd stay in Sydney and build. But then I decided I should diversify a bit and that I should also build on the Gold Coast," Harry says.

"Sydney was one type of building, and Surfers was another type. I liked the Gold Coast, I was going there, and I did nothing there. I was bored, so I built."

Years earlier, Harry had headed overseas with a friend for a look around.

"We stopped at Cancún in Mexico, and I saw all the apartments on the waterfront. I knew there was no reason why we couldn't do the same in Australia."

It makes sense then that Harry's first two Gold Coast towers were fronting water. The Nelson at Paradise Waters sat beside an inlet from the Nerang River, and Florida was on a riverside site on the southern side of Surfers Paradise.

Harry went to look at The Nelson site in 1980. "At the time I thought I was buying the land for stage two of the Atlantis project, but that land was on the other side of the road," Harry says.

The Nelson was 16 levels and had five retail areas at its base, while

Florida, which fronted the Gold Coast Highway, was 14 levels. They were being built at a time when the city was in the midst of high-rise fever. Then, in 1982, the apartment market hit the wall and a property slump began.

"I didn't make much, but I didn't lose either," Harry says.

"So, even though in those days I didn't buy land on the beachfront, I always had good positions, and I always found a lot of buyers. The problem was that those buyers didn't have money. The people on the Gold Coast in those days weren't well to do, but they all wanted to buy.

"The guys used to come to me and say things like, 'Harry, I like your unit and I'll buy it. I'll give you a block of land in Townsville as a deposit.' One chap said, 'Harry, I'll give you my boat and that's my deposit.' I said, 'I don't want your boat. I don't want anything. You want my money, and I'll organise it for you.' And so that's what I did.

"I saw the buyers' problems were money. I knew that my buildings were good value, so I thought I would give them vendor finance.

"If you talk to the builders from those days, they'll always tell you that I got to where I did because I gave the buyers finance, and none of the others [developers] could give finance to the buyers like I could. I borrowed money from the bank and gave the buyers that money."

Harry, when he'd first ventured into building on the Gold Coast, realised that because the Queensland planning rules were different to those in Sydney, he needed a lawyer 'on the ground'.

That lawyer was Gino Moro and, more than 40 years later, he was still handling Harry's property work in the city and is a friend of the Meriton founder.

They met in 1981 when Harry was undertaking The Nelson and, a year later, the Florida, when the market took a downturn.

Gino says Harry came to his office with a developer friend from California. "They sat down and Harry said he was having trouble moving apartments in the Florida building, the market looked bleak, and he needed to come up with a solution.

"His American friend said, 'Well, when you've got a building that's a lemon you treat it like a lemon and you paint it yellow.' Harry seemed to listen to this expert advice and, I must confess, I was rather relieved when he didn't take it. He came up with another solution for a changing market – if times were tough, buyers needed help, so he offered them finance and rental guarantees. Harry's solution worked – his apartments all sold."

Harry had retained the penthouse in The Nelson.

"At that time, I had probably the best house in Sydney. The apartment in The Nelson definitely wasn't the best in Surfers so I decided I should get a better apartment."

Harry took Rhonda to look at the penthouse in new Main Beach tower Silverpoint. The 32-floor tower, built in 1989, was developed by the Girvan Group in tandem with British and Japanese partners.

"Rhonda looked at it and she didn't want to look at anything else. All she wanted was this one."

The two-level apartment, bought for $2.6 million after previously being under contract for $4.1 million, spanned 900 square metres and had views in all directions – ideal for a fellow who always had an eagle eye out for development sites.

It didn't take long for that 'eye' to spot a property only 200 metres away from Silverpoint as the crow flies. It belonged to Gregory Motors and spanned more than 6,000 square metres in Woodroffe Avenue. Harry picked it up for $2.5 million and started a flurry of projects in Main Beach that saw eight towers built in little more than a decade.

Japanese companies, some of them not in the property business, had descended on the Gold Coast. An example was the SUN Group, an education business. It built a hotel topped with a revolving restaurant and also delivered a golf course, designed by Jack Nicklaus, called Lakelands. Both assets were later sold, and SUN headed home with a financial black eye that cost it more than $100 million.

The Early Years in Queensland

The Japanese retreat – in the wake of the country's economic bubble bursting in 1991 as a result of tumbling land and share prices – opened up new Main Beach opportunities for Harry.

Major sites had been amalgamated by the Japanese and grand plans had been in the pipeline – until that bubble popped.

"And then the Japanese ran away," Harry says.

He ended up buying three of their holdings – enough land for five towers. Eventually, he developed eight towers in the beachside suburb, all with resort-like resident facilities.

"Because I built them all in one area, I could easily walk from Silverpoint to the first site and later to the next seven. It was very convenient for me."

Harry says he recognised early on that there was a substantial difference between the Sydney and Gold Coast markets. Sydney was a big market with fewer fluctuations.

"You have to be careful on the Gold Coast, and this is difficult for foreigners to understand. They come here and look at the land and they think, 'Oh, that's terrific', but they don't realise that we have few people and we have little money. They see we have lots of properties that are very, very attractive. So, they think they can't go wrong if they buy a good property.

"But that's not the way it works because there aren't enough people, not enough money. Sometimes there is a big demand and then it's time to build."

Tower number one for Harry at Main Beach was aptly called The Meriton, a building close to Main Beach's Tedder Avenue retail strip.

Gordon Douglas, one of the men behind the Gold Coast-founded PRD Realty chain, had first met Harry at a conference in Sydney in the 1970s. The group went on to market The Nelson, Florida and The Meriton buildings.

"I've always liked him. He has what you might call a one-stop shop, where Harry likes to do everything in-house," Gordon says.

"He provides a lot of accommodation on the Gold Coast that others

105

can't provide or aren't capable of producing on the Harry scale. He's able to buy bigger sites, and on those you can do things better. He has the ability to say, 'I'm going to build', and he always does. He doesn't worry about the market or interest rates and factors like that."

Harry and a friend were sitting in a café in Tedder Avenue a few years after The Meriton's 1994 completion when the friend asked how many levels there were in the building.

"There are 15, from memory," Harry said (the building was 16 floors). "I wanted to go higher, but Rhonda wouldn't let me. She said we would lose the Broadwater views from our penthouse."

The follow-on from The Meriton was the Waratah, a 27-level tower completed in 1995 on a 6,600-square-metre holding bought from insurer Colonial Mutual for $3 million.

The chance to buy a whole Main Beach block came up when Japan's privately owned Niizeki Constructions decided to call it quits on the Gold Coast and retreat.

The company, headed in Australia by Sachiro Niizeki, had spent $16.5 million to acquire the 1.17-hectare site and, in 1989, unveiled grand plans for a major condominium venture.

Five years later, Harry bought the block for virtually half price – $8.6 million – and went on to deliver two high-rises. One was named Oscar on Main and the other, Ocean Sands.

One of Sachiro's neighbours was a fellow called Max Christmas. Harry says that a highlight of the frequent Triguboff trips to the Gold Coast was Saturday morning breakfasts at Thyme Café in Tedder Avenue with Max.

The late Max was a veteran of the city's property market who'd long had his own agency and became known as 'Mr Gold Coast Real Estate'.

"We'd chew the fat over everything, and he knew a lot about China. That helped me because, at times, 80 per cent of my production would go to Chinese buyers and I never had agents in that country," Harry says.

A Japanese mortgagee then presented Harry with another Main Beach 'special' in 1996. It was a blue-chip one-hectare holding across the road from the beach and, after being bought for $20 million in the late '80s, was earmarked for luxurious twin towers in a project called Xanadu.

For Harry, the chance to snare the land for $11 million was too good to refuse and he set about delivering his own pair of Xanadu buildings.

Gino Moro says that a group of nearby high-rise apartment owners objected to his proposed Xanadu and Oscar on Main developments. "During the court case, the judge decided to look at the objectors' units. He went up to the penthouse of an objector, and the objector indicated to the judge the impact on his view. The judge noticed that the objector had all the curtains drawn on the west and north sides of the apartment and asked that they be opened.

When the curtains were opened, they exposed a magnificent 180-degree view totally unobstructed by any of Harry's buildings. The view said it all, and the objection failed."

Gino says that after Harry had built seven towers at Main Beach, his then right-hand man, Peter Spira, suggested the suburb should be renamed Meriton Beach. Some of the 'locals' were still doing that years on.

Harry is, in Gino's opinion, the master of straightforward thinking, and this is exemplified by his weekly sheets.

"He condenses the complex status of construction and sales to a one-page snapshot recording the week's position on construction costs and unit sales in all his developments. He's devised that over many years and it is truly extraordinary that the multiple aspects of the Meriton business can be simply set out in an easy-to-read format each week. It's a key insight that condensing a mass of information into a straightforward format is the key to having a clear hands-on knowledge of the day-to-day operations of a complex business. I am always impressed and influenced by his straightforward way of thinking."

Gino says Harry has a keen insight and understanding of the market as it affects his development plans.

"He's always interested in listening to the views of key stakeholders, what's happening in the market and its future direction. Harry accepts that the market is king, not himself, and we often have changes to his development plans so he can meet those altered markets."

Harry's two other Main Beach deliveries – The Crest and Pacific Views – were modest in terms of size. Harry could keep an eye on work on The Crest site from his penthouse's back balcony. Pacific Views, like Xanadu, was across the road from the beach and rose on land that had housed the only service station at Main Beach.

So, Harry now had a solid foot in the Gold Coast market, and he only went on to do bigger and better projects.

More from Quentin a little later.

Completed 1983 | The Nelson, 5 Admiralty Drive, Paradise Waters.

Completed 1984 | Florida Apartments, 2916 Gold Coast Hwy, Surfers Paradise.

Completed 1994 | The Meriton, 29 Woodroffe Ave, Main Beach.

Completed 1995 | The Waratah, 22 Montgomery Ave, Main Beach.

Completed 1998 | Oscar on Main, 1-9 Hughes St, Main Beach.

Completed 1998 | Xanadu, 59 Pacific St, Main Beach.

Completed 2001 | Pacific Views, Main Beach Pde.

EIGHT

FAMILY ARRIVE FROM RUSSIA

On Sunday 8 April 1990, Harry stood with daughter Sharon at the arrival hall at Sydney Airport waiting for a flight to land from Baku in Azerbaijan, Russia, some 13,230 km away. After a 22-hour flight, eight of Harry's family members on his father's side, whom he had never met before, were disembarking to start a new life in Australia.

It would be a day of mixed emotions for Harry. He was thrilled for his father's sister, Maya, and her family, who were coming to live in Australia, but it was also bittersweet. He could do for them what he had been unable to do for his own father and mother. Again, it had not been easy, but this time he had been victorious.

Harry, over many years, and especially following the death of his father, had stayed in contact with Moshe's family in Russia. In particular, he wrote to Moshe's sisters, Rosa (Raisa) and Maya. Shortly after Harry married Rhonda in 1980, he wrote to tell Maya of his marriage, and in the same letter, he issued an invitation for them to come to Australia. Ten years later, Maya and her family landed on Australian shores.

For the first time, Harry was meeting Maya, her husband, Losif, their daughters, Vera and Lilya, and their respective husbands, Valery and Slava, Vera and Valery's daughter, Raya, and Lilya and Slava's son, Ilya.

"My mother, Maya, and Harry's father, Moshe, were very close," Lilya says.

"In 1980 Harry sent us a letter to tell us he had married again, and if we ever thought of leaving the Soviet Union, we should let him know and he would sponsor us to come to Australia.

"The letter was misplaced because it had been caught up in some old newspapers and it wasn't found for a very long time.

"Eventually, my father came across it and gave it to my mother to read. She appreciated Harry's offer, but she knew how difficult it was to immigrate to Australia and Canada from Russia.

"We had decided to immigrate as a family, but we weren't sure where that would be to," she says.

One day Maya and Lilya walked past the Australian Embassy, then Maya turned around, walked back again and walked inside. On the spur of the moment, she had decided she would call Harry.

"My mother asked for the telephone book for Sydney, Australia," Lilya says.

"She looked up the name Triguboff, initial, H. There was only one, so she called the number.

"Later we found out that it was Sharon who picked up the phone and she, of course, could not speak Russian.

"The next time Rhonda picked up the phone and she understood who was calling when Mum said her name. From that very moment, there has always been a connection with Rhonda where she could understand and communicate what we needed without speaking our language. It was incredible. She told Mum to ring back in an hour – Harry was walking the dog.

"Then we called again, and Harry picked up the phone and spoke to my mum. Harry, of course, could speak Russian," she says.

"Mum told Harry they had decided to immigrate to San Francisco in the United States, and Harry asked her who they had there. Mum told him they had nobody but that I had a friend who immigrated there, and they liked it.

"Harry told my mother not to be silly and that she should be with family in Australia. He told her to bring her whole family and that he would help.

"Next thing you know, my mother was applying for all of us to go to Australia."

The decision for Maya now was easy. Harry had reassured her that if she made the decision to come to Australia, he would make it happen. Maya and her family were to settle in the same country as Moshe's son and his family. It was exciting. There was no way Maya and her family could know how successful Harry was – but they soon found out.

"When we first arrived, my father whispered to me that he thought Harry must be a millionaire," Lilya says.

"I laughed and asked how he would know that. He said the cars were a dead giveaway. Harry drove a Rolls Royce and Sharon a BMW. We could never have imagined the extent of his wealth. Coming from a country where there isn't really any class distinction, the way Harry lived was like a fairytale.

"We were definitely the poor relations, not that Harry or his family ever made us feel that way."

For the first month, Harry's family stayed at Waratah Gardens in Surry Hills. They didn't know at the time that Harry owned the building. Harry had one of his friends, Simon Slavin, who could speak Russian, help them find more permanent homes in Bondi. Harry, taking the language barrier into consideration, also helped them into jobs at Meriton.

"It was funny," Lilya says. "The day after we arrived, Harry invited us into Meriton so he could get to know us and see where we would fit in.

"Our husbands, who were engineers in Russia, went into labouring. I worked in the hotels as a housekeeper, my sister was in the office as a bookkeeper and that's how it remained until we could speak better English.

"Of course, my mother and father weren't expected to work. Harry looked after them.

"My father had been a successful lawyer in Russia, but he could never have practised in Australia. He was also a very proud man. He wasn't comfortable with Harry paying for everything. He wrote Harry a letter and told him that his children would eventually pay back every cent and set up a schedule of payments. Harry tore it up and told him that he expected nothing.

"As soon as I had enough English, I went into rentals, then later into sales. I was in sales for 23 years before leaving Meriton in 2013. I did very well," Lilya says.

After Lilya and Vera's husbands had worked for a time at Meriton and could also speak better English, they started their own independent contracting businesses, while still doing a lot of work for Meriton. Lilya's husband went into building a successful painting company, and Vera's husband went into the gyprock trade and was also successful.

While everyone's English was improving, so was Harry's Russian. He only spoke to this side of his family in Russian. Lilya's son, Ilya, finished school and went to work at Meriton as an assistant to his mother. He was eventually a land buyer and, after many years at Meriton, started his own development company.

"I remember when we first arrived in Australia, Sharon was pregnant with Daniel," Lilya says. "She was delightful and more than happy to help us with anything.

"Rhonda is the most wonderful woman. She did everything to make us feel welcome. When I wanted to get my driver's licence, she paid for some lessons. She also gave me some clothes, and I remember when she first invited us to their home, we were very shocked Harry lived in the manner he did. The extent of his wealth was beyond our understanding.

"I remember when the whole family came to our two-bedroom unit in Blair Street, Bondi, we wondered what Harry would think. We fed him our food and we danced and laughed a lot. Harry appeared to love every minute.

"Everything we have now is thanks to Harry. Whenever we meet, our first toast is always to Harry."

Lilya and her husband, Slava, went back to Russia in 1996 with Harry and Rhonda and Harry's friend, Chris Crawley and his wife at the time, Judith Crawley.

"I took Harry to the apartment where our grandmother used to live," Lilya says. "It was in Sochi on the Black Sea, and she had long since passed.

"No-one was at home, so we went next door and Harry gave the old lady who lived there some money before we left. It was very touching," she says.

"It was an odd feeling being back. When we were finally allowed to leave to come to Australia, we came with $30 each. We had to give our homes and money to the government. We had to pay $700 each to lose our Soviet Union citizenship.

"They told us if we wanted to leave, we couldn't financially gain from that decision. We couldn't take anything. I'm not sure Harry knew what we had to leave behind but if he did, he chose not to talk about it.

"We are in the best place in the world, we are safe, we are with family, and it's all thanks to Harry.

"He is our patriarch. He is our first toast at gatherings," she says.

За твоё здоровье!

To your health, Harry!

Harry with his Russian family. L-R: Vera Grishina, Orna Triguboff, Lilya Melnikoff, Maya Dinaburg, Harry, and Ukranian-Israeli politician Natan Sheransky.

Harry celebrating his 60th birthday with Ella, Orna, Maya & Sharon, 1993.

World Tower & Meriton Tower stand tall in the Sydney cityscape.

PART 2

THE START OF A NEW MILLENNIUM

Cartoon by John Shakespeare of Harry at the top of World Tower, 2003.

NINE

WORLD TOWER

Through the latter years of the 20th century, Harry continued to build to the same methodology as always. He and Rhonda were enjoying a good life together and both were shocked when Harry was diagnosed with bowel cancer in the mid-1990s, found during routine testing.

Harry's nephew, Michael, who was living in New York at the time, suggested Harry should go to New York for a second opinion. The doctor there agreed with the course of treatment Harry's doctor in Australia had suggested, and Harry returned to Australia to begin his treatment. He barely missed a beat. In fact, once he was declared cancer free, it projected him to even greater heights. Harry was unstoppable.

At the turn of the millennium, Harry, aged 66, referred to himself as a 'young man'. Business was booming as the popularity of apartment living had risen profoundly. A variety of factors influenced this shift, including demographics, urbanisation and lifestyle preferences. At the start of the 21st century, Harry's tallest, most controversial project was underway.

In the Old Testament, a Hebrew prophet named Jeremiah was the first to say that 'leopards never change their spots'. That expression, still used today, means the older you get, the less likely you are to change your ways. Harry was about to prove Jeremiah wrong.

Harry had bought the blackest hole in Sydney and was going to plug it with the highest residential superstructure in the world. 'World Tower' would be worthy of its name.

Black hole, white elephant, take your pick. The site, bordering George, Pitt, Castlereagh and Goulburn streets, had been sitting ugly and dormant for more than 10 years. It was also filled with water due to unforgiving rains, and Harry had, for many years, no intention of dipping his toe into its murky waters. He kept an eye on the property from a distance but World Square, colloquially known as 'World Swamp', held no interest to him at all.

While World Square was considered the blackest hole in the 1990s, there were other black holes dotted throughout the streets of Sydney. There were 22, in fact, and each told a story. The same story.

"I sat back and watched the World Square site for years," Harry says. "There would be movement for five minutes and then it would stall, then movement again. Then nothing. Then it was locked down for years.

"The unions were causing havoc across the city. All the black holes were created by developers who had completed demolition, but after futile negotiations with the unions, they had downed tools, locked up their sites and abandoned their plans.

"I couldn't care less about the unions. I had fought them and won every time. They were more scared of me than the other way around," he boasts with a defiant smile.

"Go high or go home!"

In the 1800s, the block known as World Square was originally named Brickfield Hill. It was the roughest area in the city and, as its name suggests, it was one of the biggest brick-making areas in Sydney, until the 'father of Australia', as he was known – Governor Macquarie – booted the brickies out. They didn't fit in with his plans for a new open recreational space, which has become the oldest public parkland in Australia – Hyde Park. The criminality that was Brickfield Hill aside, the noise, pollution and smell were not conducive to the Governor's plans to transform the area either.

In 1906, after the brick kilns had long moved on, Anthony Hordern

& Sons' department store opened to huge fanfare. It had 52 acres of retail space and was the biggest department store in the world. The project was built by 500 men using 50,000 bags of Portland cement, 80,000 sheets of corrugated iron and 10 million bricks – enough to form a line from Sydney to New Zealand. The Horderns finished the building by covering the floors with 1.8 kilometres of pale-green carpet. They were geared up to sell anything and everything. Harry's father would have loved it.

The Hordern men, like Harry, had no less trouble with the council, which meant they were constantly changing their plans then re-lodging, then changing again and re-lodging. Samuel Hordern, who became known as the Merchant Prince of Sydney, was infuriated by the delays, even though they were still significantly less than they would be today.

Anthony Hordern & Sons traded from the building for nearly 70 years before being taken over by Waltons. The property was sold to Stocks and Holdings Limited for $8.5 million in 1970.

Around the same time as the sale, an interim conservation order was placed on the building, which remained in place for 10 years. It was leased to the New South Wales Institute of Technology until the building no longer met the appropriate fire regulations and the institute moved out.

Malaysian property giant Ipoh Garden International bought the building for $13.5 million in 1981, and the plan was to save and renovate it, much in the same way it was doing with the Queen Victoria building and Strand Arcade. Interestingly, the Tan family, who owned Ipoh Garden, also owned one of the biggest retail and commercial precincts in Tianjin, China, where Harry had lived as a boy before coming to Australia.

When Ipoh commissioned a report from the CSIRO, its findings advised that due to the state of the building's concrete and other fittings, it would be too costly to restore. It would be more financially viable to pull it down. The planning minister at the time, Bob Carr, stepped in. He seized control of the site from the City of Sydney Council and, ignoring objections from the National Trust and the Heritage Council of New South Wales, approved a $1 billion development of the site.

The old Anthony Hordern & Sons building was controversially demolished in 1986.

World Square, as it was named, was approved in 1987 and excavation began. The ghosts of the Hordern family obviously didn't approve and showed their fury by dumping an unprecedented amount of rain on the site. It caused major work delays – nearly as many as the interference by the unions.

When Ipoh submitted its development application it proposed four quarters, representing retail, residential or commercial buildings. World-renowned Japanese architect Kenzō Tange designed four buildings in the shape of a lotus flower, but they would never eventuate. The name World Square had been chosen to reflect prosperity, potential and possibilities, but the project wasn't living up to those intentions.

In 1989, Qantas earmarked nearly half of one of the office towers for its head office. In 1990, adding to Ipoh's woes with the weather and the unions, there was a downturn in the Sydney property market. That same year, Qantas pulled out of its commitment. Ipoh threw its hands in the air, locked up the site and abandoned it in 1992, leaving only a 10-storey hole in the ground for the car park.

The site, due to planning disputes, remained undeveloped throughout the early 1990s until a master plan for World Square was approved in 1996. It in no way reflected the original plans of Tange's lotus flower.

"When Harry bought the northern end of the site and associated airspace, I thought it was the bravest move he had made in the 20 years I'd been working for him," Peter Spira says.

"There were so many problems with the site, and the unions had been relentless. They caused delays any way they could.

"I remember being told that when the site was a giant swimming pool, the unions insisted the workers reach the substation by boat to turn on the electricity.

"It couldn't just be an inflatable dinghy or a rowboat either, which would be easy to manoeuvre onto the site; they insisted on a boat with a motor, driven by someone with a boat licence. It was ridiculous, but that was symptomatic of the unions at the time. Wherever they could cause a delay, they did. It was going to be our toughest build yet!"

Harry, for almost 40 years, had stuck to his knitting, but there was now a determination and willingness to change tack. He was even prepared to give up the blondes. Not wife Rhonda, of course, but his penchant for blonde bricks.

"For decades we had built affordable, boxy apartments in blonde brick," Peter Spira says. "We had a formula and we'd done well by following it. Harry remained constant with his methodology, and it made him a billionaire several times over.

"Building to the demands of the buyer was something Harry never did. World Tower was a brave, bold move, both of which fortune favours."

Maybe Harry had simply digressed all those years. Right from the very start he had wanted to go big. From the time he had visited the US with his family and saw the massive condominiums, he knew then that bigger was better. More than that though, Harry loved the southern end of Sydney. Harry's office at the time was a block away from World Square. His office today is a block away from the other side of World Square. His heart belongs to the Chinatown end of the city, and he was really excited about contributing to the revitalisation of that end of town. World Square was Harry's sweet spot, and the perfect place to have his big moment.

And a big moment it was. Not only did Harry build an award-winning masterpiece, but World Tower also signalled the start of a hospitality empire, greater expansion into vendor financing, and a relationship with the media that improved exponentially overnight.

A lot had happened in the late 1990s that heralded a new beginning for architecture and the design of residential towers in Sydney. The Premier at the time, Bob Carr, while travelling down Anzac Parade from his home in Maroubra, was less than impressed with the architecture he was seeing along the way. He started a campaign to create a design guideline and brought a lot of people together in a design summit to share their ideas.

Carr had a good relationship with Harry and was a little embarrassed when he found out that a number of the buildings he had seen were being built by Meriton. He pushed on regardless. To compensate for his unflattering assault on Harry's buildings, he included Peter Spira in his design summit as representative for the architects and developers. Other attendees included representatives from the Department of Planning, plus councils and town planners.

Even though Peter Spira tried to explain to the summit the methodology of the Meriton design, the fact of the matter was that boxy, blonde-brick buildings no longer rated highly on an architectural scale, if they ever had.

"I gave a speech in which I explained that the developers don't design the buildings," Peter Spira says. "I explained that they facilitate a design, but it doesn't always end up as the final product.

"We go to council with our plans, then they go to the town planners, and whatever recommendations are made, we change the design to accommodate those comments.

"Once that's done, we would again lodge the plans, and then we're required to advertise everything to allow anyone and everyone to comment. Those comments would be lodged with the council, and then we would be called back in to make more changes. We would then make the further changes and lodge the plans again. It would then go to another council meeting, and so on and so on …

"Councillors who had no idea about building would then call the shots. We would do whatever it took and make further changes to our design, and then we would lodge again, and it would go to another council meeting. It was a long, drawn-out struggle.

"The end result was nothing like our original design," he says, but we could probably safely say it was still a blonde-brick box."

When Harry found out that new design rules were going to be announced by the Sydney council, he went ahead and followed them for the design of World Tower in 1999 – before they became law.

From March 2000, the new rules – aimed at stopping the construction of ugly or unimaginative buildings – were set. Developers of high-rise towers would be required to demonstrate that the proposed design was the result of a competitive design process.

"While we cannot legislate for good taste, we can introduce a process aimed at encouraging and rewarding greater effort and preventing the worst," the Lord Mayor, Councillor Frank Sartor, said at the time.

Sartor had become aesthetically aware coming into the Sydney 2000 Olympics. He had spent $70 million cleaning up the streets to welcome visitors from around the world, and after all his trouble and expense, he wasn't going to let developers get away with not covering over their black holes and finishing their sites with some basic landscaping.

Sartor, for the first time, was thrilled that Harry had bought the biggest black hole because he knew he would make it presentable for the games. Harry assured Sartor he wouldn't embarrass the country, and he would have the site looking presentable, and, more importantly, safe for the games.

The new system that arose from the design summit required architects to compete with their designs to win the business. After long discussions with Harry, Peter Spira invited three architectural firms to compete for World Tower: two Sydney-based firms, Peddle Thorp & Walker and Harry Seidler & Associates, and the third from Melbourne, Nation Fender Katsalidis.

All were required to conform with the existing masterplan for the site, which set broad controls on height, overshadowing and dimensions.

Harry Seidler thought his company was a shoo-in because of his relationship with Harry, but Harry had delegated his vote to ensure fair judging. It never crossed Harry Seidler's mind that he might not win. He went with his wife, Penelope, to the winner announcement at a Sydney hotel. Bob Nation, the lead architect for Nation Fender Katsalidis, who took out the competition, still clearly remembers the winning moment.

"I came up to Sydney for the announcement with a friend, and we were all at a hotel waiting for the decision," Bob says.

"Harry Seidler couldn't believe he didn't win. He was up the front with his wife, Penelope, and he just turned on his heel and left the room when the winner was announced.

"I suppose I was deluded when I thought he might come and say, 'Well done, you young bastard,' or something along those lines, but he was furious," he says.

At the time, Peter Spira said that what tipped the balance towards Nation Fender Katsalidis was "the richness of architectural materials, its fit in the urban context and the way its scale is broken by variety".

Once Nation Fender Katsalidis had won the project, Bob Nation announced that he immediately needed to organise a move to Sydney.

"I started with a small team and set up a new identity known as Nation Katsalidis NSW," Bob says.

"Setting up the practice was bloody hard, but it was a necessity to be on the ground in NSW to work on World Tower.

"It was worth it. Right from the very first meeting with Harry, I could tell he was an extraordinary man. When I left the office, I felt totally committed to him and determined not to let him down. I felt like we were partners from day one. His recall was astounding and his involvement in the project to the level of detail was astonishing," he says.

At the time, the tallest residential towers in Sydney were The Peak Apartments in Chinatown and Pitt Street's Century Tower. They were 153 metres and 158 metres respectively. World Tower was to be 234 metres.

It was to have 74 above-ground levels and 10 basement levels. The plan was for 701 residential units, divided into three sections, each with a pool, spa, sauna, gymnasium, games room, virtual driving range and private 24-seat theatre. The pool and spa areas on levels 38 and 61 would offer 180-degree views of Sydney and were accessible from one of 15 elevators. There would be not one but two childcare centres located in the building.

World Tower would be held together with about 100,000 cubic metres of concrete, which equated to around 20,000 trucks visiting the site for its three-year construction. The 10,000 tonnes of steel and 40,000 square metres of glass would cover 125 tennis courts, 375 cricket pitches or about six full football fields.

The views across Sydney would be second to none.

"I loved working with Harry," Bob says. "There wasn't anything he didn't know about the project. He was a genius and could talk to you about any aspect of the design.

"When we had the hard conversations, and Harry was eventually happy with the outcome, he would laugh and pat me on the arm affectionately. He had little patience for any kind of inadequacy, was intensely involved and wanted the very best result. It's fair enough. I would describe my relationship with him during the build of World Tower, and still to this day, as very enjoyable and mutually respectful.

"I've never met anyone quite like him and expect I never will again. He's a remarkable man."

As well as working on the design for World Tower, Bob started to help with the people that aggravated Harry, to ease the burden on him. Most notably, the Lord Mayor at the time, Frank Sartor, and, as a bigger group, the media.

There was one journalist, namely the person writing this book, who spent a lot of time with Harry at his sites. At that time, nobody else did. They would sit at their computers writing only what they believed was historically correct. They wrote the same thing over and over again.

"The media had been so unfair to Harry," Bob says. "He deserved none of its scrutiny. They would trash him at every turn without even passing him the compliment of looking at his projects. For Harry's sake, and for my own, I wasn't going to let that happen with World Tower.

"I personally took a number of the property writers on a tour of World Tower and really got to know them.

"You could tell by the number of black holes in the city that many developers didn't take the risks that Harry did. He was happy to be the first to try anything. That should have been celebrated, not ridiculed.

"It was exciting to work with someone like Harry, and I wanted to show that to the media. I was fond of him, and his team on site were absolutely fantastic. I'm not saying that we had no issues, but it was a culture that you rarely see. Everyone was family. I was pulled into that vacuum, and they always had my back. There was no experience quite like it," he says.

Harry doesn't want to dwell on his earlier relationship with the media. Over time he has formed a good relationship with a number of journalists, and he is now invited by many to give commentary and advice on the current state of the market. His opinion is now sought as an expert.

He has worked incredibly well over the years with many journalists, including Robert Gottliebsen from *The Australian* and *Business Spectator*, Robert Harley from the *Australian Financial Review*, Turi Condon formally of *The Australian*, Lisa Allen from *The Australian*, John Stensholt from *The Australian*, Ross Greenwood from Sky News, Erin Molan from Sky News and *The Daily Telegraph*, Mark Whittaker from *Forbes Australia* and many more.

"The media unnecessarily worked against me in the early days," Harry says. "Now they work with me. It makes for a far better relationship."

Back to World Tower, and one of the issues was that the existing footings were going to be for a commercial building and they weren't suitable for a residential tower. The existing footings had an 11:1 slenderness ratio. It wasn't going to work, and it looked like they would need to be removed at a massive expense.

Bob talked to his engineer about raking the existing footings through World Tower's foyer. By doing that, they were able to reduce the existing footings to an 8:1 slenderness ratio. It's now an architectural element in the foyer of World Tower. It saved a lot of money, it secured the rigidity of the tower and helped with any kind of sway.

"Harry was willing to listen and let the experts give him the advice," Bob says. "He thought the vertical elements should have been a different colour. He thought they were too dark. He was still reverting to his blonde-brick moments occasionally, but he went with the darker colour I advised."

That willingness to embrace change helped World Tower become the 2004 bronze recipient of the Emporis Skyscraper Award, which highlights the best skyscrapers worldwide for the previous year. World Tower beat buildings including Times Square Tower in New York.

"With World Tower, Harry changed inner-city living," Bob says. "It was interesting to watch Harry change the hospitality industry with serviced apartments. That was a real shakeup for the industry."

Harry decided to keep the 74th floor penthouse for himself. There were no better views from anywhere across Sydney and the harbour, and he used it to entertain important people and visitors to the city. Harry loved it mostly because he could pinpoint all his other Meriton buildings through its floor-to-ceiling windows.

The Prime Minister at the time, John Howard, said in his speech when he opened the building in 2004: "Harry epitomises what a lot of Sydney is about, somebody who has got hope and optimism and drive and determination. He has been at the heart of expansion."

"It is the most exciting residential building I have ever done," Harry said at the time. "Meriton can now clearly compete with the world's best."

The new Meriton didn't stop there. It was also the time when Harry took bankrolling his buyers to a whole new level. He was offering vendor financing on a large scale by not only loaning money to homebuyers but to investors as well.

To fund the offer, he needed to borrow up to $400 million from the ANZ bank, one of the 'Big Four' banks. It was becoming hard for Australians to borrow money to buy investment units. The big banks had begun to tighten their lending requirements for inner-city dwellings late in 2003. At the time, mortgage lender Mark Bouris' Wizard Home Loans found that more than 100,000 Australians had abandoned plans to buy an investment property that year.

The banks' tough line on lending meant they were valuing apartments at about 80 per cent of their cost to buyers. The banks were then lending just 70 per cent of the lower valuation, which meant would-be buyers would be forced to find deposits of more than 40 per cent of the cost of the property.

"I don't think the banks realise the impact that this sudden change of lending policy will have on the entire residential real estate market," Harry said at the time.

"Two years ago, they were prepared to lend 120 per cent of the value of units because they were rising in value. Now they will only loan 50 per cent."

Harry was prepared to fund buyers into his units with two-year loans at interest rates of about 6.8 per cent, slightly below bank variable rates of 7 per cent. After two years, borrowers would be expected to find alternative financing or could sell their properties.

Harry said that investors looking to use an existing property as security for an investment unit would face cuts in the valuation that banks put on other properties.

At that time, Meriton had about 880 apartments for sale, averaging about $550,000, but many were a lot more expensive.

Harry also had his own portfolio of units, bought as part of developments over the decades. He was prepared to pledge part of the portfolio to the ANZ bank, which would then fund the loans to buyers of his units.

Harry said that despite the downturn in the property market, the difficulties of financing apartment purchases were pushing up the demand for apartments to rent.

In 2005, Harry said his decision to turn some of the units in World Tower into serviced apartments had paid dividends.

"Now, because they are serviced apartments, I get better returns than I would if I leased them out long term, and that's my strategy," he said.

"It's proved to be very successful."

Above: Brickfield Hill, George Street, Sydney, 1873. Source: JR Clarke, from the collections of the State Library of New South Wales, Dictionary of Sydney.

Below: Anthony Hordern's Palace Emporium, George Street, Sydney, 1907. Source: Dictionary of Sydney.

Harry on-site during the construction of World Tower.

Harry & builder Andrew Fletcher in the basement of Meriton Tower, 2001.

Harry & Chris Crawley looking at building models, 2000.

World Tower under construction, 2002.

Cartoon by Peter Nicholson of Harry and John Howard, published in The Australian *newspaper, 2003.*

TEN

THE GOLD COAST AND BRISBANE

Over to Quentin again to talk more about Harry's expansion in Queensland in the new millennium!

In 2002, Harry stepped into new territory and what was to be by far his biggest commitment to the Gold Coast. The location was the suburb of Southport, across the Broadwater from Main Beach. He snared a 5.7-hectare site that had been home to Sundale, for many years a premier shopping centre that, while still operating, was owned by superannuation funds linked to BHP and ICI.

Harry had been offered the property, on which the centre was still standing, in the late '90s but it wasn't a contender for him at the time. He bought it for $54.5 million in late 2002, and a year later set out to create a landscaped community called Brighton on Broadwater.

He has described the project as a 15-year adventure. When the seven-stage Brighton was completed in 2018, it comprised both mid-rise and high-rise buildings, shops, a Woolworths supermarket, and parks. Its 1,603 apartments were home to 3,000 or so people.

The last building in Brighton on Broadwater, a 55-floor tower and Southport's tallest, is named after the former shopping centre, Sundale, and was a 'fine finale' for the project.

"It's a standout building with standout views over the Broadwater and out to the ocean," Harry said on opening night. "There's no doubt it will become a landmark."

Brighton was Harry's first dual-purpose development on the Gold Coast, offering serviced suites as well as apartments. But another 'suite' venture was in the pipeline.

Harry stepped into more new territory – Broadbeach – in 2004 when he paid $33 million for highway-front land that had been owned by companies linked to a former bankrupt who'd had offices on the site. A statue of Pegasus, the winged stallion, graced the front lawn and still graces the lawns of the highway frontage to Meriton Suites Broadbeach. Meriton completed two linked Pegasus towers in 2008.

"I was originally intending to sell the Pegasus apartments as strata-title units, but the GFC made me change my mind," Harry says.

His decision to run the 405 apartments as serviced suites is one he's never regretted. The suites became what he terms 'standout' performers in a Meriton Suites portfolio that spans five major cities.

"Broadbeach has enormous vibrancy, and it's a place where everyone – from families to tourists and corporates – wants to stay," Harry says.

"The move to offer one-, two- and three-bedroom apartments as hotel suites was a winner, especially with families."

Harry twice mooted putting a third tower on the Pegasus site, backing off the first time because Rhonda vetoed the idea. When the idea resurfaced, he was talked out of it because it might impact on the Meriton Suites towers and their guests.

The Harry era on the Gold Coast entered a new stage in 2016 when he made the first of four site buys in Surfers Paradise: three on beachfront street the Esplanade. All but one of the four buys were from offshore parties.

The first purchase was of land that housed what started life in the '60s as the Apollo high-rise and was later owned by Singaporean investor Gertrude Kwok.

The 22-floor tower was demolished, and in 2017 Harry announced plans for the Gold Coast's tallest tower, the 76-floor Ocean, on the 3,833-square-metre site. He bought the property for $58 million, with part of the appeal being that it backed onto the Gold Coast Highway.

He said that Ocean's design encapsulated all that was great about one of the world's standout beachfront locations.

"Arriving at the final design has been quite an adventure for me," Harry said at the time. "I've been passionate about delivering a building that is in tune with the ocean and the golden beach that fronts it.

"Getting there hasn't been smooth sailing – the design tide has gone in, and it's gone out again. The end result has involved several months of changes and refinements, but we've succeeded."

The Ocean construction job – because of the tower's spinnaker-like design and the ground conditions – is described as the most complex undertaken in the history of Meriton.

Ocean's engineers had to come up with a unique design to solve wind assaults on the 252-metre tower. The traditional method of stopping swaying – huge water tanks on the roof – could not be used.

Meriton looked at projects around the world, and the Ocean answer came from bridges such as the Golden Gate, the Brooklyn, and Sydney's The Anzac.

The upshot was that Ocean was built like a bridge standing upright, with four mega columns running halfway up, each with cables running through ducts. In heavy wind, the cables stretch like a rubber band, therefore reducing the amount of Ocean's sway.

The tower was completed in 2022, with a Meriton Suites hotel up to level 33 and apartments above, some looking down on previous Surfers Paradise super-towers Q1 and Soul.

———

Ocean, to use a restaurant term, was just a 'starter' for Harry on the Surfers beachfront. Singaporean company Banyan Tree had decided to abort plans for twin towers on the northern end of the Esplanade and head home. They left with $75 million of Harry's money from the sale, and he quickly formulated his own plans for the land, which then housed a small tower, Bahia, along with a low-rise, Beach Lodge.

A demolition team moved in, and later in 2022 site works were underway for Iconica, which would consist of twin towers – with the North Tower taller than Ocean.

Harry says Surfers has one of the best beachfronts in the world.

"Little did I know that one day I would have the opportunity to buy the best land in Surfers Paradise," he says.

He also believes that the purchase of the Banyan Tree land wasn't just a sign of confidence in Surfers Paradise, but also a reflection on how much easier it is to do business on the Gold Coast than in Sydney.

"When the councils in Sydney drive me crazy, I build more on the Gold Coast.

"In Sydney you talk to the city's town planners and get a 'take it or leave it' attitude. That's not the case on the Gold Coast and in Brisbane, where the planners and councils are fair and, if a rule is clearly wrong, they'll change it.

"In other words, life's a lot easier for me in Queensland."

Dawn Crichlow, a city councillor for 29 years, was positive about Harry's projects, along with those of other developers. She'd met Harry in Sydney in 1965, at a time when the man who later became her husband, Desmond Crichlow, had partnered Sir Arthur George in a unit project in Clark Street. Dawn lived in one of the units.

Desmond went on to sell two blocks of Clark Street land to Harry, who built six-pack unit buildings, and Dawn, who worked in the ICI finance department, had a role in the marketing.

Harry reflects that when he started to build on the Gold Coast the council wanted to give him 'the treatment'.

"I went to Dawn (then a councillor) and she told them to lay off. She did it for many other developers as well. She just wanted progress."

Dawn and Des went on to become Meriton customers. Over time, the Crichlow name was on five titles at Harry's Brighton on Broadwater, and in 2023 Dawn was still calling one of the apartments home.

Harry kept buying in Surfers Paradise in 2023, taking his spending in less than a year to $176 million. He paid $34.35 million for three-quarters of a whole city block – known as the Chinese-owned Vomitron site – across the road from the rear of Ocean.

Harry says he and Rhonda had often visited a mini-golf venue on the property.

"The guy who ran it was always scared that the land would be sold and he'd have to find another business. I always told him he was safe for many years. Never did I think that I would buy the property!" Harry says.

Five months after the Vomitron buy, Harry signed up for another so-called knockdown job – a holding on the Esplanade that included the ageing The Shore high-rise, which had two other street frontages. The property, which cost $67.5 million, was added to the Meriton Surfers Paradise pipeline.

———

A key person in Meriton's success on the Gold Coast has been Eunice Arden-Wood, who was first employed at Meriton in Sydney to take over a bookkeeping role from Harry's wife, Rhonda. The job was the start of a 40-year stint with Meriton.

"We had this Burroughs machine in accounting at the time I started; a very old-fashioned machine, and I pestered Harry until we got computers," says Eunice.

"These had to have special programming to enable us to produce Harry's report sheets the specific way he wanted them laid out.

"Harry came into my office one day and said, 'It's easy to find a bookkeeper – I want to start property management, so I don't have to have Chinese laundry in my buildings (clothes hanging on balconies).'

"I had no idea how to do property management, and his reply was that you start with one or two units."

Eunice says she also pestered Harry to start internet advertising, which he did, and which succeeded to the point that most of Meriton's sales were coming from that advertising.

"Eventually, I ended up working in sales, and one day in the sales meeting in Sydney, Harry decided I was to go to Queensland. I was still there 25 years later."

Eunice ended up overseeing the selling of apartments in more than 15 buildings on the Gold Coast and in Brisbane.

"I found Harry to be a great motivator, and he always pushed to the maximum, wanting improvements in all aspects of Meriton's operations.

"Harry can also be unpredictable and is known to change his mind frequently. One day we're selling, the next we're not.

"He is very good to his long-term staff and has helped me out in times of difficulties. He's generous and appreciates my efforts with the Meriton family."

Harry's Gold Coast interests aren't all about holidays and building apartments, though. They extend to Griffith University's Institute of Glycomics, which is involved in research into drugs to control a wide range of medical conditions, such as cancer, diabetes, infectious diseases, inflammation and immune disorders.

Harry and Rhonda have been benefactors to the institute since 2007 and have visited the Gold Coast campus several times to look at its research.

In 2012, then university Chancellor Leneen Forde conferred an honorary doctorate to Harry in recognition not only of his services to Griffith, but also to the community and the residential construction industry.

As for Brisbane, Harry once described the Queensland capital as a backwater. He later, tongue in cheek, termed it a suburb of the Gold Coast. Many years later still, in 2007, he dipped one toe into the property market of that Brisbane 'water' and quickly followed with another.

The newcomer to the city's development industry then proceeded to make his mark big time, building what at the time were the city's two tallest towers. The Brisbanites who didn't know of Harry Triguboff or Meriton soon did as the skyline changed. The property veteran, after a near 10-year Brisbane hiatus, in 2023 lined up to change it again.

Not that life was all sweet for Harry in Brisbane. At one point he became stuck, literally, between a rock and a hard place.

Harry first set foot in Brisbane in the mid-'60s during one of the family's northern holidays. At that time, it was something of a sprawling country town. The oldest building, the Old Windmill in Observatory Park, dated back to 1828 and had been built by convicts and used to process wheat and corn for the Moreton Bay penal settlement. It eventually became a tourist attraction.

In the mid-1920s, 90 years before Harry raised the city's ceiling, Brisbane was heralding its first 'skyscraper'. Ascot Chambers was 10 levels and its name was a reference to the famous English racecourse, Ascot. The Chambers building was, to use a turf term, 'nobbled', or demolished, in 1995.

A wave of towers, mainly offices, began in the 1970s, and the building continued in the lead-up to the 1982 Commonwealth Games and Expo 88.

Harry cautiously stepped into the Brisbane market as the global financial crisis was evolving and bought a 1,470-square-metre site on the fringe of the central business district in Adelaide Street for $17.4 million.

He said at the time that the market seemed buoyant, and the city council appeared to welcome development.

"We are in some ways testing the water. Brisbane has a lot of catching up to do in the high-rise field compared to Surfers Paradise."

At the time, the Sydney market was on the up and up. "When Sydney prices go up, people sell and move to south-east Queensland," Harry said. "I want to be part of the welcoming party for them in Brisbane."

The first Meriton 'party' was the 2011 opening of Harry's 74-floor Soleil by then Lord Mayor Anna Bligh. Soleil became the city's highest building and came with 467 apartments and 10 levels of basement.

"I built in Brisbane because I thought that if I could build so many towers in Surfers Paradise, as I had done, I could build some in Brisbane," Harry says. "At that time, I was prepared to build big, tall towers, which was exactly what Brisbane suited.

"Why did I go so high? Well, I thought the apartments would get great views, and because Soleil had so many units, the land price for each unit would be lower."

While Soleil was being completed, Harry made his somewhat humorous remark that Brisbane was a suburb of the Gold Coast. He told a high-powered audience in Sydney that every time he took someone to work in Brisbane, they ended up living on the Gold Coast.

"Anna Bligh doesn't want me to tell you this, but I'm trying to tell the Chinese that the Gold Coast is the best part of Brisbane," Harry says.

"At Main Beach in the afternoon in summer, all the cars go one way – back to Brisbane."

Harry, hard on the heels of buying the Soleil site, bought a $25 million one of 1,800 square metres in Herschel Street. He used it for Infinity, an 81-floor building that took over the city's tallest-tower mantle from Soleil.

Prior to getting development approval, Harry described Brisbane as the most exciting growth city in Australia.

"The population is swelling and, with it, so is the appetite for high-rise and medium-density living close to the city centre," Harry said at the time.

Harry described the city council and various authorities as proactive and able to make decisions quickly.

"They're people I can work with, and I don't have to spend fruitless years battling bureaucracy like we do in Sydney."

In the lead-up to Infinity being given the green light, then Brisbane councillor and neighbourhood planning chairperson Amanda Cooper said the tower would provide a significant boost to the real estate industry and to Brisbane's economy.

"We are very much focused on making sure we build a world-class city. My observation is that Meriton really wants to be a part of the Brisbane economy. They have been working with us to make sure they address all the issues that are important to Brisbane as a city," she said.

Infinity was completed in 2014, but only after Harry had been caught between the proverbial rock and a hard place.

"We couldn't dig deep enough because the rock under the site was so solid," he says.

"We decided to blast the rock and to use machinery from the mines."

"We had little joy, so the city council, thankfully, allowed me to have some of the parking above ground without having to lose any of the apartments.

"That was nice of the council because, if it had happened in Sydney, I would've had to go through the whole bureaucratic process and wasted a lot of time. The council just had a chat with me, saw my problem was genuine, and realised that I'd tried my best but couldn't make my plan work," he says.

The result was that the number of basement levels was cut from 11 to nine.

Murray Herrod, the Infinity construction manager, says the rock under the site was so hard that explosives experts from Orica were called in to blast the bottom level and lift shafts.

Infinity's height was only just under the height restriction imposed by the Civil Aviation Safety Authority (CASA).

"We had to engage an aviation consultant to meet CASA in Canberra to come up with a procedure to allow our tower crane to penetrate their airspace (radar field)," Murray says.

"The Brisbane airport traffic control tower had direct communication with the project team in case there was ever a need for us to stop operating the crane in the restricted zone in times such as bad weather or fog."

Once the Infinity tower was completed, the Queensland Fire and Emergency Services used it as a test facility for running up the building and abseiling down.

Infinity was opened in 2013 by then Premier Campbell Newman, who praised the vote of confidence Harry had shown in the Brisbane market.

Harry said at the opening that both Soleil and Infinity stood out, not just because of their height but because of their narrowness. However, the tall and thin configurations did mean they could sway in the wind.

"We had to come up with some interesting engineering solutions to that problem," Harry says. "At Soleil we put the water storage on top of the building to weight it down. It's a bit unconventional but it works.

"With Infinity, it's not so much a square building as a hexagonal one with lots of views, but you don't have one big side open to the wind."

The height and wind load meant the Infinity construction plan had to incorporate the use of hundreds of 40mm high-tensile bars coupled in columns from the basement to the roof to maintain the structural integrity.

David Chandler, an independent construction consultant, visited Infinity while it was in the final stages of construction and walked from level 80 to level 50. He was known as a harsh critic of poor quality, waste and sloppy construction methods, but said he had seen none of that at Infinity.

"Meriton builds to a price, but it knows the standards it wants to achieve, and so do the company's designers and suppliers," David says.

"Harry uses independent building and quality certifiers for his projects. I'm told they have direct access to him. His finishing contractors know the standards required of the final product, and they will not accept or apply a finish to any unacceptable sub-surface or building element."

David said Meriton was running the job with one foreman and two leading hands, one coordinating the structure and one the finishes.

"Meriton sub-contractors don't need supervision or attendant labour. They know what has to be done. They self-organise and they respect the other sub-contractors."

At this time, Eunice Arden-Wood was still living on the Gold Coast, where she handled the marketing for the bulk of Harry's projects.

Then she received the 'we need you in Brisbane' call. She completed the marketing of Soleil and the selling of the Infinity apartments.

"I had to drive to Brisbane and back each day," Eunice says. "Some of those days were long. Sometimes I didn't get home until 9pm because a crash had blocked the highway."

Eunice says that many of the early buyers in the Brisbane towers were Chinese.

"One Chinese lady walked in and bought nine apartments and used Meriton's vendor finance. She later refinanced and retained them," Eunice says.

Harry wasn't shy in stepping forward when buyers later decided to exit. In one case he bought back 50 from Chinese sellers who wanted to take their money home. "They got their money quickly and didn't lose any," he says.

When he'd finished Soleil and Infinity, the council wanted Harry to build more.

"I told them the market had changed, which it had, but it later came good again."

The Soleil and Infinity projects enabled Harry's Meriton Suites hotel arm to open properties in a third city, coming after Sydney and then the Gold Coast. Between the two towers, there are 442 hotel suites.

Harry saw the move as strategically important in building awareness of the Meriton brand on the national stage, as well as offering existing customers a new and exciting destination.

Infinity and Soleil also meant Meriton could offer hotel guests the highest accommodation in Brisbane – the penthouse suite at Infinity is at nearly 250 metres and has views to match.

In 2020, Harry started scrutinising central Brisbane for a site upon which he could make a return to the city. He zeroed in on a large holding overlooking the Botanic Gardens and the Brisbane River. But there was a problem – it was occupied by an apartment tower and adjoining units, and it wasn't on the market.

Harry, undaunted, garnered some help and the long process began of persuading the owners of the 107 titles in The Gardens to sell. Some people had owned their apartments for 40 years.

A thorn in the amalgamation's side was a Queensland law that said a sale couldn't go ahead unless 100 per cent of owners agreed to it. In NSW, the rule was 75 per cent.

Success at The Gardens wasn't achieved until May 2023 and at a cost to Harry of $130 million.

"I've waited a long time to get the deal over the line, but it's been worth it – I now own the best site in Brisbane. Where else could you buy a parcel of land with unimpeded views over the Botanic Gardens and across the river?"

The new Meriton site, in Alice Street and backing on to Margaret Street in the CBD, spans 5,485 square metres. Harry quickly began work on planning two towers, one including a Meriton Suites hotel.

He says The Gardens property is quite different from any he has in Surfers Paradise.

"You have the best beach in the world running for miles and miles in Surfers. In Brisbane, you don't have any tower sites right on the river. Between our site and the river there's the beautiful Botanic Gardens, so there's just nothing quite like it."

Thanks, Quentin, for covering Queensland.

Harry on-site during construction of Ocean, Surfers Paradise, 2022.

Ocean outdoor podium pool.

Completed 2023 | Ocean, 84 The Esplanade, Surfers Paradise.

Harry with Peter Dutton at the Ocean opening event.

Harry & Rhonda walking at Surfers Paradise Beach.

CGI of Cypress Palms, 3-7 Cypress Avenue, Surfers Paradise.

CGI of Iconica, 154 The Esplanade, Surfers Paradise.

Site location and views of The Oscar towers, 204 Alice Street, Brisbane. Construction to begin in 2025.

1: Iconica, 2: Shores, 3: Ocean, 4: Cypress Palms.

Dianne Reynolds, Helen Williams & Harry, 2016.

PART 3

THE MERITON FAMILY

Harry with Di Reynolds at his 90th birthday celebration.

ELEVEN

THE MERITON WOMEN

Harry, before his actual blood family came into the business, often accredits his success to 'the women and the bricklayers', in that order.

"The women have always been clever, capable and competent," Harry says. "They're good with the money. They not only look after it; they have a big hand in making it.

"The women have been instrumental to the success of my business over the past 60 years, and many who are here today have been here for decades. You won't find that employment longevity in many other places. It's because they are also my family, and family stay together."

Sixty years ago, it was a different normal to today. It was common for women to have to use their feminine wiles to get the job done. Flirting up a storm was how the women of that generation helped Harry secure money from the bank. When they were getting ready to go for a meeting, they never talked to Harry about strategy. They would head into his office, strike a pose, and ask him how he thought they looked. That was their strategy. Times have definitely changed, although so adept was one woman that she ended up marrying the bank manager!

"It was all pretty harmless," Harry says of the time. "I remember when the women were headed to an important meeting, they would walk past the construction site a couple of times, hoping they might get a wolf-whistle or two from the construction workers.

"It gave them confidence. It was more about the women controlling the men's behaviour, not so much the men being inappropriate. The women have always been smart. It was a different approach back then.

"If you ask me, the women have always had the upper hand. We're putty in their hands." He laughs.

Harry's mother was conservative and traditional. She taught both her boys to respect women. That included complimenting them on their appearance, standing up when a woman enters the room, opening the car door, pulling out their chair, and anything else considered polite and proper behaviour at that time.

That was the acceptable etiquette in Harry's early life, and it came naturally to him. He was considered extremely charming and quite the romantic.

Harry found it confusing when things changed with the women's liberation movement in the late 1960s. He still laid on the charm in spades for the women who were 'old school' but, with the others, he found the easiest approach was to treat them like men. If they wanted all things equal, he could do that too.

In 1970, the release of Germaine Greer's book, *The Female Eunuch*, changed lives even more. It inspired women to strive for more. It was the beginning of the end of gender inequality – women had had enough of being viewed as sex objects. Many women shunned Germaine Greer and everything she stood for, but, love her or hate her, she started the feminist revolution and the women of the world took note.

"Women have always been very smart," Harry says. "Those women who worked for me in the beginning and lived by the motto 'if you've got it, flaunt it' should be celebrated, not stereotyped. They were a massive asset to my business when we were starting out.

"With the new wave, the women were more ambitious and had a different approach to business, but they were no more or less valued than the women before them," he says.

But the tide turned and the 'damsels', who never really were in any distress, became a lot more ambitious and tougher. The culture had changed and Harry, a little reluctantly, had to change with it.

He was way ahead of the curve anyhow. Women were in senior roles, he gave them opportunities that would normally only have been given to men, and he paid them accordingly. Harry, as he did with the Meriton men, insisted on getting to know the women's families and he socialised with them. Equality was alive and well at Meriton. Harry has never cared about race, creed, colour, age or class. If you can do the job, his door is open.

Harry first met wife Rhonda in the mid-1970s when the culture change was in full swing. She had come to work at accounts at Meriton and Harry liked everything about her. It helped that she was the keeper of the 'debt barometer', so any news Harry received from her was always good news about the reduction of his debt.

Rhonda, when delivering the happy news, projected the positivity, light and energy that reminded Harry of the US Marines in China all those years before. And he'd loved them. Rhonda made him happy, and it didn't go unnoticed that she was also tall, blonde and very attractive! Harry, as he did with everyone at Meriton, took the time to get to know her. She was from a large family, and he respected that she had worked hard to put her first husband through university. Harry admired her quiet poise and confidence, which was the exact opposite to the woman he was dating at the time – a loud party girl who also worked at Meriton.

Although Harry finds it hard to talk about, you can deduce from the timing that he had a change of heart about other women around about the time his brother, 51-year-old Joe, died in 1977 of a heart attack. Harry was devastated and it still shows to this day in his unwillingness to talk about it. When he talks about Rhonda at that time, however, he lights up.

"Rhonda knew how to stand her ground, but she was still feminine," Harry says. "She was level-headed, bright and seemed to enjoy my company."

Peter Spira says that the first time he saw Rhonda on Harry's arm at a function, he was very surprised. "They turned up at a dinner together and that was unexpected. Harry had been casually dating another woman at Meriton, but as soon as Rhonda's marriage was over, Harry swooped in.

"He'd clearly had his eye on her for a while. He can be patient when he needs to be. He wouldn't be responsible for breaking up a marriage, but he knew all wasn't good on the home front, so he bided his time. His own relationship had been rocky for a while, so that petered out to a natural end too.

"That first night Rhonda had his undivided attention, so I knew it was different. She was the one," Peter says.

Many of the women who have worked for Harry for decades started in the accounts department, but Margaret Rahilly – who has worked for Harry for 44 years – started in property management.

"There are a lot of women who've been here with me for more than 20 years, many of those for more than 30 years, and my Margaret for in excess of 40 years," Harry says.

"I can't be that much of an ogre." He laughs.

Margaret's daughter, Vanessa, started working part-time at Meriton when she was just 15 and she's still there today – a familiar face around the corridors for well over 30 years. She has done some extensive travel over the years too, but has always returned to Meriton.

"Like I say, my family sticks together," Harry says. "Vanessa is smart, like her mother, and I encourage family to come and work here. You expect the young ones will want to travel. All my grandchildren have. You just add it into the equation until they're ready to come back."

When Margaret started at Meriton in 1980, Harry put her in an office next to Rhonda. He thought they would be a good fit, and he wasn't wrong. They got on like a house on fire. Both were from big families, they had a lot in common and they spent a lot of time together outside of work too. Harry was thrilled because he wanted to keep these two important women in his life happy.

The first time Harry met Margaret she was managing a property in Annandale Street, Annandale, an Inner West suburb of Sydney. Wallgrove Lodge comprised 72 bachelor apartments (or studio flats) across five buildings, and it was owned by a doctor, a barrister and a builder.

Margaret worked out of a tiny office with bars on the windows. Things went smoothly for a while, but when the owners started to fight, they decided to sell. Margaret was worried she would lose her job. She had four hungry, growing kids that needed to be fed every night. She was hoping the new owner would want to keep her on.

Harry, before he decided to buy Wallgrove Lodge, spoke to Margaret who, as far as he was concerned, seemed to be the one running things. Most importantly, she knew about the money.

Margaret was quick to tell him how she kept vacancy rates low. "All the tenants had 13-week leases, so there were people coming in and going out all the time," she says.

"I had to take the good with the bad. It was a pretty rough end of town back then, but most of my tenants were lovely. A lot of them renewed their tenancies at the end of the lease, so we had great continuity of tenancy and money. The vacancy rates were low, and for those who weren't paying up, I showed Harry how I changed their locks with a screwdriver and got them out.

"If there was trouble, I was lucky to have the police station across the road. There was one huge bloke who threatened me. I got right up in his face and told him I wasn't giving his bond back because he hadn't cleaned his unit well enough.

"He yelled at me and said he'd left it in perfect condition. 'Your perfect is not my perfect!' I yelled back. 'No refund.'"

Margaret knew there would be consequences. A favourite with the bad tenants was putting sugar in her petrol tank so she couldn't drive her car.

What Margaret didn't know at the time was that Harry had already made up his mind about her. She was thrifty and thought outside the box. She protected the investors' money like it was her own. Harry also admired her for bringing up her kids on her own. She was going to fit in just fine at Meriton.

Harry, as always, was right about Margaret's potential. She could do twice as much as any man could do. He sacked his property manager only weeks after Margaret started at Meriton and gave her the job.

"It was a crazy role," Margaret says. "Harry expected me to work at Meriton during the week managing his properties, and he still expected me to work at Wallgrove Lodge on the weekends and pick up the rents there. He worked seven days a week and thought everyone else who was invested in the business should do the same.

"It didn't take him long to find me something to do with my evenings as well. It's not like he forgot I had four kids at home – he just chose to ignore it because I kept picking up the slack without complaining.

"The family then pulled together so I could go to strata meetings at night!"

When Margaret eventually went into sales, exactly where Harry had always wanted her to be, she felt ready for the onslaught she knew would come from the men. She was the first female salesperson, and she knew better than to complain to Harry when they gave her a hard time. Like everything else in his business, Harry knew what was happening, but he didn't step in. She was in a man's world now and he knew she was more than capable of looking after herself. He'd seen it for himself the first day he met her at Wallgrove Lodge.

One agent disliked Margaret because she rose to the top quickly. He did everything to sabotage her and diminish her in Harry's eyes. At the time, neither thought Harry knew what was going on but of course he did.

Margaret tells the story of when she was selling a building called The Palisades in Darlinghurst, and this other agent was selling another building down the road. They were in competition for buyers. Harry had put them within range of each other deliberately – it was best for the business, as was always the case with competition.

"There was a well-known transvestite in Kings Cross that everyone knew," Margaret says. "She was always looking for a job, but most people would walk to the other side of the street when they saw her coming.

"When she walked into my display suite, she'd been to the other agent's building first. To get rid of her, he'd told her to come to my building because there was a caretaker job waiting for her there. He told her not to leave until I'd agreed to give her the job.

"She had nits crawling out of her hair and I was almost vomiting. The stench filled the whole room. Potential buyers were coming to the door and walking away again.

"I told her the truth that we wouldn't need a caretaker for at least another six months. She started screaming at me and calling me a liar."

The Hare Krishnas – a branch of Hinduism – had their headquarters across the road from The Palisades. When the head swami heard the yelling, he came into Margaret's sales office with members of his movement and calmly encouraged the woman to leave.

"Before that happened, the only exposure I'd had with the Hare Krishnas was seeing them in the streets dancing and chanting, dressed head to toe in orange robes," Margaret says. "I'd never been so relieved to see so much orange in my life. I couldn't believe what happened next.

"They were needing more accommodation for the senior members of their faith, so they looked around and ended up buying eight apartments. The head swami was astute and had a strong head for investment and figures. If Harry had met him, he would've loved him.

"It turned out to be one of my best sales days ever!"

Better still for Margaret, the other agent sold nothing that day.

"I went on to become head of the sales team. I managed overseas investment, acquisitions and anything else Harry threw at me. I was a bit of a 'Jack of all trades' – emphasis on the Jack!" It was unheard of that a 'Jill' could do everything Margaret was doing.

Margaret's daughter, Vanessa, went on to be head of the re-sales division and still holds that position today. Harry still asks her on a day-to-day basis what is happening when he passes her office.

"Considering the size of other areas of the company, it isn't a huge income earner for the business," Vanessa says. "It still makes money, good money, so Harry still wants to know what's going on.

"I have my own page in *the sheets*, so what he doesn't ask me on a daily basis will be reported in there."

Kim Jorgensen, Robyn McCully, Helen Williams and Di Reynolds all started at Meriton more than 30 years ago. All were initially in accounts except Robyn, who has always been in conveyancing. All four say that Harry gave them opportunities they would never have been given in any other company. From those initial accounts roles, they have gone on to be the backbone of the company, and Harry trusts each of them implicitly.

Kim Jorgensen has been with Harry for 35 years. She is his first port of call every day when he comes into the office as she is the keeper of the sales journal, and that is Harry's daily bible. *The sheets* are Harry's weekly bible.

"I came out of advertising," Kim says. "I was creative; figures weren't my thing at all, but somehow in a difficult employment market I ended up in the accounts department at Meriton.

"I failed maths miserably at school, so my mother was shocked when I took a job dealing with figures every day.

"I was upfront with Harry and told him I wasn't good with figures, but because it came so naturally to him, he decided I could learn in no time.

"For the first few months I thought he was going to sack me every day. I look at where I am today and still wonder how the hell it happened. I can now pick up even the tiniest discrepancies in the sales figures. We have so many sales on the go at any one time, and the process passes through so many hands, but the smallest error – you can be sure I'll find it."

Kim has always been herself around Harry, and they have a similar sense of humour. He likes that she stuck it out at the start because he didn't make it easy for her.

"She didn't think she could do it, but I showed her she could," Harry says. "It was tough love, but I saw her potential, even if she didn't. Look where she is today.

"I've done that with a lot of the women, and it gives me great satisfaction. They didn't mind so much – they are all still here!"

At some stage over the years, all the women have been wrongly accused of something, but unlike the men, they didn't wear it. One day Harry was tearing strips off Kim for something that wasn't her fault, and she didn't take it lying down.

"I'll take it when it's deserved," Kim says, "but I'm not shy giving it back when it isn't my fault. We work too hard for Harry to take that shit, so one time, as I was walking away, I threw a few words in his direction a little under my breath because I'm still not that brave in such close proximity: 'You give me the shits.' He heard me, called me back and asked me what I'd said. 'Bloody salespeople,' I said. I still know when to draw the line and firing obscenities at the boss is one step too far. He still apologised later in the day when he realised I was given a lashing for no good reason.

"Harry did teach me to be tougher, and I developed a sharp tongue. In the old days, before James (James Sialepis who is now national sales director and Meriton Group director) took control of the salespeople, I was the one that took them on when they were getting a bit slack. Like Harry, I can't tolerate low achievers. I always used his name in vain to get them off their arses, which Harry fully supported. I have Danish blood and a red-headed mother – I take no prisoners!" She laughs.

Kim says that the building meetings back in the day used to be an absolute hoot. The boys would come off site in the afternoon and drink until their late afternoon meeting with Harry. Five minutes before the meeting, they would be having fisticuffs in the car park, and then everyone would go into the meeting like nothing had happened.

"Wednesday nights I used to go out drinking with the same lads," Kim says. "Ken McDonald would pretend to play rough and get me in a headlock. He was like a big brother stirring up his little sister and I loved it. It was all harmless fun, but you wouldn't get away with that nowadays.

"Everyone thought Harry was so brave the way he handled the unions, and it rubbed off a bit. We all wanted to be tough, just like him."

Kim says she still yells at her television screen when something bad is reported that has happened in a Meriton apartment. They don't show the unit because they can't get into it, but they show the building outside with the Meriton signage.

"Seriously, dude, what are they trying to do?" Kim says. "Sully the reputation of the building or the person who built it? Just not newsworthy. It has nothing to do with Meriton; the person just happened to live in a Meriton apartment, which is not so unlikely considering we've built nearly 80,000 of them. Tall poppy syndrome lives on."

Kim says that in the very early days, Harry never owned a diary and he never had an assistant. "Whoever was sitting closest to him, he would tell to take notes. To this day, you can never walk into his office without a pen and piece of paper.

"He might be thinking about something that has nothing to do with you and he'll ask you to write it down.

"Even now, if he feels like a cuppa, he tells the person closest to him to go and make him one. Doesn't matter who that is. Everyone knows how Harry takes his tea," she says.

Kim also remembers a time when a couple of young kids broke into one of the sites in Liverpool and stole a bulldozer. Harry didn't even try to hide his amusement. Rather than have the kids charged, he donated money to Youth Off The Streets. Not that Harry wanted to encourage bad behaviour, but they didn't destroy anything, and he did find it funny that they pinched the bulldozer and took it for a spin. It was the type of thing Harry thought he might like to do, and it wasn't worth giving the kids a criminal record over. He acknowledged at the time that it could have gone wrong, and they could have been hurt and that safety must always come first. Because the kids were fine, it was a little bit funny.

Conveyancing has been Robyn McCully's area of expertise since she started at Meriton 33 years ago.

"Sometimes you feel like Harry knows you better than you know yourself," Robyn says. "The man is cheeky. He has a cracking sense of humour, and he still likes to impress the women.

"Harry loves women, not the same way he loves Rhonda; he just loves the company of women. All the longstanding old birds here have often been to lunch with him, and he likes to make you feel like a princess. You have his undivided attention for an hour, and he spends the whole hour entertaining you.

"He took me to lunch one day in the Bentley, and he turned to me and asked me if I felt like Princess Diana. It was sweet and all very innocent," she says.

Robyn tells the story of going to court for the first time to represent Meriton. A woman had bought a number of apartments and then defaulted on her finance and was unable to complete.

"It was very straightforward," Robyn says. "There was nothing untoward, but the purchaser was saying she was put under undue influence to buy as many apartments as she did. I was involved because I was doing all the conveyancing.

"The lawyers for the other side kept trying to trip me up, and they were very aggressive. All Harry had said was to go and tell the truth because we'd done nothing wrong.

"I kept reminding myself I'd be fine if I stuck to the facts. I also knew I wouldn't be there in the first place if Harry hadn't trusted me to handle it.

"I was wrung out at the end of the day, and I had a terrible headache. I felt shattered. When I arrived back at the office, Harry had champagne waiting and he was in high spirits. We weren't finished yet, but he was making a fuss to cheer me up. I was too exhausted!

"Harry asked, 'What's up, love? It'll all be over tomorrow.' And I said, 'They were mean to me.' There was no other word for it. 'Mean to you,' Harry repeated, then said, 'You go home and get a good night's sleep. It'll all be fine, you'll see.'

"The next day, I was giving evidence and Harry walked into the courtroom. He came and sat as close to me as possible. The exasperated groan was audible from the opposing counsel. Harry loved a fight, and nobody wanted or expected him to be in the courtroom. He put them off their game. He continued to stare the other side down. If you've ever been stared down by Harry, you know how it feels!

"Having him there gave me the confidence I needed, and they went a bit easier on me with the boss in the room. That meant much more to me than anything else he's ever done for me. I've never forgotten it. Again, he was looking after his family.

"I'm sure we all have similar stories because we all feel that Harry has given us opportunities we would never have had anywhere else.

"It's extraordinary when I look back over the years at how progressive he was, and he didn't care what anyone else thought of his choices. He had confidence in you and, as far as he was concerned, nothing else mattered."

Helen Williams has been with Harry for 32 years. She started out in 30-day accounts, then worked with the subbies on seven-day accounts while also helping out in payroll and a bit of HR. Harry threw a lot at her because he knew she was capable and had the capacity to multitask. Even Helen was surprised when Harry offered her the role of contracts manager.

"One day, Harry rang and told me the contracts manager had suffered a nervous breakdown and wasn't returning to work," Helen says.

"Like it was no big deal, he asked me to take over the role. At the time, there would've been no other woman in the country with the role he was offering me. It was a man's world.

"Everybody said I wouldn't be able to handle the subbies, and Rhonda was really concerned because she thought if it didn't work out then I was putting my position at Meriton at risk.

"If Harry thought I could do it, I was going to give it a crack. He didn't see me as a woman; he saw me as the best person for the job, and that was good enough for me.

"That was over 30 years ago, so the subbies have had a long time to get used to me."

There were a lot of trades and contractors at the time that had been with Harry for years, and they had learned never to question his motives or decisions. This one they were concerned about. They had dealt with Helen when they did their accounts, but this was a very different role.

"Initially, none of the subbies thought I could do it," Helen says. "It just wasn't a woman's job. It wasn't easy in the beginning, but Harry always stood by me and reassured me that I could do it."

Helen needs to get a minimum of three quotes, and then the decision of who gets the job always sits with Harry.

"Harry signs off on anything over $25,000," Helen says. "That's the majority of our quotes, so he's having to sign off every day. I spend a lot of time with him.

"We try to be fair with the spread of jobs between the old and new suppliers, but Harry is loyal, and he generally likes to use the same guys. He gives them continued work, as he has throughout the years. That's particularly the case with subbies who've been with Harry from the start and are on to the third generation. Harry likes to make sure they have future work.

"Harry and I work very well together, and I've always been so grateful that he gave me the opportunity. He pushed me in a way that wouldn't have happened anywhere else. He took a personal interest – I wasn't just another number.

"He trusted me, and the loyalty is mutual. I'll be forever grateful for the opportunity, and I think that shows in a lot of women who've been here for so long. We were way before our time, and that's thanks to Harry."

When Di Reynolds started working for Harry he said to her, "I don't know if I like you." Di speaks her mind, so it was likely that Harry didn't like that. Thirty years later, Di laughs about it.

"It wasn't personal," Di says. "I think he saw in me a woman who might challenge him, and that's what he wasn't sure he liked.

"So, here I am 30 years later, and more important than liking me, he trusts me. He sees my ability to keep a broad eye on the business, and he likes that."

Harry, of course, does like Di, and she has longevity to show for it. As with the other longstanding women of Meriton, he has a real soft spot for her. When Harry married one of those women, you would think that it would cause some tension, but it only brought them closer.

"To this day, Rhonda still has an office next to mine," Di says. "She doesn't use it much, but it's there if she wants it. She'll always have a place with us. Before she married Harry, Rhonda was one of us, and that's how it will always be."

Di is now the group administration manager at Meriton, but she feels a bit like a 'Di of all trades'.

"Titles at Meriton mean nothing," Di says. "If Harry asks me to do something that's outside the realm of my role, I never question it. Every year my position evolves to incorporate whatever it is that Harry wants me to do. That could be anything totally unrelated to my business within the business. He doesn't care; he just wants the job done by someone he trusts."

Harry doesn't think about how that adds to someone's workload. He envisages the right person for the job, and he gives it to them to do. If you're at Meriton, you adjust to that way of working. The more work you do, the more responsibility you're given, and the more work Harry gives you.

During COVID, Di had more responsibility dropped in her lap. Because Meriton was in an essential industry, they continued to keep their doors open, although there were small periods of time when construction work also had to cease.

"Where I live wasn't within the 5km rule. The first thing I did when I heard we were going into lockdown was organise a room in our Meriton Suites above the office," Di says.

"I had a quick coffee with my husband, packed a bag, and I was out in a couple of hours. My husband understood it was what I had to do, so he was fine with caring for our older kids. I didn't go home again for three-and-a-half months. That's how invested I am in the company. I couldn't work from home mostly because I'm a cheque signatory."

Harry sees Meriton's management of COVID as one of their most successful times in the business. Di was responsible for making sure Meriton worked within the Public Health Orders.

"We did everything to protect our workers, both in the office and on site," Di says. "We took people's temperatures before they entered the building, we had hand sanitisers all over the place, and we moved desks around to incorporate all the safe-distancing restrictions. We did everything to the letter of the law.

"As we were an essential industry, we could continue to work most of the time. We had a committee because the restrictions were changing every day. Harry wanted it to be business as usual, but there were times even we had to pause work."

As an example, for two weeks from 19 July 2021, the NSW Government introduced new restrictions to pause all construction across the Greater Sydney area for two weeks. That applied to Mcriton as well.

"It was probably the only time in Harry's life he had to do as he was told," Di says. "It didn't make it any easier when I was the one who had to do the telling! It was the first time in 30 years that I felt our relationship was stretched. COVID wasn't a good time for Harry and me. It was the only time I thought he might say it was time to part ways.

"But it was just a blip. When things were back to normal, I could tell Harry appreciated that I'd left my family for all that time to be there for him and the company. It was a stressful time, but it made us stronger, if anything."

Everyone that has contributed to this book has mentioned Harry's driving, and Di was no exception. Cars or boats, the driving has never been good. God bless Pablo, his driver. Harry always said that he would give up driving when he was 80. The other drivers on the road should have celebrated that birthday! As for the water, boat owners used to go and grab their quant or barge pole (used to move boats away from their craft) when they saw Harry coming.

"My gosh, the driving was scary," Di says. "I remember one time I had to go to Harry's house because he wasn't well. As the day wore on, he started to feel a bit better, so he rang and told me to come over to go through some accounts. Big boxes of them.

"I put everything into a taxi and headed over. We went through the accounts, and then Harry said he would drive me back to the office because he said it would take too long to get a taxi.

"We loaded up the car – a new Bentley – and he starts driving like a maniac down the 'S' bends of New South Head Road," she says.

That is a winding road between Edgecliff and Vaucluse, where Harry lives. In the famous City2Surf race, part of New South Head Road (between Rose Bay and Vaucluse) is called 'heartbreak hill' because it's so steep and winding.

"It was that section of road where Harry suddenly sped up," Di says. "He had glimpsed a taxi, and he was driving erratically while blaring his horn, trying to get the driver's attention. I was sitting there wondering if it would be rude to put my hands on the dash to brace myself.

"Fortunately, the taxi driver pulled over – he really wasn't left with much choice. Harry turned to me and said, with a sniffle, 'Sorry love, I'm not feeling well. I'll go home to bed. I probably shouldn't be on the road.'

"No kidding, Harry! He was so keen to get away, he almost drove off with all my things still in the car," Di says. "He didn't need to apologise. I'd never been so relieved to get out of a car in my life."

The fact Harry cannot drive anything with an engine makes him more human. It's about the only thing he cannot do well. Take one for the team, Harry – driving is something everyone in your life does better than you!

"I'm totally committed to Harry and the company as a whole," Di says. "I love the times Harry and I go out to lunch and we don't talk about work. He's very personable and asks about my family and how they're all doing. It's a different Harry at lunch."

Di is one of Harry's favourites. Even during her interview for this book, he was looking for her. She's the only person, when called, who didn't get up and leave immediately. She told him what she was doing, and he agreed she could finish up. When he thought he had given her enough time – 10 minutes later – he was paging her again. "I better go this time!" Di laughed.

Another person coming up to 30 years at Meriton is Magdalena Riviere, who started in 1995, straight out of university. Like Vanessa, she took off a couple of times to do some travelling.

"I started in a relatively junior role, but after I'd travelled, I was invited back to head up property management," Magdalena says.

"I feel like Meriton has been such a huge part of my life, and I wonder where the time has gone. It's gone by in a flash. I don't know anything else or anywhere else."

Harry had reached out to Magdalena because he was going to start keeping his stock and building to rent.

"When I started, there were a bunch of buildings under construction," Magdalena says. "We were getting ready for those to come on board.

"Suddenly, they all completed at the same time, and we had 300 apartments to manage, then another 300 apartments, and we grew in a very short period of time. That smaller portfolio grew to 9,000 apartments with 22 people managing them. Victor Toscano is head of leasing, and I do the property management. Now, I delegate and deal more with people than properties. My day-to-day job is really managing my team.

"Harry and I have a mutual trust, and he has given me a lot of leeway to do whatever needs to be done to get the job done. His business is my business, and my business is in an area that makes him a lot of money.

"I've noticed that he trusts all the women to get on and do their jobs, but I feel he watches the men like a hawk!"

Magdelana feels like she is part of something that is evolving and constantly changing.

"I like being part of something bigger than myself," she says. "It's been such a huge learning experience, and I feel like I've been here my whole life. Harry is a huge part of that.

"Even though I think I have the best job in the world, I still wonder after being here so long if I missed something along the way. There's a whole other world out there, and I feel like a protected species here.

"But Harry kept sending me challenges, and I had to rise to the occasion, so I've never been bored," she says.

As with Helen Williams, Magdalena's job in the beginning, in any other company, would only ever have gone to a man.

"Harry has always been way ahead of his time," Magdalena says. "He never had any doubt that women were as capable as men. In fact, I think he thinks they are more capable.

"I think the women are more secure in their roles at Meriton, and some of the men have more of a fear of losing their jobs. They do whatever they can to stay in Harry's good graces. The women pretty much just tell him how it is."

In 2023, for the first time in nearly 30 years, Magdalena thought she might move on. There was conflict. A couple of the men thought she shouldn't be in her role. Word got out that she was feeling unsettled, and Harry called her into his office and asked her what was going on. He couldn't understand why she cared what anyone else thought because at the end of the day, it only mattered what *he* thought!

"He told me that whatever was unsettling me, we had to change it," Magdalena says.

"I didn't build this company only for myself. I built it for all of us, and that includes you," Harry told her.

"In a few words he made me feel valued and that he had my back. I remember going home that night thinking there was so much said in that short conversation. It made me think more about what I wanted to achieve and how I was so included in that equation. Those words helped me reconcile what I was dealing with and helped me come to some kind of resolution within myself.

"I did make the changes, and I did speak up. I addressed those I needed to address, and I got the resolution I needed. It was Harry that made me see what I needed to do.

"It is amazing how much can be said in so few words that so influence the direction of your life."

And that is why Harry is the chief of conflict resolution.

"I'm only too well aware that I have the ability to listen more and think differently," Harry says.

"I can hear about a problem and offer a resolution in a split second. It doesn't matter what the problem is, business or personal, I know instinctively the best way to fix it. I don't need to banter on for hours. I tell them this is what you must do, so do it.

"That's not part of the genius people talk about; that is because I'm all about the people. They always come first, and I've done my best to be there for all of them. I am a master in humanity. It is instinctive. It has always been about the people.

"I have solved millions of problems in my life for all kinds of people.

It's the most satisfying thing I do. I know how to put people's minds at ease. It's a gift."

Last but not least, the woman who spends the most time with Harry in the office is his executive assistant of 20 years, Loreto Escobar. Those who have been at Meriton a very long time agree that Loreto has been the best EA Harry has ever had. The common consensus is that they really get each other. They also like each other, and that leads to the strong working relationship they have.

It wasn't always that way though.

"I started in reception, and I didn't even meet Harry until my second week," Loreto says.

"One day he called me into the sales meeting. I walked into the room and it was full of people. They were all just sitting there staring at me.

"Harry started firing questions at me: 'What's your name? Where are you from?' It was my first encounter with him, and I was absolutely terrified.

"At the time, I lived in Blacktown and I was actually living in a Meriton apartment in Reservoir Road, but I didn't realise it. Harry was quick to point that out.

"Over time, if Harry's assistant was sick, he would call me up to his office and I would make calls from his desk for him. Call me crazy, but when one of his assistants didn't last long, I put my hand up for the job, but I really didn't know what I was getting myself into," she says.

Harry gave Loreto the job. She had her own office, which was the first sign of how important the job was, and initially she continued to type letters and do the usual calls. Then Harry saw that Loreto was capable of so much more. Like the other women, he was going to bring out the best in her and tap into her potential.

"For a whole year he tested me at every turn," Loreto says. "He was putting me through my paces, and it was really hard at first. In those early days I made mistakes. Lots of them. I wouldn't cop it though when I was blamed for something I didn't do.

"Early in the piece Harry blamed me for something that wasn't my fault, and he started yelling at me. I spoke back to him.

"I wasn't being disrespectful, but I was standing my ground. I have self-respect and I wasn't going to accept it. I don't take shit! He apologised, and he was more careful after that," she says.

"Those early days were really stressful, but I was determined to make it work. It was a once-in-a-lifetime opportunity.

"Where I used to be terrified, I get a thrill out of it now." Loreto smiles. "I thrive on the adrenaline rush. When Harry changes his mind at the last minute, he doesn't ever worry about the consequences, he just wants me to fix it. He doesn't want to know the details; he just wants a resolution.

"I've had unbelievable last-minute requests, but I love that part of my job. It's very satisfying. Jaws drop when Harry asks for the impossible, and when I pull it off, nobody can believe I did it. That's why I love my job."

Loreto just smiles when she talks about his temper. "It's generally not directed at me these days, so it's water off a duck's back," she says.

"I see a different side to Harry when we go out for lunch. He's such a gentleman. I love it when he talks about when he was young. He remembers in such detail. He has a really wicked sense of humour – he's so entertaining and fun.

"He calls every woman he likes 'the girlfriend', which is all in good humour. Problem is, he has so many of them now that I never know which one he's talking about."

Loreto spends more time with Harry than she does her own family, and over the years she has become quite protective of him.

"Everybody wants a piece of him, all of the time," Loreto says. "He loves it, but I have to make sure he has some breathing space. He's still his own worst enemy because I get him comfortable, make him a cup of tea and leave him to his thoughts. Then as soon as I'm out of the room, he bypasses me to reception and starts summoning people to his office.

"I even try to spread out his lunches so we keep his weight in check. I don't fuss over him too much, but I do consider his health and how his crazy schedule affects it."

It's not a one-way street. Harry reciprocates by showing an interest in Loreto's life too. Her husband, Anthony, is a fireman. Harry loves hearing stories about Anthony's job. What kid didn't want to be a fireman at some stage when they were growing up?

"They get all the women too." Harry laughs. "Look at how lucky Anthony got!" he says.

Harry also shows an interest in Loreto's son, Jack.

"He's always asking about him," Loreto says. "When I was pregnant with Jack, Rhonda told Harry that he wasn't to scream at me and that I was to leave early. Before I had Jack I would stay until all hours. He got into the habit of not screaming at me, and when I came back after maternity leave, he stopped it altogether," she says.

It had nothing to do with habit. Harry realised during Loreto's maternity leave that life was a whole lot better when she was looking after him.

"It was so hard leaving my tiny baby at daycare," Loreto says. "I went back to work, but I was constantly checking in on Jack. I knew Harry appreciated me being back, but it was hard to say goodbye to my beautiful boy every day.

"Harry knew it was hard though, and he was always checking in on me. To this day he doesn't like it at all when I'm not around. I hang out in his office a lot!"

What Loreto finds most amazing is how Harry takes the responsibility for everyone on his shoulders. He knows that providing a job for people becomes tenfold when those people have to provide for their extended families.

"It's extraordinary how personally invested Harry is," Loreto says. "He takes an interest in everyone. He really loves people. He doesn't do idle chit-chat well. I always know when he's done with someone. They're usually trying to impress him and his eyes glaze over and I try to wrap it up.

"I tell people to keep it short and sweet and not to push it if he says no. Sadly, many don't heed the advice and they persevere, thinking they can change his mind. The devil comes out and fireworks light up the room.

"No means no to Harry. End of conversation. Just leave!" Loreto says.

"But he protects me as well. When I had my gallbladder out, I woke up to find one of the most senior doctors at the Prince of Wales Hospital hovering over me. Harry had him check on me.

"When I was living in one of our buildings at Waterloo and there weren't enough buses, Harry lobbied to get more, but I think that one was so I wouldn't be late for work.

"Any way you look at it, we spend a great deal of time together and I enjoy every day because I never know what to expect. There's always something new and exciting happening. You forget sometimes who he is because he has no airs and graces. Harry is definitely not a snob," she says. "Harry doesn't like snobs."

"I see all these women every day," Harry says. "I'm not like other bosses. I let them wander in and out of my office whenever they want. Mostly they wait until I call them, but they've had the open-door access to me for so many years, sometimes they just walk right in. It drives Loreto crazy because I don't allow her to stem the flow.

"But I love working that way. Driving Loreto crazy, that's an added bonus," he says with a laugh.

There is also a special mention for a kid who started at Meriton when she was 20 years old.

Harry has a bit of a soft spot for Eleni Tritsiniotis. He calls her the 'Coca-Cola kid'.

"She had the most junior role at Meriton when she first came here as a kid 20 years ago," Harry says.

"She used to fill the fridges with soft drink, hence my nickname for her. She was funny and I liked her immediately. Over the years, she's made her way through the ranks and is now my document control manager for architecture and construction.

"My relationship with her is still the same as it was all those years ago and I sometimes still call her the 'Coca-Cola kid'. I tease her and she pretends to take offence, but no offence is taken. She's a big part of my Meriton family because she's spent more than half her life with me," he says.

Meriton Christmas party, 2016. L-R: Dianne Reynolds, Helen Williams, Harry, Robyn McCully, Kelley Carson, Evelyn Barrios.

Harry and Margaret Rahilly.

Harry with Kim Jorgensen.

Helen Williams, Harry & Dianne Reynolds, 1996.

Helen Williams, Harry & Dianne Reynolds, 2022.

Rhonda, Loreto's husband Anthony Wallgate, Harry, Loreto Escobar, 2008.

Orna, Harry, Margaret & Rhonda at the Property Council of Australia Awards, where Harry was inducted into the Hall of Fame, 2015.

Above: Meriton staff celebrating Australia Day at the Ferrython, 2020. L-R: Kelley Carson, Harry, Eleni Tritsiniotis, Kim Jorgensen.

Left: Cindy Martin & Margaret Rahilly at the opening event for Macquarie Residences, 2014.

Celebrating over 20 years with Meriton on International Women's Day, 2023. L-R: Sharon Bruchhauser, Kim Jorgensen, Loreto Escobar, Orna Triguboff, Dianne Reynolds, Helen Williams, Eleni Tritsiniotis, Jeanette Lloyd.

The Meriton women, International Women's Day, 2023.

TWELVE

THE FAMILY

Harry loves the big picture and things are always revolving around in his head.

"I don't have the luxury of dedicating all my time and energy to dealing with one thing at a time," Harry says.

"On any one day I am dealing with multiple projects across the eastern seaboard. I'm dealing with red tape with governments and councils, dealing with legal issues, having meetings with architects and designers, and dealing with multiple issues that pop up from any other area of the business. I'm also a big supporter of the Jewish community. I have a large extended family now, and I must make time for the wife.

"My people at Meriton are also my family, so I help them deal with their issues as well, whether business or personal. I know their families well.

"It is a full life. Sadly, gone are the days where I could have a one-track mind." He laughs.

One of the family members who has been around Meriton the longest is Harry's daughter, Orna. She has been sitting in on meetings in Harry's office for 50 years, since she was at school. He likes that she has a broad knowledge of the entire business, garnered after all those years of 'sitting in'. Orna, no matter how busy she is, sits quietly, listens and/or takes notes. If she is familiar with the context of the meeting, she'll join the conversation.

Orna plays down the importance of her being there by saying that Harry just likes her to observe.

"I remember when I used to pop into the office for five minutes to pick something up only to still be there an hour later," Orna says. Harry would tell her to sit down and learn something.

"Who knows, you might be able to help the business one day," Harry would say to her.

And so, after all these years, it is their tradition. Orna is now in the office four days a week and much of that time is spent in Harry's office doing exactly that – helping the business and still learning.

"I don't expect to be running anything in the future," Orna says. "But at least I'll be across a lot of things, so I'll be able to input my knowledge to those who need it."

There is a special bond between Orna and Harry. Orna is the only one in the family who doesn't call Harry by his name in the office. To her, he is first and foremost her dad, and that's what she always calls him. When the room is not full of people, Harry will take her hand while he's talking to her, and he will look directly at her. Not with the eyes that bore into your soul when he's unhappy with you, but with gentle fondness.

Sharon chose a different path. She worked at Meriton for a while but then she married Gary and had three children.

"It wasn't all smooth sailing there for a while with Dad and Gary," Sharon says. "Dad didn't like that Gary wasn't marrying me as fast as he would have liked. He let us both know in no uncertain terms.

"Dad was used to people doing what he told them to do. I stayed clear of Dad and the office and, when Gary and I did get married, I had my heart set on starting a family. I never really did go back into the office full-time. I still go in for meetings and my boys are working there, so I'm still around," she says.

Sharon has always been around. Although it was sometimes hit and miss, she says her dad made an effort to entertain them when they were growing up.

"Growing up, on the weekends we used to go to the jobs. Our first foray into the building industry was walking up the gangplanks and climbing up ladders. Dad had a sandpit in the back of the ute for us to play in.

"Dad liked boats, but he didn't know much about them. When we were young, he used to hire these little boats and then pass them on to us to drive ourselves. Orna and I were terrified. He didn't show us how to drive them – he just expected us to drive them with no instruction.

"He bought a bigger boat when he and Mum divorced because he thought it was a really good thing to do with the kids. He found out what it was like to drive with no instruction. Every second weekend we got beached somewhere." She laughs.

Harry never farmed the girls out during school holidays. He always took them into the office.

"We loved sitting on the switchboard with Marie," Sharon says. "It was one of those old switchboards with the cords you pull in and out and crisscross over to the different extensions. We loved doing that. We also used to make buildings out of paddle-pop sticks. It was definitely fun."

Harry also helped the girls with their homework, particularly maths and French.

"They both came naturally to him," Sharon says. "He loves languages and anything to do with figures."

Even after Sharon was married with her own children, Harry would still organise holidays for them.

"I remember one time Harry asked us to go to Western Australia for a holiday," Sharon says. "We were taking all the kids, and we were thinking we would have a bit of time at Margaret River, then some time lying in the sun on beautiful beaches on the west coast. We couldn't wait.

"But … Dad loves mines, so all we did was go to 12 different mines. We slept in all these weird little pubs that had beds with squeaky springs. I don't know when that became his idea of a holiday, but he wasn't always like that.

"We used to have fabulous holidays in Fiji and Surfers Paradise when we were young. Dad loved the sun and swimming so he would sit by the pool and swim and read. Somewhere along the way he lost the art of relaxation and thought 'holidaying' was a waste of time.

"Dad loved bowling and putt putt in the earlier years, and we had so much fun," she says.

Sharon and Orna had a lot of fun growing up, but they were also made to understand the value of money from a young age.

"I was 15 and Orna was 16 when Dad sold us our first apartments," Sharon says.

"Obviously, he backed us financially, but he made us go to the bank, get a loan and go through the whole process ourselves. He was insistent on us knowing what was involved in paying back a loan – he wanted us to know the financial responsibility.

"And that respect for money has come down the generations. My children also understand the value of money.

"I didn't know my grandparents, so I'm also very grateful my children have known their grandparents so well. I'm thankful they have had such a close relationship with Dad and Rhonda.

"Now Dad is great-grandfather to my grandson, Archie. They love each other very much. They play with trucks together and Archie loves concrete trucks. He loves going to the building sites, and he will stand there for hours just looking around with Dad."

Ella, Orna's daughter, also takes her children out on site, and she loves that they are such a close family. She makes specific mention of Orna and Harry's close relationship.

"Mum is very close to Harry, and vice versa," she says. "They have a very special relationship, and the thing they have in common, which clearly Mum gets from Harry, is that they're both capable of doing 10 things at once.

"The cute thing that Harry taught Mum was the benefit of an afternoon nap. When she was young and they arrived home on the weekend after being out at site, Mum and Harry would have a little nap and they still continue to do it today, to recharge their busy minds."

Harry has always said that sleep is food for the brain. "You cannot fire on all cylinders without it," he says. And when he says 'fire on all cylinders', he does it like no other!

"There are no formalities at Meriton, and it's always been that way," Orna says. "It's all very fluid because Dad knows in his own head exactly what's coming next and who he needs. It just takes everyone else time to catch up.

"For example, Dad might consider a conversation he's had earlier in the day where he was advised that laundries could be smaller, allowing extra space for the kitchen or the bathrooms.

"He thinks about who this will directly involve, and he calls all those people to his office to discuss it and get their views. Ella is very involved in design now, so she'll be there with head of architecture Frank Ru. James Sialepis will be there to discuss how it might affect sales; Matthew Thomas will be there to represent Meriton Suites; Brad Goodman is there in regard to costings; Charbel Rabie is there in regard to building changes; and Albert Chan is there because Harry likes his ideas.

"They'll all be in his office within three minutes. They talk it out, discuss it from their perspectives, and a plan of attack is put in place. It might get a bit heated, but there's always a solution. If anyone needs to come back to Dad, it's done in a short period of time. And that's how decisions are made," Orna says.

The next time Harry will see anything about it is at the end of the week when it'll be included in *the sheets*. That's where Harry will see it has been actioned, and if it hasn't, come Monday morning he'll want to know why.

Orna has been at Meriton a long time, but she still finds it exciting when there's a lot of activity going on in Harry's office.

"It doesn't matter what you throw at Dad, he knows exactly what's going on, even if it's coming at him from all angles," she says.

"Nothing gets by him. His capacity to prioritise in his head within seconds is a gift, but he sees it as just being the way his brain works."

Orna is right, but Harry certainly doesn't see it as a gift. In fact, at one point when it was particularly busy, he told his HR manager at the daily senior management meeting to 'find me someone who can do everything I can do'.

Ella immediately spoke up, "What part of what you do, Harry?"

"All of it," Harry responded. "I know everything about every area of the business so it can't be that hard to find someone else that can learn."

That was one of Harry's pearler unpredictable moments. The room went silent. He had no idea what an impossible task that would be. He had set his human resources manager up to fail … miserably.

"What are you all looking at?" Harry asked. "What they don't know, I'll teach them."

Of course, it never happened because such a person doesn't exist. No amount of teaching would ever give Harry what he wants or needs. The other problem is that a person who thought they could be Harry would have a huge ego by default. They wouldn't be happy being told what to do. They would want to shake things up and Harry would hate that.

Harry's senior management team members have each honed their skills to work the way Harry prefers. He needs colour and that comes in variety. More people, more ideas, more interaction. The last thing Harry needs is an experienced operator from a large conventional business coming in and talking to him about the thing he hates most – setting goals and drafting business plans. But what Harry couldn't find in one person he has found in his four directors.

The Triguboff family, Harry's 90th birthday celebration, Sydney Town Hall, 2023.

Harry & Rhonda in the 1980s.

Orna & Harry in Israel, 1980s.

Harry receiving the Member of the Order of Australia, 1990.

Michael, Harry & Sharon in China, 1997.

Celebrating Orna's PhD graduation from Sydney University, 2003.

Sharon, Orna & Rhonda at Harry's 80th birthday celebration.

Harry being awarded an honorary doctorate by Griffith University, QLD, 2012.

Harry with family & friends departing for a sea plane ride for Harry's 86th birthday.

Harry holding Asher, 2015.

Harry & Asher on Father's Day, Gold Coast, 2015.

Harry holding Talia, 2016.

Talia, Rhonda & Orna, 2017.

Asher & Rhonda, 2019.

Talia, Harry & Ella, 2022.

Miki, Archie, Ella, Asher & Talia, Israel, 2023.

Archie ready to build, 2024.

Talia and Harry & Rhonda's dog, Susie, 2018.

Harry and Asher, 2019.

Miki Hendler, Ariel Hendler, Dorren Triguboff.

Family dinner, 2018.

Harry & Orna.

Rhonda, Miki & Sharon, 2020.

Harry, Talia and Rhonda, 2022.

Sharon & Harry, 2023.

Harry with Hendler family at opening of Ocean, 2022.

Harry & Rhonda, 2022.

Asher giving a speech at Harry's 90th birthday.

Nir, Ella and Asher on-site at Trilogy, Macquarie Park, 2024.

Rhonda & Harry with Miki, Poppy & Archie, 2024.

Left: Orna & Harry on site, 2023.

Middle: Orna, Harry, Rhonda & Sharon on Sydney Harbour for Vivid festival, 2024.

Bottom: Gary, Daniel, Michael, Asher, Nir, Harry & Ariel, 2017.

THIRTEEN

THE DIRECTORS

When you start a jigsaw puzzle you logically dig out the edge pieces first and join them together to create the border, providing a clear framework for the big picture.

James Sialepis, Matthew Thomas, Albert Chan and Brad Goodman are the four sides to Harry's jigsaw, and all the other pieces interconnecting them create the big picture. Three directors have their own areas of the business to manage, and one is a generalist across the business.

Aside from Harry's biological family, these four directors have a big stake in the giant cogwheel that is Meriton.

"My directors spend more time with me than anyone else, and I must share my wisdom. It's very important for the future," says Harry.

By 2024, James had been with Harry for 28 years, Matthew for 20 years, Albert for 15 years, and Brad is the newcomer, starting at Meriton five years ago.

In 1998 James, then a cheeky 21-year-old kid with a big smile and a bigger personality, was handed the keys to a $100 million project in Hornsby. He was told by Harry to, 'Show me what you've got!'

Until then, James had been working on different sites as a sales assistant. For two years he had been responsible for making sure the sales units were clean, the lights were on and the doors were open. He made sure the sales agents had all the necessary collateral, and he would sprint the lunch run for the selling agents to the little corner shop. During the inspections, he listened and learned. James was a natural.

"When I started at Meriton, I was bottom of the pecking order, so for the first two years I never even met Harry," James says. "There was no reason for me to go to head office as I was always on site.

"Once the construction process is done, which Harry loves, he no longer goes to site. He hands over to the sales agent and monitors the sales from his office. We never crossed paths."

Harry had only heard good things about James from the other sales agents, so when there was a need for an agent at Hornsby, Harry decided James should do it.

Harry wasn't concerned at all about handing over such a huge responsibility to a kid James' age. At around the same age, Harry had run a successful carpet factory on his own in Israel. If James had what it took, it was time for him to step up.

"Harry was giving me a huge opportunity, and he wasn't wrong in thinking I was up for the challenge," James says. "I worked every waking hour to prove to him he'd made the right decision. It wasn't without its challenges, but I was determined to succeed.

"I literally went from an assistant to a senior sales and project manager overnight."

Ten years later, James was the national sales director, and he was working full-time in head office. He spent more time in Harry's office than his own, and he not only headed up sales but was responsible for the management of the marketing department as well.

"I would never have been given the opportunity anywhere else," James says. "When Harry puts his trust in you, he asks you to repay it by working hard and by doing the best for the business. If I'd been the wrong choice, Harry would've worked that out pretty quickly and I would've been shown the door. No matter your qualifications and experience, if you don't click with Harry and you're in the inner circle, you are on borrowed time."

James, even after so many years, says he still has to pinch himself that he is in that inner circle, working for the greatest captain of the property industry of our time.

"I've learned more from that one man than I would've ever expected in my lifetime. It's a great gift," James says. "I was very proud when he invited me to be a director of Meriton."

As far as James is concerned, the game-changer developments were not in the inner city. It was in the suburbs like Mascot, Dee Why and Pagewood where Harry had completely changed buyer perceptions of apartment living.

"It was amazing to see people head to suburbs away from the inner city to buy apartments," he says.

The city dwellers were already converts, but those on the outskirts of the city were still sitting on the fence. Those who hadn't yet made up their minds which way to jump then turned to Pagewood Green, Mascot Central and Dee Why. Buyers were more than happy to take one of the oversized four-bedroom, low-maintenance apartments with every possible convenience because it was a promise of winning their weekends back to spend with their kids.

At the opening of Mascot Central, Harry stood proudly and admitted that it was one of his best. "This is the new way for family living and to accommodate everyone. I think we have built the biggest car park in Australia, in the world maybe," he boasted.

James says it is amazing how Harry changed people's views on apartment living. Harry always knew it was only a matter of time, even if nobody else agreed when he first started out.

"We had people relocating to Pagewood Green from Rose Bay and Double Bay," says James. "Before Pagewood Green, you would never have heard about families from the inner eastern suburbs, with their kids in private schools, boasting about moving into an apartment development in Pagewood. The same on the Northern Beaches with our projects in Dee Why.

"It's absolutely fantastic to be a part of this and see where the buyers are coming from. It's what makes Harry extraordinary. He is the master of vertical living."

In 2002, Alex Alexiou, then manager of Tiffany – the twin towers above the train station in Bondi Junction – said the feedback was that a lot of people wanted a furnished apartment. Harry realised he could add $200 a week onto the rent for a furnished unit. When the tenants' lease finished, he began to change the units into serviced apartments. And that is when it all started. That is when Matthew Thomas joined the company, at the inception of Meriton Serviced Apartments.

"Bondi Junction had 26 rental apartments being used as serviced apartments, and the stock increased from 26 to 40 when I started," Matthew says.

"At World Tower, Harry had decided to keep the whole top section of the building and that was the first time anywhere that two-bedroom and three-bedroom units came into the hotel sphere."

Traditionally, hotel rooms were always 45 square metres. World Tower was the first building to see whether you could run a hotel with a larger-sized product. Back then, Harry was only testing the market and wouldn't commit a whole building to serviced apartments.

"We didn't have a lot of the technologies that other hotels had, so we were a bit on the back foot. But we caught up, it was successful, and we evolved from there," Matthew says.

"Now we have 23 Meriton Suites properties across Sydney, Brisbane, the Gold Coast, Canberra and Melbourne, making us the biggest hotelier in the country."

A real Harry moment that was a challenge for Matthew was when Harry decided he wanted to open one of his hotels on the Gold Coast before the completion of the building.

Harry wanted to totally complete the first 35 floors of the hotel and fill them with guests while he was still building level 50 and above. He decided 15 floors was enough of a buffer. The guests didn't seem to mind at all, so he kept going and completed the remaining 25 floors while guests holidayed below.

"Of course, it worked! Nothing better than the Meriton Suites experience with a little scaffolding thrown in," Matthew smiles. "Only Harry could get away with it. Only Harry would have tried."

When the COVID pandemic broke out in Australia in 2020, some of Meriton's hotels were used by the government for quarantine and medical facilities. Harry was pleased he could offer people more space than a small hotel room and they could be more comfortable during such extenuating circumstances.

"We lost a lot of staff who knew our product and processes," Matthew says. "Coming out of COVID, we had a few staff but then we had to recruit at the same time as 200 other hotels in Sydney. It was a scramble but a huge opportunity for anyone with no skills to get into the hotel industry.

"You basically needed two arms and two legs, and we would train you. We were literally hiring people who'd only done a few shifts at McDonald's and had never stayed in a hotel, let alone worked in one.

"It was amazing that many of those people came with a huge willingness to learn and a fantastic work ethic," he says.

That is why Harry says that COVID was one of the most successful times in the history of his business. His profit margins were terrible, but it wasn't about that. He helped so many people in so many ways and was able to give people opportunities to work immediately the restrictions were relaxed.

"I think we had the right people come and work with us," Matthew says. "Okay, we still had the people who applied for housekeeping roles who wanted to work from home, but generally we found some fantastic people.

"Our staffing task was made harder by the fact that there were a lot of government handouts, so many people chose not to work at all. Borders weren't open, so we didn't get the visa people. We relied heavily on our training program to attract people into the industry. It was all a bit crazy, but it was also a brilliant opportunity for unskilled workers.

"Harry has good reason to be proud of that time. Our hotel business stayed afloat when all tourism halted and many hotels closed their doors. We pivoted to provide quarantine and health accommodation, which meant we managed to maintain some staff and income until the pandemic was over.

"Harry would've been cheering on every one of those people who came to Meriton Suites after COVID. He would've loved that he was training them and giving them skills – pushing them to be the best they could be.

"Harry is all about the people, and we certainly have a lot of them at Meriton Suites. Some are transient, like many visa holders in this business, but many are loyal to the brand. They might move around to other Meriton hotels, but they stay loyal to the brand," Matthew says.

Albert Chan has been at Meriton for 15 years. He had a number of roles before becoming the general manager in July 2024. Albert had already been an executive director for the past three years.

Albert started his career at Meriton leading teams in one of the hotels. He moved to more senior positions within Meriton Suites but rarely had a need to spend time at Meriton head office.

"Harry has made a huge impact on my life, and it's very special," Albert says. "Always my objective is to take work off Harry's plate. There are things I can do for Harry that he doesn't need to be involved in."

Albert says it was challenging when he first started at head office. He went in as head of operations and nobody really knew who he was. Harry didn't really know him either, although Albert had been at Meriton for years. Albert heard a lot of, "Who's the kid?" and "Who's Albert? He's not going to last!" Nobody wanted him to be involved in what they were doing, so it took time.

"I didn't have a rapport or relationship with Harry when I came over to head office," Albert says. "But I came with fresh eyes, and I think that made a difference.

"Harry has always seen me as the ideas man. I see myself as the person who finds better ways to do things. For the first 12 to 18 months, I became the 'fix-it man'. After that I became the 'ideas man'. It was all about how I could make or save Meriton money.

"We now have our own insurance company, our own electrical company, and we own our cranes rather than rent them. All those things have saved us money," he says.

Albert now feels like he has a connection with most of the people in the office and he is happy to fill Harry in on everything he needs to know.

"Harry wants to know about everything, but he doesn't have to be involved in the nuts and bolts of fixing the problem," Albert says. "Tell him the problem and then tell him when it's resolved. I'm good with people, so I take responsibility for relationship management in the business. If there is conflict, I will manage it, but Harry will always know about it. Mind you, Harry doesn't see me as a fixer. He sees me as an ideas man, but that's fine.

"I tell him that if he isn't happy with someone, I'll sort it out. If it cannot be sorted, I will find him someone else. It's one less thing he has to worry about. Because people have access to Harry, they just expect it, but there are times when he doesn't have to deal with some things. I feel privileged that Harry, and even his family, have confidence in me. I learn quickly, and I have good common sense. I'm really good with people. I feel like that is my greatest strength."

Brad Goodman is the new kid on the block, having only worked at Meriton for five years. He started just when COVID hit and came into Meriton as chief financial officer, with a lot of experience under his belt.

"The thing I first noticed was that Meriton is different to how anyone else would run a business," Brad says. "It's certainly different to my previous roles.

"The most amazing thing is that Harry tries to keep everything simple. That way, everybody understands what we're doing and that in turn saves a lot of time."

The most extraordinary thing about Meriton is that the business can pivot. It can always make money because of that. Brad believes that today it would be very hard to replicate what Harry has done.

"The hotels didn't work during COVID, so Harry handed over some to the government and to the hospitals or rented them out long term," says Brad. "I'd never seen anything like it.

"Harry has set his business up in such a way that he always has options. There is always a need for housing and accommodation, and he can fill any demand in any situation.

"And he's always open to new opportunities and change. He asked me the other day if we could bring somebody in to talk about artificial intelligence. That's a world far different to Harry's world, but he's still interested in how he might bridge any gap."

Brad's main responsibility is to get *the sheets* to Harry every Friday. What is really impressive is that Harry initiated the concept of *the sheets* when he first started in business 60 years ago. It may be a more sophisticated version today, but it is extraordinary that Harry can run his whole empire with snapshots compiled into a wad of A3 sheets of paper that he can take home and read over a weekend.

"Getting *the sheets* to Harry every Friday is imperative," says Brad. "It helps him to evaluate every area of the business and that in turn helps him make decisions moving forward.

"Harry's grandson Daniel also gets a copy of *the sheets* to take home on the weekend, so he is across the whole business as well."

Daniel says that Harry is very happy with Brad because he has such a clear understanding of *the sheets*. He's very involved and competent with them, and to Harry that's imperative.

"There are three of us now poring over *the sheets* every weekend, and that gives Harry a lot of confidence that we contribute to, and understand, his bible," Daniel says.

Harry also discusses succession with Brad. Even though he is more than happy to keep his own seat warm for the next 10 years, he knows it needs to be talked about.

"The one thing we're clear on is that Orna and Sharon will take ownership of the business, but they will not run it," Harry says.

"Both had their own ambitions and followed their own paths, so they're not across the day-to-day mechanisms of running such a large business. The next generation is more involved, and I have strong management experience in my directors," he says.

"The only thing I hope for is that Meriton will stay in the family and not get carved up. No one person can do what I do, so they will all have to work together as harmoniously as possible to make that happen.

"For now, I'm calling the shots, and I will continue to do so. I'm still in the prime of my life and, thankfully, I still have good health," he says with conviction.

Daniel says that Harry will be at the helm for a long time yet.

"Harry has every intention of staying at Meriton until he's at least 100 years old," Daniel says. "He's in excellent shape and there's no reason why that can't happen."

Although not a director, Walter Gordon, Harry's head of town planning for 20 years, also features strongly in Harry's day-to-day life.

"I applied for the role and within two days Harry wanted me to start," Walter says.

"He wanted me involved straight away and told me that I was to go to the builders' meeting every day. Harry and I built a rapport quite quickly and to this day we are very close. I'm the one who had to push the approvals through and that has become more and more difficult over the years.

"When I first started, I was getting approvals quite quickly because the planning system wasn't so complex. Construction now is faster than I can get approvals. It's the bane of our existence," he says.

Walter goes to lunch with Harry up to three times a week. They pop downstairs for a sandwich when Harry doesn't have a lunch out.

"Harry is more like a father figure to me than a boss," Walter says. "I have adapted to the way he works and it has rubbed off. I get more impatient than he does these days.

"Harry taught me to get straight to the point because there is no time for waffle. He has taught me the best life lessons and they have held me in good stead."

Walter says no one will ever come up to Harry's level.

"He is so focused and he never listens to the noise around him," Walter says. "He has an inexplicable way of getting things done and getting the result he wants.

"Without warning, Harry just announces on any given day that we are going out. Not just anywhere but to see the Premier or to see the Prime Minister.

"At first, I think they wondered who I was and why I was there, but now they are warming to me, and they're used to seeing me with Harry.

"He just decides at the last minute to take me with him. Sometimes, I feel like the son he never had. There are days that end with Margaret and I having a scotch with him. It's an unusual relationship, but it is also the best relationship.

"I have had the best life at Meriton and an extraordinary friendship with Harry. I could never have been as happy anywhere else and, like Harry, I love what I do," he says.

National Sales Director, James Sialepis.

Group General Manager of Meriton Suites, Matthew Thomas.

General Manager, Albert Chan.

Chief Financial Officer, Brad Goodman.

FOURTEEN

THE NEXT GENERATIONS

Three of four of Harry's grandchildren work in the business, and Harry says that not only do they all get on extremely well, but they have all found their niche.

"My youngest grandchild, Miki, Sharon's daughter, has worked in the business and hopefully she'll return, but being a new mother to little Archie and newborn Poppy is her priority, as it should be," Harry says.

"My oldest, Ella, Orna's daughter, came back after she had her children and she brought her husband, Nir, with her.

"Ella is the creative person in the family, so when she was initially at Meriton she was the marketing director. Now, unsurprisingly, she has found her way into new developments, specifically architecture and interior design.

"All the grandchildren get on very well," says Harry. "While Daniel is a generalist, I see the roles of Ella and grandson Ariel in the business as no less significant. They are becoming experts in their areas of choice, which is important to the business because they are totally focused on a specialised area.

"Each of my grandchildren and great-grandchildren are individuals. No two are the same, and I'm very happy about that. Of course, the great-grandchildren are too young to come into the business, but they might one day, and they will be interested in different aspects of the business as well."

Don't speak too soon, Harry!

Ella and Nir's children, Asher 10, and Talia eight, love it when their mum and dad take them to the office and around the sites. Things could change, but right now, both would like to one day work at Meriton.

"It's not a matter of if, but when," Asher says. "I'll definitely be coming to Meriton."

It seems Asher has inherited his great-grandfather's sense of humour. More than that, he has his confidence.

At Harry's 90th birthday, Asher stood up and gave a speech in front of nearly 500 people. He was nine at the time. He talked about what life must have been like when Harry was that age.

"There would have been no computers, just paper and pencils," Asher said in his speech. "There would have been no iPhone or WhatsApp for communication, instead letters and telegrams, and no Google-Earth, instead an atlas. There would have been no taxis or Ubers to get around with, instead bicycles, rickshaws and donkeys."

But it wasn't tough for Harry. He thought he had the best childhood, and today Asher is having the best childhood but in a very different way. And, if you remember, when Harry was nine, he was also known as Asher, so Harry and Asher have a lot in common. As do Harry and Asher's mum.

Harry always respected that Ella wanted to hit the ground running. It didn't faze him at all when she told him she didn't want to go to university – degrees mean nothing to Harry. He knows there are areas of the business where they're required, but it just meant it would take longer for them to come to Meriton.

"A good brain and street smarts don't always come with a degree," Harry says. "I don't care about that at all. There are people in very senior positions at Meriton who don't have a degree, and they're the very best at what they do in their field."

Ella says she wasn't interested in the theory and just wanted to be learning on the job.

"After school I worked in event management and marketing, and then I went off to travel the world," she says. "When I came back to Sydney, I could truly appreciate why Australia was 'the lucky country', and this was where I wanted to settle down. I went straight to Meriton and took a role in the marketing department. Saba (the Hebrew name for grandpa) was happy that I was finally working at Meriton, and I was excited to be learning from him.

"I was in awe of how Harry approaches each issue as a new opportunity. He's an incredible problem-solver and never takes no for an answer. It's been an exciting place to work, as each day is unpredictable, with Harry making ongoing changes and improvements, all the while keeping the company moving at a fast pace. He keeps everyone on their toes."

Ella is back at Meriton, and she is involved in both architectural design and interior design.

"Rhonda used to take me around with her when I was quite young to pick tiles and carpets for the interior of the units, and Harry would take me around the job sites," Ella says.

"I really loved it. When I was director of marketing, I used to love writing and designing our collateral, but later I wanted to be more hands on with the actual design and construction of the buildings, rather than working with pictures of the final product.

"When I'm not looking at plans or visiting sites, I do my best to sit in on as many management meetings as possible, to be across all areas of the business.

"Working with my cousins, my husband, Nir, and our longstanding staff makes Meriton feel like a small business, no matter how much the company grows," she says.

Daniel, Sharon's eldest son, has been working with Harry for more than

10 years. He started in new developments and Harry is thrilled he took an interest in understanding *the sheets*. He is now the deputy managing director.

Daniel agrees that Harry hasn't run the business by being concerned about five or 10 years down the track and says that Harry is only thinking of problems on the ground that need sorting out.

"It's been a hugely successful methodology because it allows us to move quickly in any given situation," Daniel says.

"I could never have planned for the past 10 years I've spent at Meriton. Because Harry makes every minute count, you feel that the business has achieved more in that time than most would in 100 years. It's been a massive learning curve."

In fact, when Daniel started a Bachelor of Business at UTS, he still wasn't sure what he wanted to do.

"A good friend of mine was doing Property Economics at UTS, and at that stage I was doing a couple of days at Meriton. I hadn't really connected to the business yet, but I was looking at this course and all the subjects and realised all the content was valuable because I'd seen it happening at Meriton. I switched courses and that was definitely the turning point where I was learning the fundamentals of a business like Meriton. It all just connected."

Harry was happy when Daniel decided he would go straight into Meriton from university. Daniel had never had a job before, so he had nothing to compare it with and, until then, he had only seen Harry as the doting grandfather.

"I have fond memories of going to the sites with Harry. He used to take me, Ariel and Miki and he let us run riot. He would let us ride up and down in a cherry picker and we would laugh ourselves silly," Daniel says.

"We would get filthy from jumping around in the mud, and then when Harry was ready to leave, he would open the door to the Bentley and tell us all to get in. Our shoes were covered in mud and the plush carpet in the Bentley would be filthy when we got out. He was never angry – he was pleased to see us having fun."

Miki says that was fun, "but I remember most that he always took us to Twenty-One in Double Bay".

Twenty-One first opened in 1958 and the Triguboff family has frequented it since 1961. Harry and Tommy Gluck used to go there to discuss their first building in Tempe.

"It's been a tradition for our family for all those years," Miki says. "We love tradition."

Daniel remembers their time at Twenty-One as well, but in the office Harry was totally different, and it was all about learning how to work with him.

"There was quite a lot of friction in the beginning because I didn't know how Harry worked or how he liked things," Daniel says. "There was always irritation when learning took time, so you had to grasp things quickly and make decisions accordingly."

Harry can make split-second decisions involving millions of dollars because he has the confidence to know he is always right. Daniel learned early in his career that Harry would much rather have decision-makers in his midst than fence-sitters.

"I always have the final say," Harry says. "If their decision is wrong, I will yell a bit and then we'll fix it. They learn. I would much rather they have the balls to make a decision than fluff around trying to decide what decision they are going to make.

"If they're good, they will start thinking like me, and they will make fewer wrong decisions and more right ones."

While Daniel is involved across the whole business, brother Ariel plays an important role as well.

An area of Meriton's operations in which Harry doesn't spend as much time is the refurbishment of the older buildings. He understands it is a huge part of his business and he places great importance on everything being maintained to a very high standard. He is confident to leave the day-to-day running of that area of the business to Ariel to manage.

"Refurb is highly technical with a lot of detail," Ariel says. "For example, you might work with a lift company for 18 months with a refurb. It's not a quick process, and the detail is painstaking. Harry likes things to happen quickly.

"I surprised myself that I would want to become so involved in such finicky work. It's a lot of dealing with third-party consultants, and I really found a strength I didn't know I had in negotiating contracts.

"As a family member working at Meriton, I spend the least amount of time with Harry. He and I are both perfectionists, so I know, and Harry knows, what he wants to see with the refurbs, so I just get on with it.

"New developments and construction are Harry's greatest loves in the business, so that's where the rockstars hang out.

"I see Harry a lot because my office is close to his, but I'm not a member of that particular band."

One of the greatest actual rockstars of all time, Bono – lead singer of rock band U2 – has been quoted as saying, "I have two instincts. I want to have fun and I want to change the world. I have a chance to do both." That is Harry and Bono singing from the same song sheet. So, well done, Ariel. The terminology 'rockstars' is very appropriate.

"I do spend time with Ella, which I love," Ariel says. "She's absolutely one of the rockstars in new developments, but she lends her skills to refurbs in regard to painting, furniture and overall revamp.

"She's so passionate from the design aspect, and it leaves me to concentrate on the technical side. We work very well together."

Harry loves to see his grandchildren working in harmony. That's important to the future of Meriton.

Prior to Ariel taking a shine to refurbs, he was bouncing around in the business and trying to find his niche. Harry insisted he look at all areas until he could find a place where he would feel most involved and happy.

"There were areas of the business I could never see myself in, but then I found refurbs, and it really has become my baby.

"I think that Harry likes that I've found my place and that I love what I do," he says.

It wasn't always that way. It was a tough transition when Ariel headed straight to Meriton from university.

"Harry was getting impatient and always asking me when I would be finished with uni," Ariel says.

"When I did start work at Meriton, he was hard on me in the beginning because I had no idea what I was doing. He provided little guidance because he wanted me to figure it out for myself. It was definitely tough love!

"For the first six months, I think Harry wondered what I was doing, but he said nothing. He was willing to watch me fumble around being lost until I figured it out.

"And, fortunately, figure it out I did. I feel comfortable at Meriton now. I know exactly what I'm doing, I know I'm good at it, and at long last, as far as Harry is concerned, I've found something that is totally my bag. He trusts me and leaves me to my own devices to run my own show.

"It's a cool place to be."

The architecture and construction team includes Daniel Hendler, Frank Ru, James Sialepis, Matthew Thomas, Albert Chan, Brad Goodman, and construction head Charbel Rabie. Ella is vital to this team and is involved in all design aspects.

Daniel started in new developments when he first joined Meriton 10 years ago. Today he works across the board in the business, but new developments are a big part of his day.

"I don't naturally gravitate to the creative areas of the business, like Ella," he says. "While she's involved in attracting the buyers to our properties through her design contribution, I make sure it's a financially viable proposition for buyers.

"That's why everyone in the family has their own niche in the business. A bit of Harry has rubbed off on all of us and, fortunately, we have different strengths. Harry might not spend as much time with Ariel, but he's thrilled he has such an interest in refurbs. When you consider how many buildings we have, that is a huge part of the business, and he has made it his own. Harry doesn't have to worry about that side of the business."

A year after Daniel started full-time at Meriton, Harry not only gave him his own project to manage, but he also made sure he was financially invested. He was 25 at the time.

"We had a big masterplan at Epping on the old Channel 7 site and there were a few blocks of land left," Daniel says. "The first project I tackled was 41 apartments, and I had to totally manage it from start to finish.

"I had to pay for everything myself, including buying the block of land from Harry. It was a huge opportunity and not one that others would be given just a year fresh out of uni. It was a massive challenge, and I was really thrown in the deep end, but I was also really excited."

Daniel had been enrolled in Harry's school of progression. He had to cover decisions on every aspect of the build from the ground up. Harry made it clear that he would not be there to back him up with grandfatherly words of advice. He had to put his progress in *the sheets* like everyone else, and he was critiqued by Harry accordingly.

"I would say that Harry was definitely proud of me doing the development on my own," Daniel says.

"At the opening of the Epping masterplan development, which happened before the last few stages were complete, Harry said in his speech that I was doing the next block of units by myself, and he was staying out of it. I'm sure I saw his chest puff out as he said it."

When Daniel had the first project under his belt, he almost immediately looked to doing a second. He had learned a lot from the first project, and he instinctively knew what needed to be done for the next one to better the process. A block of land came onto the market independently of the sites Meriton owned, and he bought it and went on to deliver a building with 47 apartments.

"As with the first building, I was able to contract to the Meriton construction team, and I paid wages and overheads anytime I used any Meriton people," Daniel says.

"It was a fabulous experience. I put up my own money and then I went to the ANZ to negotiate finance for the construction costs."

Daniel, after completing his first building, had a better understanding of how to expedite the process. He was thinking like Harry.

"I had learned from the first build what areas I needed to be most invested in and what areas I could delegate to others. There was one area of the build I managed on the first project that I entrusted to the Meriton contracts team for the second," he says.

"Helen and Christine (Law) had the relationship with all the sub-contractors, and I realised early in the piece just how important those relationships are.

"Helen had been dealing with some of the subbies for more than 30 years, so her experience in that area of the business is invaluable. It was commonsense to draw on that."

Like Harry, Daniel was looking at the bigger picture. He was showing early signs of being a chip off the old block.

Once the second project was completed, Harry told Daniel he now had to decide if he was going to stay on his own path and get bigger, or stay with him at Meriton. Daniel chose the latter, and although Harry didn't say much, Daniel was sure he was thrilled with his decision.

"I decided Meriton was my future, and I feel I've had a hand in helping run the business ever since," Daniel says.

"The more I understand and the more I get involved, the more I love it. Now, like Harry, I take *the sheets* home with me on the weekend and go through everything. I know Harry will test me."

Harry has said of Daniel on numerous occasions: "He's very smart and now he totally understands, and contributes to, the intricacies of *the sheets*. That is the most important thing."

Daniel, Harry and Ariel at World Tower, 2017.

Harry and family with former Australian Prime Minister Scott Morrison at the opening event for Meriton's Pagewood Green development, 2018.

Daniel Hendler.

Ariel Hendler.

Daniel, Ella & Harry on-site at Meriton Suites, King Street, Melbourne, 2021.

Nir Lizor.

Ella Lizor.

FIFTEEN

THE ARCHI-CONSTRUCT FAMILY

If Harry sees potential in anyone in the Meriton family, and it might not be an area of the business they are working in, he will fast-track them, like he did Daniel.

"I did the same with James, Matthew and Albert, and now I'm doing the same with my head of construction, Charbel Rabie," Harry says.

Charbel has had his title for a little over a year, taking over from David Cremona, who held the same position at Meriton for 26 years.

Harry simply says of David's departure that "it was time".

"David was talking about leaving because I think he felt he didn't have a big enough hand in the decision-making process," Harry says.

"I've said it before, if someone is not happy and starts shaking the tree about leaving, then it's time for them to go.

"David and I were probably the most alike in many ways, but I'm still the boss, and I make the decisions.

"Over the years, David made a tremendous contribution to the business, especially with our quality. He sorted out sub-contractors in regard to quality and he moved the roughies on," he says.

David says he learned an enormous amount from Harry. "It was incredible working for someone like Harry," he says. "I learned so much and there is no-one like Harry and there never will be again.

"I felt, at this stage of my life, I could thrive in a role where I was able to have more decision-making responsibilities. I felt ready for the challenge of being more accountable for my choices. Meriton has one decision-maker, and there is no question Harry has made his brand a massive success. I would like to have a crack at making that kind of difference."

Charbel and David started their construction relationship with Harry in almost exactly the same way.

"My first dealings with Harry were when Ken McDonald asked me to work on Harry's renovations at his home, so I saw him every day," David says.

Almost word for word, Charbel says of his experience, "My first dealings with Harry were when Ken McDonald asked me to work on installing *Our Big Kitchen* in the basement of Yeshiva College, and I saw Harry nearly every day when he dropped in."

Charbel started with Harry in his early 20s, and he is now 34. David was almost the same age as Charbel when he became construction chief. Harry had no qualms about promoting Charbel to that role.

"During the last 10 years of my head of construction role, methods of building changed, and Harry allowed me to implement them. I'm most proud of setting new quality standards," David says.

"Harry, although tough, would never put anyone's welfare at risk, so I agree with him that the management of COVID was also a huge tick for Meriton.

"I remember it was a Saturday in July, 2021, and I received a call from Brian Seidler, the executive director at the Master Builders Association of New South Wales. He said, 'I have to let you know that the Premier has just shut down the construction industry.' 'On what grounds?' I asked.

"Brian said there had been some COVID cases on construction sites and the numbers were growing. He said the Premier was under pressure."

For the next two weeks, Harry and David campaigned to keep the sites working. David spoke to Ray Hadley on 2GB Radio and Harry spoke to Sky News and Channel 7.

"We had all the right processes in place," David says. Being in construction, we were used to dealing with risk and we understood how to mitigate it.

"There was no good reason to shut us down. We had better systems in place than the government.

"We knew almost immediately if someone had the virus and who they had been in contact with on a two-minute, 10-minute and one-hour basis. If anyone had been in contact with someone with the virus, we would send out an SMS and send them home to monitor for symptoms. If they were free of symptoms after three days and had a negative test, they could come back.

"We continued to work, and we had very few cases of the virus at Meriton. More than 90 per cent of our people were fully vaccinated.

"We had a big hand in keeping the building industry alive and working. It was one of my proudest moments at Meriton, and I know Harry agrees it is also one of his."

Charbel had been in his role for a little over a year when Harry said he was very pleased with his progress.

"It's very different coming off site and working with Harry in the office every day," Charbel says.

"One day you're working on your own little patch, which in terms of other developers is still huge, but then the next day you're a major player in the overall Meriton picture.

"I wasn't a builder anymore; I was contributing to major decisions that affected the company as a whole. When Harry called me into the office to speak to me about the role, it wasn't to discuss the opportunity – it was a given I was already sitting in the chair.

"There was no honeymoon period. There is no such thing at

Meriton because we move so quickly. Harry has expectations, and when he throws you in the deep end, you either sink or swim. There is no grey area treading water – you either fit or you don't.

"It was a big change to be in the inner circle on a daily basis. The others have been with Harry for years, and they're used to his level of expectation. You have to get with the program really quickly, and now, like everyone else immediately around him, I believe he trusts in my ability.

"It's rewarding because Harry never takes all the credit for the success of the business himself. He always says it's a team effort. He always says it is about 'his people'. He's first to recognise the contribution his team makes. And it's not only those at the very top.

"Harry will talk to the most junior person on site and ask them, 'What's happening?', like he does with all his senior people. He's actually interested in what the kid on site thinks about the project. I was that kid once, and look where I am now. Harry saw something in me all those years ago when I first started at Meriton that I never saw in myself. People stay because he's so involved," Charbel says.

Harry is always at the forefront of change which, in turn, means everyone who works for him has to keep up.

"It was very different when I started back in the 1960s," Harry says. "Demand, and where that demand came from, was very different. Initially, it was about affordable options, so it was about what I wanted to build and how much it would cost. I built what I thought buyers needed, not always what they wanted. It kept the price down. You couldn't get away with that today.

"Buyers have big expectations, so you have to give the market what they want. They're not interested in my opinion of what I think they should have. The market is king, and I listen to that," he says.

"I hadn't realised how unimaginative my blonde-brick, medium-density designs were because I built for purpose, not aesthetics. Then I found out I could do both. I would always think big but when World Tower was finished, it was the tallest residential tower in the country, and it was a steel and glass architectural masterpiece. I did that, with help of course, and you can't go backwards from that greatness, nor did I want to."

As we know, Harry had always been told that apartments would never be a preferred option in Australia. Now all the magnificent buildings are filled with people loving the way they live.

"My people at Meriton had to adjust to the changes as much as me. We now had an army of external architects to ensure that with change came beauty, and more importantly, life functionality," Harry says.

"Each and every building is a badge of honour. Families now live, as a preferred option, in Meriton developments in Mascot, Pagewood, Waterloo, Zetland, Rosebery, Epping, Macquarie Park … and the list goes on. That was never supposed to happen in Australia."

Not only did Harry change the landscape with beautiful, iconic buildings, but he also changed the landscape on how Australians think.

"It's exciting and fun working with a lot of different architects," Harry says. "They all have a healthy ego like me, which is terrific. I'm always in good company." He laughs.

But never a truer word was spoken. Harry believes there is a big difference between having an ego and being egotistical.

"Ego with a touch of arrogance is essential when you're designing a masterpiece," Harry says.

"You need to have confidence in what you're doing, and an ego gives you that.

"Egotistical is being excessively conceited and self-absorbed, and that is a different thing altogether. We don't have a place for that at Meriton.

"It's very good we work with more than one architectural firm because the talent across the board is sublime, and you can see that in all our buildings. Beautiful architecture offers the greatest art show on Earth."

Harry's head of architecture at Meriton, Frank Ru, says that managing all the different architects is a major part of his role.

"Design is obviously the priority, but relationship management is also a huge part of that role now," Frank says.

You can't argue with Harry when he comes up with brilliant new ideas in relation to architecture and design. To bring them to fruition is not always possible. Until, of course, it is. After Harry plants the seed, his team walk out of his office shaking their heads. They know they must find a way.

"If Harry thinks we look defeated, we get a pep talk in the way only Harry can give," Frank says.

Harry's view is that, "I don't hire you for you to tell me something can't be done. I hire you to resolve it for me. If you can't make it happen, why do I need you?"

Harry includes everyone in the tough conversations. Directors, design team and grandchildren. He never excludes his own blood because, at the end of the day, they work for him and there is no preferential treatment. At home he is 'Saba', which, as Ella mentioned, means grandfather in Hebrew, but in the office, he is the boss, regardless of hierarchy or heritage, and he never lets anyone forget it.

"Harry loves watching us all pull together to make something happen," Frank says. "When he sees we are all working well together, it gives him confidence about the future of Meriton. And Harry never stands on the sidelines. He's happy to get in the ring and fight with us to make things happen."

Frank says his role has changed enormously since he first started at Meriton.

"I've come a long way since that first day I was sitting with Harry, three of his directors and the head of architecture discussing my possible role.

"Considering most of Meriton's senior management were in the room, it was all pretty casual. Harry didn't look up from what he was reading at first, but when he did, he asked his team, 'Who's this guy?

What's he doing here?'

"They told him I was there about the architecture role. He asked, 'Why? Do we need people?'"

Harry was winding Frank up to see how he would react. Frank took it in his stride because he had worked with a Chinese billionaire of a similar calibre, so it took a bit to spook him.

"They tell me you're good," Harry said to Frank.

"I think I'm okay," Frank replied confidently.

Harry then asked Frank to write him a list of what he could do.

"Write it down now," Harry said. He always goes on gut, so he hadn't read Frank's resume. That was a job for someone else before the applicant landed in his office.

Harry turned to everyone at the table after five minutes and said, "He thinks he's pretty good; he's still writing!"

Harry then went out for a walk around his different departments, and when he came back, he read Frank's list.

"He was clearly impressed with what I could do," Frank says.

"He can do this," Harry said. "He can also do that," he said. "Very good."

Harry then turned to Neil Warner-O'Connell, who was head of architecture at the time, and said, "If you want him, you can hire him."

"At the time, I'd been offered another role," Frank says. "The one with Meriton was going to offer the less-predictable lifestyle of the two, but this was Harry Triguboff. Who says no to the biggest property player in the country?

"How many times in your life can you say you've worked for someone like Harry? Anywhere in the world, if you say you work for Harry Triguboff in Australia, it means something. Even though the onboarding was a little unusual, it was a glimpse into what would come next, and I was drawn to the job and to Harry.

"Now I know what Harry wants. Near-impossible scenarios every single day and an expectation we deliver every time."

Frank explains the normal development process with other property developers in simple terms: "The developer starts the process, works out how much they have in capital, and then how much they'll need to borrow from the bank.

"They might have 20 per cent and then they need to borrow 80 per cent. They'll develop to a point and then they start the pre-sales.

"The developer then sells on the market rate at the time. Once they sell 60 per cent, the bank has confidence that the rest of the development will sell, so they fund the construction costs. That means the developer cannot change a thing because they must build to satisfy the bank. They complete on the bank's terms and repay their loan to the bank. The profit they make will probably dictate their future success in the property development industry."

Harry, however, doesn't have to go through that crippling, controlling process with the bank. He can do and change anything he likes because he pays for every aspect of the job, development and operating costs with his own cash.

It gives him full control of his product and his price. It is a rare model and that is what makes him so resilient. He can always change the usage of a building to whatever he wants it to be at the 11th hour, and that is where Frank's team comes in.

"We have to make changes quickly and, while we are acclimatised to that, it's very stressful for external architects," Frank says.

"Harry doesn't care about sensibilities; he cares about profit. If something is going to work better for him financially, he'll always take the road less travelled or, more to the point, the one not travelled at all.

"It doesn't matter what he does, the demand is there. You need shelter, so it's not something that will be superseded or that will ever be obsolete. The model he created is amazingly robust."

Frank is from a Chinese background and, like Harry, did his final years of school in Australia. Also, like Harry, he was raised in China until he was 15.

"We have a lot of cultural similarities," Frank says. "I worked with one of the top 10 richest people in China, so I understand the mentality – as much as anyone can.

"Harry isn't actually too dissimilar to the old-fashioned Chinese billionaires. They don't really care what you think, they just want the result, and they're unapologetic about it.

"People give Harry the licence to do things most other people wouldn't get away with, purely because he is Harry. He made the apartment industry in Australia. He started the apartment movement in this country. If you think about it, he started strata. Harry has an amazing ability to persuade in everything. I know there are times when I say in my head that something is impossible, but I never say that to Harry. I'm no longer an architect; I am expected to be a miracle worker."

Frank thinks that what Meriton did in relation to above-ground parking in one of their buildings on the Gold Coast was amazing. The City of Gold Coast Council had never allowed more than a couple of levels of above-ground parking in any residential buildings. When you have to bury car parking underground, construction costs a fortune. Harry wasn't going to dig nine levels down when he could challenge the above-ground regulations. No other developer could do this because they don't have the time or resources to put everything on hold while they fight.

"I thought it was amazing that we were able to increase the above-ground allowance, firstly from two levels to three levels and then to four levels! We had already doubled more than what was considered acceptable to the council," Frank says.

"Harry's attitude is, 'if they can double, they can double again'."

He wrote to the mayor, who said it wasn't possible to go any higher above ground for the car park. Because Harry has the luxury of being able to sit on a project while he fights, he waited and eventually he had seven levels above ground approved for the parking. It was a remarkable result.

"Of course, it wasn't only a victory for that first building," Frank says. "It was Harry's new baseline. That first building had set a precedent. The council was never going to be able to tell Harry again that two levels was the rule. He had changed that."

Frank, when he started at Meriton, worked with head of architecture Neil Warner-O'Connell, but when Neil was feeling the pinch, Harry insisted the portfolio be split in two and that Frank should manage the other half.

"Neil didn't want to be demoted, so they created two separate titles," Frank says.

"Neil remained as architecture head, and I was made design head. That lasted three or four years. Neil then left and a number of other architects came in to manage the other half of the portfolio. None of them lasted very long, mostly because of the volume of work they were expected to manage.

"I was used to the way Harry worked, and we understood each other well, so he told me I should manage the other half of the portfolio as well. He wasn't asking me if I could manage it, he was telling me I could. End of conversation. So here I am."

Stuart Marsland, principal of Rothelowman Architects, said of Harry's first building in Melbourne that it was probably a good thing he had some distance from Harry.

"I, of course, had heard the stories," Stuart says.

"We had a few rollercoaster meetings, but you can't argue with success at that level. If we had a good relationship with Harry, there would be more opportunities, so I respected Harry's processes, and he was respectful of mine.

"Harry's first contribution to Melbourne was going to be one of the best buildings in the city. Harry understood that it had to be a marriage of what he'd like and what the city needed, and he had absolutely no issue with that.

"The structure of the building included the most intricate piece of pre-cast concrete we've ever done. It wasn't just there for window dressing; the structure actually holds up the entire building," Stuart says.

One time Harry went to the site and travelled up in a lift with Stuart. Suddenly, the lift stopped. Inside were four of Harry's senior people and the builders.

"We were in a cage, and we were freaking out," Stuart says.

"Harry had jumped up in the air when it happened, like that would help, and he was poking fun at us for being nervous. We were stuck there for about 15 minutes because someone had turned the electricity off. Harry wasn't at all concerned about the risk. He had protocols in place, and he wasn't at all worried they might let him down.

"The night of the opening of the building, I asked Harry if he'd seen the new Meriton signage on top of the building. I wasn't suggesting he go and see it there and then – it would mean crossing a six-lane highway at peak hour to see it properly. Harry, without any consideration of the traffic, strode out onto one of the main thoroughfares in Melbourne to find the best vantage point. We all tried to stop him, but he was a man on a mission.

"When he made it to the other side, he turned around and smiled, giving the signage the big thumbs up, while we all held our breaths as he navigated the traffic back to us. 'Very good,' he said, with a pat on my arm."

When COVID hit, Harry decided to close construction works down in Melbourne. It was a Meriton Suites hotel, and nobody knew what the future held for hotels, so he closed the site down.

"The hole for the two-storey basement parking had been dug," Stuart says. "Then Harry told us to stop construction. We could leave a hole in the ground for a month or two but no longer, so we filled it in. Works stopped for six months."

This project was the first where Harry had agreed to use locally based builders; he'd signed off on the contract with Hickory in Melbourne. He was also building his first tower in Canberra at the time, but that one was close enough to Sydney for him to use his own builders. He already had his own established people in Queensland too.

Harry, for his first building in Canberra, used Rob Mirams, from Fender Katsalidis Mirams Architects in Sydney.

"At first, Harry spoke to me through his advisers," Rob says. "It took a couple of meetings before he'd talk to me directly. He showed huge trust in his advisers by having them sift through everything I had to say first.

"Allara Street in Canberra is a very different project to the one we're doing now for Harry in Carlingford. Canberra was built for purpose as a Meriton Suites hotel. We're building a community at Carlingford.

"There's a big skate park near Pagewood Green where my son skates," Rob says.

"I've walked up the hill there and looked down on Pagewood Green, and then we go down there for lunch.

"So, I'm using what Harry has built and I don't even live at Pagewood Green, although we did do a couple of designs. It's a big nod to Harry's model. There are kids and families everywhere, and we expect the same at Carlingford.

"When you think of a lot of organisations that flounder because they don't have a leader driving the boat, it's almost old-fashioned to work how Harry works because people don't set companies up like that anymore with a sole leader. I can't think of another company that works like Harry. All the other development companies across Australia get to a certain scale and then become a public company, so they have a huge management team.

"Because Harry's so enigmatic, people in the industry look at him in amazement trying to understand how he did what he did because a lot of people would like to emulate him and haven't been able to. What has he done that they didn't do? How did he do it all? Harry tries to baffle people into thinking he's right. And that's how he gets great projects through. I think the councils secretly love Harry and Meriton because they get things done. He just baffles them with Harry speak," Rob says.

"Every site tells a different story, so you have to try to work out what works for the site. I don't think anyone in Canberra has a pool on their roof. It's been placed there on Harry's hotel so you can look over Canberra. The site always gives us some gems of wisdom on which way to go."

Harry believes Canberra needed to be on Meriton's radar because it was drawing nearly three million visitors a year. He bought the 1,734-square-metre block off-market for $23 million in 2019. It is his 23rd hotel. The serviced suites portfolio today is worth nearly $8 billion. Meriton Suites, at last count, had nearly 9,000 bedrooms across Victoria, NSW, the ACT and Queensland.

It is a good thing Harry literally had the rug pulled from underneath him by his father in Israel. He was never destined to run a carpet factory for his entire life and, just as Harry can see potential in others, his father could see that he had greater potential as well. As Harry says of his father, "He is my very greatest hero because he believed there are no limits on anyone or anything in life. He taught that to me.

"I am very grateful to him. He didn't only give me that gift, it has been re-gifted time and time again, by me, to the whole Meriton family. My success is their success."

Meriton staff and family at the Urban Taskforce Awards, 2018.

Harry wins Developer of the Year at UDIA NSW Awards, 2024.

Harry during construction of Soleil, Brisbane, 2012.

Harry with Brian Seidler, Executive Director of Master Builders, NSW.

Harry "on the jobs".

Harry at work, 2024.

Head of Town Planning, Walter Gordon.

Head of Construction, Charbel Rabie.

Head of Architecture, Frank Ru.

SIXTEEN

A JEWISH COMMUNITY

When Harry started Meriton, he ran it like a Jewish community – keeping the family together and being all-inclusive. He is the first to admit he isn't a religious man but when it comes to Judaism, he is more a traditionalist than devout. He observes the High Holy Days on the Jewish calendar, he attends synagogue, albeit infrequently, and he has proven time and time again that you don't need to be orthodox to be a proud patron within the Jewish community.

"That's why we have rabbis," Harry says. "They are the keepers of religious law and the Torah. Of course, Judaism is a religion, but it is so much more. It is the most community-oriented religion there is. We are all about the people, and I definitely see myself as a leader within our community.

"I respect the rabbis very much and spend a lot of time with Rabbi Dovid Slavin. We say prayers in my office many afternoons when he comes to visit. I will always make the time. Tradition is important."

Remember when Harry talked about standing next to his father while he was given the honour of reading the prayers at synagogue? In his teens Harry didn't see what all the fuss was about, but he does today.

Daughter Sharon says that at the central synagogue they have a holy ark where the Torah scrolls (bibles) are kept. It is a big honour at

A Jewish Community

the end of the holiest day of the Jewish calendar, Yom Kippur, to be asked to open and close the curtain over the ark.

"Every year, for years, Dad had done that with Frank Lowy, but with Frank now in Israel, Harry does it with Frank's son Steve," Sharon says. "They have to stand for a very long time, but Harry doesn't care."

You have to wonder when he is standing there if it reminds him of standing next to his father all those years before. He had been so honoured to be asked to read the prayers.

As mentioned, Sharon doesn't work at Meriton, and Miki is also not currently working at Meriton. Both are very proud to be Jewish and involved in community organisations.

Miki says the Jewish community fills her with pride. "I think Jews are very proud to be Jews."

Harry has treated everybody like they are part of his community. Ken McDonald says it is extraordinary how invested Harry is in his family, in what they have all been doing, and how he was keen to have future generations of McDonalds come and work for Meriton.

"Harry wanted to keep the family together," Ken says. "He saw it as his personal responsibility to put food on the table of every single person who worked for him. He used to hold my newborn and speak to him as if he were his own child. 'One day you'll come to work with me at Meriton, young man.' That's exactly what has happened," Ken says.

Ken, from a big Scottish family with no Jewish ties, has also established a strong relationship with the rabbis.

Harry's support of Rabbi Slavin's *Our Big Kitchen* was to see food put on the table for everybody. The charity kitchen, the brainchild of Rabbi Slavin and wife Laya, sits under the synagogue and new conversion centre in Flood Street, Bondi.

It is all activity when you walk down a steep driveway and through the big double doors into the massive commercial kitchen. All the volunteers look like investment bankers. That's probably because they are.

George, the Greek guy running the kitchen, is pushing the bankers to get their food into containers so it's ready for pickup at noon.

"Volunteers come from all walks of life," George says.

"I came from 10 years in jail, and the Slavins gave me a second chance, one I thought I'd never be given. I've never looked back. I've been here a long time now.

"I love the kitchen and everyone here is my family. I'm a lucky man," he says with a grin.

The whole kitchen has the most incredible vibe, and everyone is happy. They are thriving on the responsibility of helping people in need by making sure they're fed.

There is plenty of fun involved as well. Many of the volunteers come from a corporate program, which involves companies such as Macquarie Bank, Microsoft, Atlassian and Optus. One morning it might be Macquarie Bank. After lunch it could be Microsoft.

The groups of volunteers are put into five smaller groups, and at the end of the morning, in MasterChef style, their food is judged. The team that comes up with the best dish using their allotted ingredients wins the day.

George judges the best dish with the head chef. Everyone is laughing and excited. Soon all the tasty food that was cooked that morning will be picked up and distributed to those in need of a good feed.

The food is not only heading out to the Jewish community. *Our Big Kitchen* supports hospitals, the Salvation Army, St Vincent de Paul, Youth Off The Streets, the Ted Noffs (NOFFS) Foundation and many more.

But again, it couldn't have happened without Harry's support. Not that Rabbi Slavin ever expected Harry to pay for his big idea, but he still needed to build on the land Harry owned.

Where Rabbi Slavin envisaged the kitchen being built was on a solid rockface in the basement. They would have to excavate, and he certainly didn't have those skills. While he was very happy to get his hands dirty and help, he also needed professionals. Rabbi Slavin didn't ask Harry for the money, but he needed trades and contractors, and he was given the green light to approach Harry's people.

Ken McDonald, who was retired, basically became the foreman and was on site every day, happy to donate his time and skills. That made Harry comfortable, but he still couldn't help himself. He checked in on the site on his way to the office nearly every day.

As far as Harry was concerned, he still had skin in the game. More importantly, he wasn't butting out when construction was involved and, most importantly, it was a project that was all about putting food on the table; a cause close to his heart.

What had been Rabbi Slavin and Laya's brainchild, was now Harry's baby too.

Having such a close relationship with the Slavins also saw the birth of the Sydney Academy of Jewish Education (SAJE), a conversion centre that has opened in the same building.

According to Orna, Harry has said that, "It will be the greatest achievement of my life" to see conversion made easier. Orna, a rabbi herself, is on the board and very involved.

"Conversion is next to impossible," Harry says. "It takes too long, expectations are unreasonable in regard to learning Hebrew, and it's burdensome instead of being a good experience. We are aiming to simplify the process so people coming into our community have a strong, enjoyable, positive experience."

Shalom Norman, who runs the Harry Oscar Triguboff Institute in Israel says, "The Harry Oscar Triguboff Institute in Israel supports many causes but the one closest to Harry's heart is ensuring the survival of Judaism.

"We had to introduce an easier process in Israel and then have it filter down to the rabbis in Australia.

"We want people to become Jews, not scare them away. We want our community to grow, particularly here in Australia. SAJE is now making conversion less challenging and complicated. Those wishing to convert are now enjoying the process, and it is especially important for inter-marriages."

Even Ariel has said that if he marries a non-Jewish girl, he would ask her to convert, mostly to make his grandfather happy.

"Mum and Dad would also love me to marry a Jewish girl, but I've met a lot of non-Jewish girls and they've been really lovely, and I dated one for a few years.

"I don't know what my future holds in relation to that. If it came to it, and it was a non-Jewish girl and we were serious, considering marriage and children, I would ask her to convert. I would tell her that it wasn't that important to me, but it would be very important to my grandfather, and that he is very important to me.

"I know Rhonda isn't Jewish, but Harry and Rhonda decided early in the piece they wouldn't have children. When children are involved, and the religion comes from the mother, conversion would be important to Harry.

"If the new conversion centre makes the process simpler and conversion can be achieved in less time, that would be a massive win," Ariel says.

Harry's nephew Michael feels exactly the same about conversion as Harry. Even though his daughter is marrying a non-Jew in March 2025, his daughter's fiancé is in the process of converting through the SAJE.

"Even though their children would follow my daughter's religion, as a family unit I think it's very important that the father be involved in the Jewish community as well," Michael says.

"I know my grandchildren would be Jewish, but I want their father to be as well. I think I'm doing him a favour insisting on it because if the rest of his family are members of the Jewish community and he isn't, he's missing out. It has nothing to do with religion.

"Unfortunately, until now, conversion has concentrated more on religion than the community, so it's fantastic that is now changing here in Sydney."

To meet Michael, you would say he has Harry's sense of humour. Michael insists he is more like his father, Joe.

Michael has a home close to Harry in Vaucluse and a house in Berrima. He says the house in Berrima belongs to his wife and that all he's responsible for is moving manure around.

"But that's okay," he says. "I've been well-trained for that. I'm an investment banker so I'm used to shovelling shit!"

Come on, Michael, it is a little bit like Harry's sense of humour.

There's no doubt that Michael is very fond of Harry. Joe died when Michael was just 22, and he and Harry grieved together.

Michael was never headed for Meriton. He is an academic and studied law like his father, but for years he also pursued other studies. He loved academia then, and still does.

"I didn't eventually follow my dad into law either," Michael says. "I was interested in criminal law, but my father said that working in criminal law 'you wash your hands in dirty water'. He didn't approve.

"The night before my last law exam, my father had a heart attack. It was a relief when he was out of intensive care after three weeks and was getting ready to come home. Right before he was due to leave, the hospital rang and said he'd had another heart attack.

"This time he died. If it'd just been five years later, he would have required nothing more than a stent," he says.

Harry played a big part in Michael's life after his father died, but even before that, Michael spent a lot of time with Harry.

"The brothers didn't always agree, but they were very close," Michael says. "Dad always told me that Harry was the quiet one. Dad was the sportsman and Harry always had his head buried in a book."

Harry's recollection is a little different. Harry says he did everything he was told to do to 'keep the mother happy'. Being quiet didn't come naturally to him.

"I respected my mother," Harry says. "She loved tradition and loved her Russian roots, which she drummed into me from a young age. When she told me to do something, I would do it. She was the mother. You did as you were told, even if you didn't like it. Tradition back then wasn't really important to me, though I didn't complain, but at the same time I was totally in awe of the brave new American world.

"The US Marines were so exciting. They brought light and frivolity into war-torn China. I would sit for hours watching American movies and listening to the Marines joke and laugh about their lives back home. It was so exciting that I thought one day I would go to America," he says.

Harry learned to respect everyone regardless of race, colour, social standing or religion. He loved the African Americans because of their bravery and their ability to live in the moment.

"When I found out I had colon cancer in my early 60s, Michael was living in New York," Harry says. "He convinced me to go there for a second opinion. It was a waste of time because the doctor in New York only confirmed what my doctor here in Sydney said, and he even agreed with him about which would be the most appropriate treatment. I asked him to discount his fees because he hadn't added any value.

"I was only half-joking! I understand we were talking about a serious topic, but I had been uplifted sitting in the waiting room surrounded by African Americans. It reminded me of the beautiful days in China when I was young. If the trip did anything, it made me feel positive about the future. Brave!" he says.

Harry and family at the construction site of Ammunition Hill, Israel, 1998.

Harry and family at the Ammunition Hill Memorial Garden, Israel, 2023.

Opening of the Moshe Triguboff Auditorium of Moriah College, Sydney, 1994.

Passover seder, 2018.

Harry hosting a luncheon at his World Tower penthouse for Israeli delegates, family and longtime friend Joseph Brender, 2023.

Harry praying with Rabbi Dovid Slavin, 2022.

Harry with Frank Lowy, opening the arc at Central Synagogue, 2023.

Children cooking for charity at Our Big Kitchen, Bondi.

Harry Triguboff AO in his World Tower penthouse apartment.

PART 4

HARRY, THE MAN

SEVENTEEN

HOW THE MIND TICKS

Aldous Huxley, controversially banned from many bookshelves around the world and one of the most gifted English writers of all time, said, "The secret to genius is to carry the spirit of the child into old age, which means never losing your enthusiasm."

Harry has never lost his enthusiasm, and the spirit of the child is still very much present, but that is only a small part of his genius. For centuries, the common belief was that a genius had a bigger brain. It wasn't until one of the most famous geniuses of all time – Albert Einstein – died in 1955 that researchers discovered his brain was the same size as a person of average intelligence. So, brain size was a total myth. Around the same time, researchers did prove that the brain of a genius has a greater capacity to 'pack more in'.

When it comes to that genius theory, Harry is the leader of the pack – more in! He has the rare ability to not only absorb information and retain every detail, but he then compartmentalises everything and can draw on it at a second's notice. It doesn't matter whether it happened yesterday or 80 years ago, it comes to front and centre when he needs it. Every single detail.

Regardless of Orna's close relationship with Harry, she and all the family understand that under Meriton's roof they will be treated the same as everyone else. They are part of the extended family, and there is no special treatment. There is one difference in that they all report directly to Harry, and they all have offices closest to Harry.

"That is more by coincidence than by design," Harry says.

"The offices directly surrounding mine are smaller. One person, two max. Open plan works best for architecture, marketing, interior design, construction, finance and serviced apartments because they are the biggest teams. They need more room, so they are in the open-plan areas across the three floors.

"That said, I do call on Daniel the most, so it's good he is close by. I'm still teaching him, and he has a greater overview of the business because he spends so much time with me.

"Daniel could tell you in detail about projects like Pagewood Green, Macquarie Park, Zetland and Mascot Central because they have been going for years and Daniel has been involved since day one," Harry says.

At the end of a busy day, when Harry walks out the door, his office is spotless. Again, discipline.

"Dad doesn't leave the office until he has gone through every single piece of paper on his desk or on the boardroom table in his office," Orna says. "He has either put things in his bag so he can read them at home, or he gives them to Loreto to file, or he's put them in the bin.

"When Dad walks out of his office, he always looks back at his desk to make sure there isn't a shred of paper on it. He is structured and he'll never leave anything behind to deal with the next day. His head is clear for the next round tomorrow," she says.

Harry says he makes huge decisions on the spur of the moment involving multi-millions of dollars, "mostly because I can".

"I don't have to answer to anyone and there is no better statistical evidence and science for change than analysing Meriton's own data on a day-to-day basis.

"When I make decisions quickly, which is most of the time, they're not reckless.

"It's not like the issue is being looked at for the first time. By the time it comes to me, many of my best people are across it. Their input is already there to help me make the decision.

"I'm always confident that I make the right decision. Sometimes the decisions are sheer *chutzpah*." Harry smiles, using the Yiddish word for fearless, brave and gutsy.

Sheer brilliance is what it is, but Harry puts it down to good old commonsense. Only Harry would use the word 'common' to describe how he operates.

How many people can change their thought process and mood with the intake of a single breath? Harry does it all the time. He can be in the office juggling numerous conversations, on numerous different subjects, and offer a resolution to all of them within minutes. He may have started out yelling, but once he realises that there are no actual monumental issues, he relaxes and finishes with a laugh and a joke. Harry's demeanour goes beyond unpredictability; it is quite unnerving, frightening even, until you acclimatise to the speed. The pace at which Harry's mind works is just not natural.

There would be no other company anywhere in the world that would operate quite like Meriton. When you walk through the doors, you slip into another dimension. Orna explains it best when she says, "It's organised chaos in the best possible, most efficient way."

Even being with Harry discussing his book, the exit directives take a little getting used to. You turn up expecting to get some time, but he's not always in the mood. After no time at all, Harry is done.

"I've had enough," he says. "I'm bored talking about this."

'This' is Harry's life. It just so happens that this day it takes a back seat to more pressing matters in the business. He doesn't have the time to sit and chat about his book today. On other days he will sit, deep in thought, and talk in-depth about his life. On those days he laughs at the memories and is relaxed, charming and funny. Those are the good days.

Until you're sitting in front of him, you never know which Harry you're going to get. If he tells you to get out after five minutes, you leave and you don't send so much as a pout in his general direction. But in true Harry style, he's already read the room, and without even lifting his head he yells, "And take that sour look on your face with you!"

At other times, Harry is the quiet assassin – he says nothing at all. You get the message that he's moved on from you when he picks up the phone to summon other people to his office, or he just starts talking to someone else in the room about a totally different subject, or he starts doing prayers with the rabbi. Nobody is immune to that treatment. Not his directors, not his family, not his wife. Harry speaks to everybody the same way, and nobody takes offence.

Still, you might think you're getting with the program, until you're not. It doesn't matter how long you've known Harry, you can't ever make the mistake of thinking you have him pegged. Don't ever get comfortable. That's when you're at your most vulnerable.

Generally, though, you can forget about undivided attention if the room is full of people. Harry isn't going to focus on one thing when he is in his element barking orders to all corners of the room. If it happens to be just Harry and Orna, time is a little less limited. If Harry gestures to the couch and there are no other people in the room, time is on your side. There will still be interruptions, but that is when you sit opposite the relaxed storyteller and what you hear is priceless. Because of how Harry's mind works, always be prepared to expect the unexpected!

With nearly every decision that's made in the company, the buck stops with Harry. It doesn't mean other senior managers or family members don't make decisions, or don't have the authority to make decisions, but Harry just wants to know about it, so he's always prepared for what change might come with it.

"It's commonsense to work that way," he says. "The property market is volatile and unpredictable, and it can change overnight.

"Sometimes we change the usage of a building at the last minute to meet market demand. We won't sell any more but change it to a build-to-rent because the market is demanding more rental stock.

"We can spin a redesign on a sixpence because of the way the business operates. If I have all the up-to-date information I need, we can get on to it straight away. I don't have to wait for anybody."

Harry loves nothing more than people asking him about his goals and his long-term plans.

"I've never had a single goal in my life and, as for long-term business plans, they can never work in the ever-changing property market that is Meriton's home.

"It's bad enough I have an agonising wait on approvals without bringing that culture into my business.

"I almost ruined my business once by going public. I lost control. I spent my life waiting on decisions, and it was almost the death of Meriton.

"When you're not the decision-maker, and you have to run everything past a board of people – that is the worst. I hated it when my company went public because I had to suffer through the dreaded meetings where I had people who knew nothing about property trying to tell me how to run my business.

"Worse still, you have the meeting, and you're forced to follow an agenda that dictates what will be discussed and in what order. The meeting will then go totally off the rails because nobody thinks like me.

"A week later, the minutes are distributed. The only purpose the minutes serve is to repeat, in writing, the agony of the meeting the week before. Nothing from that meeting is any longer relevant to me. I've moved on. A week is a long time at Meriton, particularly for me.

"The only minutes that matter are the ones right now. That's why I bought my company back from the shareholders at an inflated price. It was worth every cent to have the buck stop with me in regard to all the decisions."

Harry still calls meetings the same way he did when he first started his business 60 years ago. A loudspeaker system was installed in his business from day one and it exists to this day. If Harry wants a meeting, he calls either Julia or Brittany on reception and asks them to send the relevant people to his office immediately. Seconds later, there's an announcement over the loudspeaker system instructing the required people to, "Please report to Mr Triguboff's office."

When you know Harry is in the office, and mostly you know because you can hear him, your ears are pricked in case you're called. No matter what you're doing, even if you're in a meeting with external people, you drop it and go straight to Harry's office. Everyone is used to Harry operating that way because most of them have worked for him for decades, and it's now second nature to them.

When you arrive in the inner sanctum, there are already people there, and a lot of them. You have to wait your turn. Harry will triage you as to whether you join the queue or jump it.

As mentioned, Harry has an open-door policy. His executive assistant, Loreto, has long given up trying to control the flow because Harry is constantly asking Julia and Brittany to send people to him.

Harry doesn't care if you hear what's going on in any other areas of Meriton either. He is huge on transparency and sees it as providing knowledge to you about other areas of the business so you can learn. He never pigeon-holes anyone. So, if you go into Harry's office to talk about accounts, and you sit in on a meeting about design, you're learning about what happens in the business elsewhere. Harry is a huge believer that knowledge is power.

Another reason Harry does this is because sometimes he thinks that some people would be better suited to other areas of the business.

As quick as he can make decisions, he can read people. There are people at Meriton no longer in the job they had when they started. Harry decided they were better suited to something else. Something that didn't even match their skillset, yet he knew it would be a better fit, even if they didn't know it themselves.

"Sometimes they fight it," Harry says. "Like I did when I was in South Africa working in textiles, and the boss told me I was of more value to him in accounts, not on the floor.

"I didn't study textiles for four years to handle the money, but it was the best thing that happened to me. I was really good with figures and the boss saw that in me before I did. I had a real knack for business."

Even Rhonda started off in bookkeeping when she first started at Meriton, but Harry picked up that she had a real talent for interior design. That's where she was revered for her creative designs – bespoke, sophisticated elegance. Buyers loved her interiors.

You can count on one hand the events that have occurred that Harry perceives his most significant. Being threatened by and then beating the unions was top of the list of his greatest achievements, but he was even prouder of the way Meriton handled the pandemic that began in 2020.

The essential industries had to maintain their pre-pandemic working arrangements, while everyone else was working from home, so not even the pandemic messed with Harry's routine. He still went to work every day and everyone at Meriton did the same.

It would have been one of the only businesses in Sydney in the thick of the pandemic that was still working as normal. The rest of the city was deserted. Walking into Meriton during COVID was like being in a pre-pandemic bubble.

"When you're talking about a virus that was killing so many people, it was the first time in my life I wasn't the one making all the decisions," Harry says. "I was guided by the experts, and I did as I was told to protect my people. It was a very foreign concept to me.

"I immediately made all the relevant changes to the office and installed the appropriate protections, but I never forced anyone to come to work. Building had to continue and the Meriton family came to work every day without complaining," Harry says.

"We all had the relevant shots, and we all stayed at work. If someone became ill, they would stay home. We did everything that was required of us by law, and we kept working."

Even though some of Harry's staff came down with the virus, he continued to go to the office every day and was the first to insist that those infected by the disease stay home. If any of Harry's staff lived in an area that was going into complete lockdown, he would put them up in one of his apartments in the city so they could keep working.

"I think it was very good we kept working," Harry says. "I think it was better for our mental health to stay together. It was important to keep the family together.

"They chose to come to work, and I was so proud of how responsible they were about protecting one another. We did regular testing and if anyone had a temperature, symptoms or a positive test, they were immediately sent home.

"Of course, we had cases but, fortunately, nobody became very ill. I contracted the virus myself, but I was asymptomatic and felt totally fine. I only found out I had the disease because when the borders opened to Queensland, I had to be tested 72 hours before flying, and my test came back positive. I immediately went home and stayed there for the prescribed period.

"When it comes to your health, you do as you're advised by the experts to give you the best possible outcome. I never questioned that vaccination was the right way to go. I had all my shots as soon as I was able, and I still have them as soon as I'm eligible."

Not only did Harry do everything to keep his team safe, but he also took it on the chin when his after-tax profit in 2020 fell from the previous year's $356 million to $19.4 million.

"I had little to complain about," Harry says. "Many other people lost their lives, those of loved ones and/or their livelihoods. I knew we would recover quickly, but I didn't expect it to rebound as quickly as it did."

Harry switched 1,200 units from Meriton's serviced apartments business in Sydney into longer-term rentals as occupancy plummeted during the pandemic. When those leases expired or people wanted to leave, he took each unit back and put it into the serviced suites pool.

"Four of our buildings were used by the government for special health accommodation," Harry says. "Meriton Suites housed quarantine accommodation at Zetland, Mascot, North Ryde and the Sydney CBD for overseas travellers returning to Australia.

"I was happy to do it because staying in a large Meriton apartment was far more comfortable for those in quarantine than a tiny hotel room. Two weeks in a confined space is a long time.

"I felt we were contributing substantially to easing the problem, and that's all you can really do when things are out of your control."

Harry has always been acutely aware of his responsibility for the livelihoods of the thousands of people who depend on Meriton.

"My priority was to get as many of my people and their families through the pandemic and to make sure they had everything they needed to stay well and keep food on the table. In such a dire situation, the money was always secondary.

"I am very proud of how well we survived. I felt sorry for my nephew, Michael. He doesn't work for me, but he was the only one who went to his office, and he was floating around on his own. I told him he could have an office at Meriton with me, so he wasn't lonely. Michael is still running his business from Meriton. He never left after that!"

Harry doesn't like to talk a long game – he never has. He trusts his gut in the moment – he always has.

He wanted no part in the drudgery of mapping out a 10-year business plan when one of his early partners suggested it. It was to be a plan that would outline the tasks and milestones that needed to be accomplished to meet agreed goals over the next decade.

"Problem is, I don't set goals," Harry states matter-of-factly.

"The further you look to the distance, the more the view becomes blurred, and you lose clarity.

"To stay ahead of the game, you must be in the moment. That requires versatility, flexibility and the general ability to adapt and adjust quickly.

"That is why Meriton is so great. Considering the size of the business, we can change things in an instant to meet the market. There is no other company in the world our size that can do that," he says.

Harry's company was in its infancy when he decided there would be no more partners. After floating the company, only to privatise it again a short time later, he decided no more shareholders either.

There was no place in Harry's life for the risk averse. He intended to take many risks, not that he saw them as such, but the ability to make decisions quickly without referring to others was imperative.

"It's no news to anyone that the property market is unpredictable," Harry says. "I'm pretty good at being ahead of the game, but you must be ready for the unexpected. That might mean a complete about-face."

Harry, instead of selling, will retain apartments to create more rental opportunities. He might take apartments originally planned for sale and change them to serviced apartments. He might even completely change the layout of apartments with regard to the number of bedrooms.

"It doesn't matter what the market needs at any particular time, I can give it to them quickly. That's why I've never regretted going it alone," Harry says.

"Partners and shareholders just get in the way and slow things down. What others perceive as a risk, I see as necessity and act accordingly. I've been advocating for apartment living for 60 years and, finally, commonsense has prevailed and almost everyone seems to be on board the high-rise train. We just need the councils to speed things up and then it will be full steam ahead.

"Verticality is now the Great Australian Dream. Up, not out," he says.

Harry has always backed himself and trusted his instincts. Those instincts have never let him down.

"I'm sharp, healthy, and I have no mobility issues," Harry says. "I fully intend to remain in the business for at least another 10 years. Call it my 10-year business plan, if you like." He smiles.

Harry at the office.

EIGHTEEN

DOWNTIME

For someone who abhors setting goals and working on long-term plans, Harry's discipline gives him structure around the unpredictability of work life as well as routine for his other pursuits.

"I'm extremely disciplined, which helps me stick to my routine as much as possible," he says. "Even if something unexpected comes up, I decide if it's important enough to rattle my day. Routine gives me clarity because I always know what's coming next."

Routine also extends to his physical health. Harry, remarkably for his age, walks and swims nearly every morning and he plays billiards every night. He checks in on one or more of his project sites before turning up to work every day and there he takes the stairs between the floors of his offices, instead of the lift. Even at a far younger age, you'd need a certain level of athleticism to pull that off.

As guests arrived at the magnificent Sydney Town Hall to celebrate Harry's 90th birthday in 2023, many moved to the left or right of the iconic grand steps to use the brass handrails to support themselves as they ascended the famous stairs. Not Harry. With unwavering execution, he strode freely and unassisted up the centre of the steps with the strength and gait of a man half his age. When people called his name, he turned around mid-stride to acknowledge their birthday greetings, and then effortlessly continued his ascent to the top of the stately staircase.

Journalist Jessica Sier, from the *Australian Financial Review*, even referred to Harry as "bounding up" the grand steps in her coverage of the event.

Later, Harry strutted his stuff on the dance floor, first with wife Rhonda, then with his daughters, then with some guests, and then with more guests. He showed no signs of being in a hurry to get off his feet and even supported Rhonda's back before dipping her in an awe-inspiring pose.

Years of physical exercise have trained Harry's body to not let him down. He is undoubtedly one of the most robust, sturdy and vigorous nonagenarians in the world, though he would never consider himself a sportsman.

"I don't do 20 laps of freestyle anymore, but I still do 20 laps of breaststroke," Harry says proudly. "I don't walk as fast as I once did, but I still walk unimpeded and at a brisk pace.

"Had I been a sportsman, I don't think I would be as physically versatile and agile as I am today. I would probably be hobbling around on a stick as a result of sustained injuries during a sporting career. I love sport but have always much preferred it from the sidelines."

The powers that be at Scots College would agree. At school, Harry showed little interest in sport at all. He was the greatest cheerleader for his friends but didn't compete himself.

As legend would have it, Gareth Dyer, head of the Office of Heritage and Tradition at Scots, says that in Harry's day, all the boys had to stand in front of their peers in the old auditorium and give a three-minute speech on any subject they chose.

"Most spoke proudly about their sport," Dyer says. "Harry couldn't follow suit, but he would stand up and talk about his early life in China and his unbelievable experiences as a child growing up in a war-torn country.

"In return, his friends would cheer him on, totally transfixed by a life so exotic and worldly. They had never met anyone like Harry, and they were in awe."

High-Rise Harry

Today, Harry still walks with his friends every Sunday and then has breakfast with them. His dear friend Joseph Brender joked, when asked to contribute to this book, "Save yourself some time and write a modern-day biography on Napoleon and call it Ditto!"

Then, with an exaggerated sigh, he joked again, "If we must talk about Harry, let's have lunch at Beppi's after the Australia Day long weekend. Clear your afternoon!"

Sadly, Joseph died in his sleep suddenly on 23 January 2024, aged 92, three days before Australia Day.

On first meeting Joseph years ago, you could see immediately why he and Harry were friends. They were philanthropists and leaders in the Jewish community and shared a lot in common. They were both recognised for their contribution to the community. Joseph, founder of the Katies clothing chain, was a giant of industry, like Harry. As Rhonda is to Harry, Joesph's wife, Gerda, was his world.

Less than two months after Joseph died, Harry nearly died himself! Harry's live-in house manager and friend, Elizabeth Cunningham, immediately knew something was wrong when Harry's face blew up like a balloon. He also felt in himself that something wasn't right. He agreed that his friend and doctor, Willy Steinberg, should come to the house and check him out.

"As soon as Dr Willy saw him, he told him he had to go to the hospital," Elizabeth says.

"Then Harry insisted on changing his clothes, and by the time we arrived at the hospital, the doctors and specialists Harry knew were already there. Willy had put the call out."

Elizabeth has been working for Harry and Rhonda for 24 years, and she lives-in and manages the waterfront compound of properties with Rhonda.

"I'm originally from the bush," Elizabeth says. "My father was a dairy instructor at the biggest agricultural college in Australia, Gatton

Agricultural College in Queensland.

"We lived on the college grounds before we went to our own dairy farm in the Lockyer Valley between Brisbane and Toowoomba. We had 40 cows, which we milked, and we used to grow potatoes, sweet potatoes, corn and lucerne. Later, I worked on cattle stations, where I learned to ride horses and look after the calves.

"I came to Sydney when I was 20 and, after working for Soul Pattinsons, I worked for Veteran Affairs as an orthotist and prosthetist. There was four years training for that."

Elizabeth was with Veteran Affairs for 20 years before the Commonwealth Government gave it to the state governments. At 54, she was retrenched and went back to Queensland but returned to Sydney and ended up with Harry and Rhonda.

"After I was retrenched, I decided to go back to college and do a full-time photography course at Hornsby TAFE," Elizabeth says. "I lived at Lindfield and used to pass through Wahroonga to get there. My friend lived at Wahroonga and had this little quirk that she would look up all the jobs in the newspaper. She told me she had found a job that would suit me perfectly.

"It was a job as a pet carer and to cook light meals for the husband at night. I took the next day off school and wrote a letter of application and then caught a bus into Meriton to drop it off. I was concerned I might miss out if I waited for the post.

"The next day Rhonda rang and asked if I'd like to come in for an interview, which I did, and then about four or five days later she rang and asked me if I'd like to come in and meet her husband. I thought I had the job," she says.

At that stage, no decision had been made. Another woman was also being considered for the role. After Harry met both, Rhonda asked Harry which one was getting the job. Harry said it was going to Elizabeth and that he hadn't chosen her, the pets had.

"Only the dog was interested in the other woman, but the dog and the two Burmese cats were interested in Elizabeth," Harry told

Rhonda at the time.

"Clearly, as far as the animals were concerned, Elizabeth was frontrunner. Who was I to argue?"

Harry and Rhonda, over the years, have had several German Shepherds and cats. Their latest dog is Susie, a Standard Poodle, who has not only made a place in both their hearts, but in Elizabeth's as well.

"Harry didn't love the German Shepherds like he does Susie, and vice versa," Elizabeth says.

"Susie puts in the effort and makes a fuss of him when he gets home, and she is genuine about her feelings. She's not just looking for food. She is the only one who has ever been allowed to sleep on the bed. Harry loves her to bits."

Elizabeth has taken on a lot more responsibility as the years have rolled by. She manages the five people who work at the house, and she takes a lot of the home responsibilities away from Harry and Rhonda.

"Rhonda needs to be there for Harry when he needs her, and my contribution to the business and helping ease the housing crisis is to make life at home as simple for Harry and Rhonda as possible," she says.

"Any conversation not about Meriton gets short shrift. Harry's man cave at home is just an extension of the office, and he spends a lot of time in there.

"We talk all things Meriton when he gets home, and if there is something about the house we need to discuss, we get it out of the way quickly and then go back to all things Meriton."

On a Saturday afternoon, Harry will be in his man cave going through *the sheets*.

"When he is out of his man cave, he doesn't have to worry about anything," Elizabeth says.

She and Rhonda manage the staff, the contractors, the grounds and the wildlife.

"We have lots of birds, water dragons and Koi fish," Elizabeth says.

"It's only lately that Harry has paid much attention to the wildlife. These days he is the first to notice when the water dragons are out of hibernation in spring. He lets me know when the birds are around to be fed.

"He is enjoying the house much more now than he has in the past. Before, it was just the house, and Rhonda and I looked after it. Now it is a home, and he loves being here.

"The three of us get on like a house on fire. He understands I'm not a 'yes' person and I'll always have my own opinion.

"I won't say what Harry wants to hear to keep him happy. There are times when I need him to do something for me, particularly when he is not well, so he needs to take me seriously.

"That said, I never cross the line. I know he is the boss, but he also knows that I free him up of any concerns here at home so he can get on and look after his empire.

"There is good, mutual, healthy respect and that's why the three of us have been able to live together for so long."

So, when Harry almost died back in March 2024, he did what he was told to by Elizabeth and Dr Willy Steinberg. Dr Willy immediately diagnosed Harry with a pericardial effusion – fluid around the heart. He wasn't in good shape. Harry says the doctors told him he could die.

"They told me I had a 50/50 chance of survival," Harry says.

"They wanted to know if I wanted them to take all measures to keep me alive. Of course I did, even if it meant being in a wheelchair, as they suggested might happen.

"They started treatment and, fortunately, all went well with no side effects, like dying." He smiles.

In two hours, Harry felt back to normal.

"Whatever they did was very clever," Harry says. "Good doctors are essential for longevity."

The next day Harry was still in hospital, but he was back doing *the sheets*.

"I can work efficiently from anywhere. I felt better so I decided I should work."

It had been a tough couple of months. When he had his own drama behind him, he spoke fondly of friend Joseph Brender.

"He was my very great friend, but I still wasn't keen to join him so soon. We had a lot in common and he will be sorely missed by me and the whole Jewish community.

"He was a very great man, you know."

It was pure joy having lunch with Harry and Joseph years ago at Beppi's, a regular lunchtime haunt for them both. Harry said he had invited Joseph to join us because he had received some bad news, and he thought we could cheer him up.

There is actually a private dining room at Beppi's called the Joseph Brender Room, and Joseph came bounding through the door with a huge smile and introduced himself.

"Thanks for letting me crash your lunch," he said with a firm handshake.

Harry then arrived, sat down and lunch was ordered. It was an entertaining lunch. They ribbed each other all through it, as friends of so many years can do.

The owners of larger-than-life personalities, very proud Zionists, and giants in the Jewish community argued over who was greater – Sir Winston Churchill, loved and admired by Joseph, or Napoleon Bonaparte, loved and admired by Harry.

Harry teased Joesph that Churchill just copied everything Napolean had done a century before. Of course, Harry didn't really believe that – he was just winding Joseph up. The International Churchill Society compared the two great leaders in *France and the French – A Tale of Two Statesmen – Churchill and Napoleon* and concluded that Churchill, like Napoleon, believed in the ability of men to shape their own destiny, and consequently in the power of great men to achieve great things. Indeed.

With his friends, every five years Harry has a party to celebrate a landmark birthday. Some have been a huge affair like his 90th birthday bash at Sydney Town Hall. Others have been more intimate. One such occasion was his 80th birthday, which he had at home in Vaucluse. The Cuban-themed event was no less lavish than others, with fire-eating cocktail waiters and Cuban music and dancing. There was a firework display on the harbour and, much later, Cuban cigars and whisky being enjoyed by many of the men – and some of the women.

On Harry's 85th birthday, Delta Goodrem was the lead entertainment. She was fabulous. She danced on the tables and had everyone on their feet. It was a magical night.

Travel is another hobby that Harry has enjoyed with friends over the years, although it's not such a big deal for him today. It seems to be the six-letter words that Harry loves the most in fact: empire, Rhonda, family and travel. The latter love has taken him around the world many times over, most trips in style and other trips, not so much.

Many trips were shared with friend Chris Crawley and his wife at the time, Judith.

"I was an articled clerk when I first met Harry in 1967," Chris says. "I managed to secure Harry as a client and I went on to do a lot of legal work for him personally, and for Meriton. Our friendship has lasted nearly six decades and, for many of our holidays, we just fell into a pattern and travelled together.

"Although I have four brothers, Harry was best man at my wedding to Judith in Dürnstein in Austria," he says.

"We always knew Harry would still work while we were away though. It didn't matter where we were in the world, *the sheets* would magically turn up and Harry would pore over them for hours before we headed off to enjoy the day. Once business was taken care of, and multiple phone calls had been made, we could go out and enjoy ourselves."

The sheets even made their way to Sharon's wedding in Venice. In fact, Harry wrote his speech on the back of them.

"I was so worried about what he was going to say," Sharon says. "It was very typical that he would use *the sheets* as his stationery. I was waiting for him to thank the bricklayers instead of the bridesmaids!"

According to Chris Crawley, it was just as much fun planning the trips as taking them.

"Harry and I took many journeys to Israel, where I witnessed his generosity to the Jewish nation. The first trip was taken after the Yom Kippur War of October 1973.

"Harry is always in a rush. He was giving me the guided tour to see as many historical places in Israel in the shortest possible time."

In later years, Harry took Chris to visit the carpet factory that he had so proudly made a success, and he took him to the graves of his parents and his childhood nanny, Anna.

"In 2000, Rhonda, Judith, Harry and I travelled to Israel for the dedication of The Berel Ginges Computer Centre at The Hebrew University of Jerusalem, which is sponsored by Harry. At the celebrations Harry's daughters and their families also attended. It was an extremely memorable occasion. All the ceremonies and meetings were with the leading Israeli officials at that time.

"On one occasion in 2007, I attended, of course with Harry, a one-on-one meeting with the President at the time, Shimon Peres, and we had another private meeting with Ehud Barak, who was the most decorated soldier in Israel and later also President," Chris says.

"These are wonderful memories and would not have happened but for my friendship with Harry."

Harry is not a skier and never has been, but that didn't stop him going to Aspen, Colorado, in the US once in the thick of winter. It is hard to imagine Harry enjoying the freezing cold in the alps because he generally hates the cold – he is an Aussie sun-lover through and through. One of the only times Harry actually ventured out into the cold in Aspen was when the group decided to take a day trip to Vail.

It was a memorable day out, although Harry's legendary driving skills did come into question, yet again.

Harry insisted he should drive the large Chevrolet SUV, which was, of course, left-hand drive. Come on, Harry! A huge, unfamiliar monster of a car, left-hand drive on the wrong side of the road on ice? That was surely a disaster waiting to happen.

Fortunately, a disaster was nipped in the bud.

"Harry hopped in the driver side of this tank of a car, I was in the front passenger side, and Rhonda and Jude were in the back; Rhonda was sitting directly behind me," Chris says.

"Harry started the engine, turned the wheel to the left to leave the portico of the hotel, totally misjudging the width of the SUV, and he ran straight into the back of the car immediately in front of us.

"Rhonda tapped me on the shoulder and asked if I'd seen the parked car in front of us, and I reminded her that it was a left-hand drive and Harry was at the wheel. Thank God Harry didn't ask to drive again for the rest of the trip!

"Another year, we all travelled to the States, and we went from Los Angeles to Las Vegas, where we visited Harry's old friends Tommy and Kitty Gluck," Chris says.

You remember Tommy – he started building units with Harry right back at the beginning. After Harry decided 'no partners', Tommy went to Los Angeles to have a crack at the market in the States. Harry assisted Tommy financially to set up his business in Beverly Hills. The business name, Happy Homes, was a bit cheesy, but Harry thought it was a terrific representation of Tommy, who was always happy.

"We had breakfast with Tommy, who had a sweet tooth and loved the odd cigar and good whisky. At this breakfast, Tommy enjoyed a large piece of chocolate cake, which he quickly washed down with a glass of Glenfiddich!

"He died of a massive heart attack the very next day," Chris says calmly, as if death was a given because Tommy chose chocolate cake and whisky for breakfast. RIP Tommy Gluck.

The couples later travelled to Sochi, St Petersburg and Moscow in Russia.

"A highlight of the trip to Russia was going to watch the Bolshoi Ballet perform," Chris says. "Unfortunately, on presentation of our tickets, we were told they were for the previous evening.

"As it turned out, it was a happy accident. That night there was a private box available and, of course, it made the experience so much better."

In Greece, Harry and Chris chartered a luxury motor yacht called *MV Atlantis* so they could travel to islands such as Milos, Santorini, Paros, Antiparos, Mykonos, Delos, Hydra and Folegandros without the need for hotel accommodation.

"Before we embarked on the high seas, *the sheets* were waiting for us in the hotel in Athens," Chris says. "Come hell or high water, Harry was not leaving without them."

Over the years they travelled to South Africa, staying in safari lodges in the Kruger National Park, where little monkeys pinched the food off the breakfast tables. In Paris they enjoyed the hospitality of the President's box at the Roland Garros French Open. And while Harry enjoys his creature comforts, if you're going somewhere for the experience, then roughing it a bit is okay too.

"I go more for the experience than the luxury," Harry says. "I do the tourist thing, but I like to dig deeper and go to places that are a little off the beaten track. When I travel with the family it is more to larger cities, and it's at those times I go off looking at all the development going on.

"I have been to all corners of the Earth, and I've seen extraordinary and beautiful things, but some also sad," he says.

A visit to Buenos Aires in South America was one of the more memorable trips.

"We were warned not to walk anywhere with any jewellery on display," Chris says. "One morning I received a phone call from hotel management to say that Rhonda and Harry had been mugged and were at the hospital.

"Jude and I immediately raced to the hospital. The thieves had cut Harry's hand when pulling off his watch. Harry was adamant that he'd dressed down in shorts and a polo shirt and thought he'd be fine. I explained that I didn't think they were looking at his legs!"

Harry doesn't consider a watch jewellery, but rather a necessity. He has a lot of them, and you'll never see him without one on his wrist.

"They bandaged his hand, gave him a tetanus shot in the backside, and sent us back to the hotel. He didn't venture out again unless we were all together," Chris says.

Ella also has fond memories of travelling with Rhonda and Harry to Europe and the United States.

"Wherever we went we always had a driver to take us around the city," Ella says. "It was like a game of I Spy – Harry always had me looking around for cranes and construction sites.

"Of course, while we weren't hunting down sites, Harry always had *the sheets*, sales reports and other reporting sheets faxed through to the hotel. He also made his daily calls to check in with the office. Work never stopped," she says.

"I felt lucky to get to see the world at such a young age."

Harry and Rhonda have also travelled extensively throughout Australia, sometimes with the Crawleys and sometimes it was just a boys' trip.

One such trip was to Kununurra in far-northern Western Australia. Harry and Chris stayed at El Questro Station.

"We arranged to go fishing and took a light plane to the lower Ord River. We landed on one of Kerry Packer's properties and proceeded to Macka's Barra Camp," Chris says.

"When we arrived at the camp, both of the comfortable fibreglass fishing boats had left early that morning. We'd brought an esky with chicken sandwiches and champagne for lunch.

"By then the ice in the esky had melted, the sandwiches were soggy, but we still ate them and washed them down with a glass of champagne. We then boarded a flat-bottomed 15-foot dinghy with a small outboard motor. The boat had a shade cloth suspended on four posts over the body of the boat.

"Macka, the proprietor of the business, said that as it was afternoon it was unlikely we could catch any barramundi, but it was best to try in the shadows near the shoreline. He said that the others who were out fishing earlier hadn't caught anything. At this point in time, we were in the middle of the river, so I suggested Macka help Harry bait a hook, and he then headed to the back of the dinghy to cast his line.

"Within a couple of minutes, Harry caught his first barramundi – and he'd never caught a fish that size in his life. Of course, we went back to the camp and ate it."

Harry was grinning ear to ear after having the great Australian experience in the bush in the middle of nowhere and was super happy about his big catch.

Harry has shared thousands of stories over the years about his travels, but he is always happy to come home.

"I love to travel with my family and friends and enjoy the experiences together.

"I don't travel as extensively as I used to, but I still make sure I go to Israel at least once a year. There is no place in the world like Australia, and I never take that for granted.

"My country is my hero," he says.

―⋅―

Harry has a close network of friends. Aside from Joseph Brender, he has his Sunday walking league that includes Willy Steinberg, Bill Roney, Patrick Corrigan, Alex Abulafia and Yossi Eshed. They meet every Sunday morning for a walk and breakfast, without fail. Even when the weather is absolutely foul, they will still meet for breakfast. Willy and Bill are doctors, Patrick is an arts patron and collector, Yossi is the CEO of the Zionist Council of NSW, and Alex is the CEO of Bell's Pure Ice.

Naturally, they call him 'Iceman'.

Willy Steinberg is not only Harry's doctor; he is one of his best friends. Willy says that although they both immigrated from China around the same time, give or take a few years, he didn't meet Harry until the late 1980s.

"I met Harry through my cousin, Paul," Willy says. "Paul rang one day and said that Harry caught his leg on something at a building site and it wasn't healing. He asked me to take a look at it.

"I sent him to my partner, John Chong, and he patched up the wound and it healed well. A few months later I was sitting at Georges at Double Bay having a coffee and Harry and my cousin walked past. They were headed to the movies with their wives. We said a quick hello and they kept walking.

"One day, out of the blue, my cousin rings me and says that Harry wants to go to a French restaurant in Oxford Street and he'd like me and my wife, Trish, to join him. Claudes was a big deal in those days when it came to fine dining. Small, intimate, expensive. We had a lovely evening, and we went on to be close friends from there," he says.

As it turned out, Willy already did the Bondi to Tamarama walk on the weekends and Harry suggested he join him. It is now a ritual they all enjoy.

"Harry used to drive to my house in Bulkara Road, Bellevue Hill," Willy says. "He would leave his car, get into mine and then we would pick up Paul, my cousin, and Bill Roney. Our group grew to six and we would have our walk and then go to Gusto at Bondi for breakfast.

"We were very protective of who could join our group. Our gang is now Harry, me, Yossi, Alex, Patrick and Bill.

"For Harry's 91st birthday, not being a big five, we went to World Tower and had lunch, just the six of us. He is always very thoughtful and inclusive with his friends.

"Beppi's is one of our great meeting places. A lunch with Harry and Joseph was always epic."

Harry has a lunch routine, and he sticks to it. He makes sure he is back in the office by 3pm – always. These days he tries to head back by 2pm because there is always so much to be done. When Beppi was alive, he was their fourth amigo and lunch was even more fun. Beppi was a sublime host.

"On arrival, Harry would ask for a scotch for all of us," Willy says. "Then he would ask Beppi what the specials were for the day. An antipasto platter would magically appear, and Harry would order a bottle of Penfolds Grange Hermitage 1989, with a price tag of $1,500.

"Then, with main course, we would have a Henschke Hill of Grace 2018 at $1,000 a bottle. Once main course was finished, Harry was gone. Joseph and I stayed on and ordered crêpes Suzette, sambuca and vodka.

"We'd get hammered. Harry wouldn't drink as much but it should still have affected him. It never did! Joseph and Harry were as alert as when they first sat down. I was legless – so legless that I fell over in the garden bed in my backyard and I couldn't get up.

"Trish was at golf, so I just had to stay there until she arrived home.

"I was still blurry-eyed when I met Harry days later for our walk. Harry, of course, was in fine form," Willy says.

Willy and Harry both love dogs. Willy's Cavalier King Charles Spaniel, Rex, is sadly no longer with us.

"Harry understood how much I was going to miss him," Willy says.

"He has been through his own canine loss with a number of his dogs, but he always gets another. I just don't think I could ever replace Rex. We think differently on that level.

"Since knowing Harry, he has had Amadeus, a German Shepherd, Caesar, another German Shepherd, and his current dog is a Standard Poodle named Susie. He loves all animals. In fact, one day he turned up to lunch and he was very hungry. On asking him if he'd skipped breakfast, he nodded before explaining why.

"My Caesar was having surgery this morning and he had to fast, so I didn't want to be mean and eat in front of him," Harry said.

And there it is. That soft side that many people don't think Harry has.

Downtime

Harry still cheers from the sidelines at sporting events as he did with his friends at Scots. Even today, Harry still catches up with his friends from school. Alan Ridge, Tony Dowe, Colin Davidson, David (Taffy) Thomas, Hugh Rawston, Ian Lambert, Peter Howarth and Terry Clune, to name a few, attend Harry's birthday parties, and he has lunch with them at his penthouse at World Tower regularly.

There was one bloke called Ian Sharrock who was in the same year as Harry at Scots College. Both men concede they were not close, but there was mutual respect and always recognition when they crossed paths. Sharrock was a boarder and Harry was a day boy. A country bloke through and through, Ian lived his whole life in the South Western Slopes region of Young – about 375 kilometres from Sydney. Between Sydney and Young is the small town of Crookwell. Charlie Fenton, another Scots old boy, is the publican at the country pub in Crookwell, and Sharrock, at the ripe young age of 91, stopped off there not so long ago for a schooner and a chinwag.

Charlie, about 30 years Sharrock's junior, brought up the subject of Harry, knowing Sharrock and Harry were about the same age, and he told him a friend was writing his book and shared his details.

"Even though Harry was a day boy, and I was a boarder, you always knew when he was around," Sharrock said.

"He was a cheeky lad and well-liked, but day boys and boarders still pretty much kept to themselves back then. I don't think he'd even remember me at all."

Not true. Harry remembers him well. His recollection was immediate.

"Nice bloke. Head prefect. One of the country boys I liked and admired. Loved his chooks," Harry said.

Damn right he loved his chooks!

"I started off selling chook eggs to earn a crust," Ian said. "Then it was meat chooks, and it went from there. We then diversified and we did okay. Clearly not as well as Harry. He's a pretty amazing bloke. Still so full of beans. Good on him. The fact he remembers me at all has made my day," Ian said.

Sadly, not long after speaking to Ian about Harry, he died peacefully in his hometown of Young. Harry remembered him fondly. Rest in Peace, Ian.

These are memories from over 70 years ago, and Harry has no trouble remembering every detail.

Harry specifically loves football, tennis and any major sporting events, like the Olympics or world championships.

Swimming legend Dawn Fraser, when she hit the pool at the Melbourne 1956 Summer Olympics and won the gold in the 100 metres freestyle, became Harry's hero. The better she did over the years, the more of a legend she became.

"We met and became great friends," Harry says. "She introduced me to her rugby league football team, the Balmain Tigers, and they became my team as well."

After a game, even in the early days of his business, Harry would head for the changerooms and give the players £1,000 each when they played well. That was a lot of money back in the day, but it was his way of helping keep the players motivated to win.

Later, when the Balmain Tigers amalgamated with the Western Suburbs Magpies in 1999 to become the Wests Tigers, Harry became the inaugural major sponsor for the newly formed club in the new millennium. Some affectionately referred to the team as 'Trigger's Tigers'. He continued his tradition of going to the changerooms after the game, peeling off some big notes and giving them to the players.

"I met Harry in 2003 when I first arrived at Wests Tigers as coach," Tim Sheens says.

"I was waiting to meet him in his boardroom, and when he appeared in a nice cut of a suit, I was surprised when I looked down that he had bare feet. Shoes and socks had been discarded, and while I was a little taken aback for a second or two, I immediately felt we had an affinity. Over the years we've had great conversations about football, and he understands the heart of the game," he says fondly.

From that first meeting, Tim Sheens became 'Coach', and that is what Harry has always called him. When he introduced Tim to anyone, he said, "This is my coach." When Harry found out that Tim was doing a 100-kilometre round trip to Concord every day from Penrith, he gave him a good deal on one of his apartments in Homebush so that he didn't waste training time in the car.

"I was indebted to him," Tim says. "He saw it as a way to keep my head in the game if I wasn't faced with that massive drive every day. I could have walked to work from my new apartment. It was brilliant."

In the same spirit, Harry paid for the lads in the team to have a new kitchen at the club, so they didn't have to waste training time by heading out for lunch. A chef was brought in to ensure they kept to a healthy diet.

"He thought this type of measure kept everyone's head in the game, not just mine," Tim says.

Harry and Tim not only have football in common, but Tim also loves property and worked in real estate and property development for 10 years.

"Back in the day, when I played footy, you had to have a day job as well," Tim says. "You wouldn't have survived otherwise. I would have injuries from football on the weekend and I still had to front up to work on Monday. I took on as much additional work as possible, including doing the end-of-lease cleaning of apartments before or after work. I think Harry and I share a similar work ethic. Push through at all costs."

In 2005, when the Wests Tigers won the Premiership, defeating the North Queensland Cowboys, Harry wasn't the major sponsor that year. According to Tim, he may as well have been the way the team included him in the post-match celebrations.

"Whether he was sponsoring us or not, Harry was Harry to everyone at Wests Tigers. No surname necessary. He had more rights than most to celebrate with us," Tim says.

"I glimpsed Harry at the entrance of the tunnel to the changerooms. He was standing with a group of people. I went and grabbed him, literally because of all the excitement, and I told him to come in. Technically, he wasn't involved with us at that time, but he'd been good to the club, and he was always involved in some way, financially mostly, when he received no recognition for his contributions at all.

"I said to my trainer at the time to go and get me one of the balls from the game. There are usually three; one on the field and two on the sidelines. One of the NRL officials went and grabbed a ball from the referee, so it was definitely the game ball. I then had all the players sign it, and I gave it to Harry. It was a huge deal for us to do that with the Premiership ball, but everyone agreed that Harry deserved it.

"I'm told the ball is in his office," he says.

It is in Harry's office, in pride of place in a glass cabinet. In fact, there is Wests Tigers memorabilia throughout the Meriton offices. The best of it is in Harry's personal office.

In 2012, after Harry had returned to Wests Tigers as their major sponsor, the then Premier of NSW, Barry O'Farrell, officially opened Harry's Vantage Towers at Rhodes.

"Harry's a bloke who came here without much, saw the opportunities here, was determined to work hard and has created opportunities for other people," Barry O'Farrell said at the time.

That day, Harry proudly took the Premier, Tim Sheens and the players on a tour of the building. It hadn't been totally completed, so Harry took his guests to the top floor in the hoist. Wests Tigers star Benji Marshall was grasping the railing, looking more than a little green. He was terrified of heights, of how high he was going, and what contraption he was riding in to take him there.

"Only I would get a major sponsor called 'High-Rise Harry'," Benji said at the time as he grasped the railing tighter.

"I love Harry, but he is looking at me right now thinking I'm the biggest wimp in the world," he said in a shaky voice.

Harry nudged Tim Sheens and said, "I think our Benji needs to keep his feet on the ground."

"Did you hear that?" a journalist said to his photographer. "Harry reckons Benji is a prima donna."

And that, right there, is how rumours start. Of course, Harry meant it literally, not figuratively.

In 2023, primarily because of similar unsubstantiated rumours, the club was drowning in controversy. To say it was affecting the players' game is an understatement.

Harry was thrilled when his team showed a glimpse of brilliance when they defeated the North Queensland Cowboys 66–18 in May 2023. As he was no longer allowed to flash cash around to individuals in the changerooms, Harry sent the club $100,000.

Six weeks later, it was payback. The North Queensland Cowboys defeated the Wests Tigers 74–0. Harry probably should have asked for his money back.

A couple of months later, Tigers chairman Lee Hagipantelis confirmed that Tim Sheens had "taken the decision to leave the Wests Tigers of his own volition".

Surprising? Probably not. Tim Sheens was said to be constantly taking bullets for the incompetencies off the paddock. Someone had to be the scapegoat for the team's poor performance throughout 2023, and the top brass weren't going to have fingers pointed at them.

"I don't even want to talk about it," Harry said in frustration at the time. "There is one bad decision after the other. It's just hopeless.

"Getting rid of Sheens and fast-tracking Marshall wasn't the answer. You don't let all the experience and passion that Sheens brings to the club walk out the door when you're in crisis.

"They want my money, but they never ask my advice. I know a thing or two about business, and their business is failing. I'm not going to keep rewarding their poor choices. It's not how I do business," he says, changing the subject, only to return to it minutes later.

"You need to fight with this," Harry says as he pummels his chest over his heart, "and you must fight with this," he says as he taps his right hand to his head in agitation.

"Sheens brought that to the club. They ousted the wrong man!"

And we all know what happened next – the CEO and the entire board of the Wests Tigers were sacked. Harry wasn't surprised at all.

"They say it like it's a shock," Harry says. "Blaming the coach for all their misgivings certainly didn't end well for them. But you look to the future. I've been in the game long enough to know that it's never too late to turn things around.

"Pretty simple advice for the new brigade – pick up the ball and run with it. Fresh legs can change the game," he says.

Harry is happy to see things have changed at the top. His mate Barry O'Farrell became interim chairman of Wests Tigers, and the 'Rumpelstiltskin' of the game, Shane 'Richo' Richardson, became CEO, locked in on a four-year term. Richo is a wizard when it comes to spinning wooden spoons into bronze statues. He has helped take a number of teams from rock bottom to premiership.

"One of the first things I did when I arrived at Wests Tigers was contact Harry for a meeting," Richo says. "Barry O'Farrell knows Harry, but I wanted to sit in front of him so he could get my measure and hopefully appreciate from our meeting that I'm all about the game.

"Harry wants us to win. Sheensy gave him that, and now it's up to us to support Benji to do the same. Barry and I can do that.

"I want to have a relationship with Harry because, seriously, it's extraordinary to be in the company of such a remarkable business giant who's happy to offer his advice and experience in ways to better our club.

"We appreciate the financial contribution Harry has made to the club for all these years, but his input on how we take the club forward as a business, a successful winning business, will be invaluable," he says.

While his footy team sorts itself out, Harry is still upbeat about other sports. He attends the Australian Open tennis in Melbourne every year and says that the 2020 Olympics in Japan, postponed until 2021 due to the COVID pandemic, was the best sporting event ever, considering the circumstances.

"Our athletes were incredible," Harry says with huge admiration. "The restrictive circumstances they had to train under during the pandemic and their acceptance, persistence and tenacity to keep training when the games were delayed a year, was totally inspirational.

"Then when they did compete, they were unbelievable. They understood how to win in the most extreme of circumstances."

Harry, perhaps, has a better understanding of 'extreme circumstances' than most. He went through years and years of fighting the unions and councils, so he understands that you always need to dig a little deeper to find extra resilience.

He also understands how physically and emotionally draining that can be, and he respected the athletes all the more for it.

"While we were at home watching them achieve and claiming their victories as our own as Australians, they were actually the ones out there being victorious," Harry says.

"I felt so much pride and excitement watching them compete. It signalled a return to normality. People were excited again. They were talking about the number of medals, not the number of cases," he says, referring to the COVID pandemic.

When the Olympians returned from the games, Harry gave each medal winner $5,000 a medal to show his appreciation – $645,000 all up.

Australian Olympic Committee president John Coates thanked Harry at the time for his generous donation, saying, "Harry is hugely proud of what our team achieved in Tokyo, and for him to say thank you in this way is very generous and most unexpected."

Olympic champion swimmer Emma McKeon had the biggest payday after winning seven medals at the games. Her bank account was bolstered by $35,000.

All Harry wanted in return was to meet his 'golden angel'. He spent an hour with McKeon discussing the highlights of the games and viewing her medals.

Harry has an appreciation for all people and is certainly no snob. He has brought up his family the same way.

"I abhor people that are snobs," he says.

"I know the man is gone and I shouldn't speak ill of the dead, but I will always remember a dinner I went to one night with Alan Bond in attendance. Bond was blowing his own trumpet standing in the centre of a posse of wannabes. Chest puffed out, he was holding court.

"Looking back now, at the time of his grandstanding, he was flat broke. He didn't have two pennies to rub together.

"I loathed how dismissive he was of the people he didn't consider his social equal. The man was an outrageous snob for someone without the wherewithal to carry it off.

"Out of respect, I won't gloat, but I put him in his place! He was the true definition of a snob," Harry finishes, with more than a hint of contempt.

There was no love lost there.

He did, however, have respect for Kerry Packer. The two men didn't know each other well but each showed an interest in the other. Like Harry, Kerry wasn't impressed by anyone who had the bad taste to talk about who they were and how much money they had.

A story that is now folklore is the time when Kerry, the world's biggest gambler, was sitting at a blackjack table next to a Texan oil baron.

The Texan was banging on about who he was, how brilliant he was and bragging about his $100 million worth.

Kerry, sick of listening to him, turned to him and offered to "flip you for it". Nothing will make a man run faster than realising he could lose everything on the toss of a coin. Good thing he ran, too, as Kerry was on a winning streak that night.

Although Harry likes that story, he's definitely not 'High-Roller Harry'. On the rare occasion that you see Harry in a casino, he will be on the main floor at the minimum-bet tables, splashing out no more than $50 for the entire evening.

"I like that Packer had the guts to bet big, but I don't have an addictive personality," Harry says. "I'm not a person to leave my luck to chance."

The thing that Harry came to respect most about Kerry, like many other people in Australia, was the speech he gave at the Corporate Tax Inquiry in 1991.

"There is nothing wrong with minimising tax," Kerry said at the time. "I don't know anybody who doesn't minimise their tax."

When told he was doing it in a spirit that was contrary to the law, he took offence.

"Well, I just got through telling you what I thought about that," Kerry said with control before putting the boot in. "… I am not evading tax in any way, shape or form. Now, of course I am minimising my tax, and if anybody in this country doesn't minimise their tax, they want their heads read because as a government, I can tell you, you're not spending it that well that we should be donating extra."

Thumbs up from Harry! Kerry had said what everyone else was thinking.

Harry has little interest in substantial others. He has no interest in competing financially and hearing about all the toys they have; it bores him.

"Outside my friends that I've already mentioned, I do like Lindsay Fox very much," Harry says. "But I like to talk business. I would like to hear how successful people operate, but all they want to do is gloat about their toys. I have no interest! I could buy most of them 10 times over.

"I like the people who surprise me. The ones who have something interesting to say that engages me. They can show me in a short period of time their own big picture, and that I enjoy."

Harry likes to tell his stories, not for motivational purposes, but because he enjoys sharing experiences he's had throughout his life. He likes to make people laugh, and he has a tremendous sense of humour. Most times he doesn't even know he's being funny. He will turn to you with a serious expression and ask why you're laughing. And then he'll laugh too. Sometimes, when he is being interviewed and has a large audience, he spontaneously makes people laugh. It even catches him by surprise.

Harry can remember, in the minutest of details, events and life experiences that happened decades ago, and he uses those to entertain people at functions and during interviews. And the apple doesn't fall far from the tree.

Orna also remembers her first little school on the North Shore of Sydney with great detail and affection. She smiles broadly as she talks about the memories of more than 50 years ago.

"When Sharon and I were young and living in Lindfield on the North Shore, there was no Jewish school that side of the bridge," she says.

"There was a small synagogue near where we lived, but no school. Along with nine other couples, Mum and Dad helped start the Masada Jewish Junior School in Lindfield. All the other parents were either Holocaust survivors or had come to Australia from Israel. There was a small room attached to the North Shore synagogue and that was where my Jewish schooling really began.

"I absolutely loved it there. It was my introduction to school, Judaism and the close-knit Jewish community, which I found beautiful.

"It was the sweetest little school. It was tiny. I was in year one and we were all in the same room with the year twos and threes. We had one teacher looking after all of us, and she would go from one corner to the next to teach each different grade. We had four students in each grade.

"Everyone was friends with everybody. I remember being six years old and being invited to a 10-year-old's birthday party. I couldn't believe it! It was so exciting.

"We would kiss our teacher hello and goodbye, and it was like a real family. It was the very essence of Judaism and the very essence of Dad and the importance he placed on the Jewish community," Orna says.

In most other schools at that time there was definitely no fondness for the teacher or their disciplinary tools of terror. Kindergarten kids were beaten with the cane, the strap or the edge of a ruler from their first day of school. Harry wasn't having that for his girls. They weren't treated like that at home, and he wouldn't have them treated like that at school.

When the family eventually moved to the eastern suburbs, where there was a much larger Jewish community and a much bigger Jewish school, Orna and Sharon were both sent to Moriah College.

"It was somewhat of a culture shock," Orna says. "Because it was a much bigger Jewish school, people grouped more into their own little cliques. I wasn't used to that. We had all mixed together at Masada. What was familiar was that it was still a strong community but on a much bigger scale. You really stuck to your peer groups in your own year. It took some getting used to."

It probably explains why Orna, like Harry, is comfortable speaking to anyone. Her roots at Masada have made her all-inclusive. Just like Harry, Orna is comfortable in the presence of all people and enjoys meeting people from all walks of life.

"I love it when Dad is walking along the street and a Wests Tigers fan recognises him and comes up and thanks him for supporting their team," Orna says.

"Dad will always take the time to stop and talk to anybody. He loves people. I really enjoy the spontaneous conversations," she says.

You would think that, being as busy as everyone is, an hour for lunch at the Meriton offices might be stretching things. In this day and age, more people eat at their desks or skip lunch altogether. Not at Meriton. Harry encourages everyone to take a break for an hour between one and two o'clock and he won't disturb anyone during that time.

He believes everyone needs to have a break in the middle of the day to regenerate for the afternoon, especially if there are any after-hours events.

One such event was the opening of 180 George Street, Parramatta. Sky News Australia presenter Erin Molan was master of ceremonies. She is one of Harry's favourites, not only because she is strikingly beautiful, but because she banters with him, and they bounce thoughts off each other with ease. They formed a bond during an earlier interview Harry did with Erin and he insisted she be given the gig.

Erin is quick-witted and easily went off-script to fit in with Harry. During his speech he covered things that Erin was supposed to address. She turned to him and said, "You can't cut my fee, Harry, just because you did my job for me."

Harry laughed, but for a fleeting moment he probably thought he should. You can't put ideas like that in his head, Erin. And like so many people now who have a Meriton story, Erin told her own.

When she was going through a tough time personally when her marriage failed, she stayed at Meriton Suites in North Sydney. When her next partner's relationship broke down, he also stayed at the same Meriton Suites.

"We worked out that we passed each other on the driveway," Erin says. "I was coming in distraught from my breakup, and he was leaving still numb from his.

"We both agreed that, in the circumstances, Meriton Suites provided a sanctuary during hard times."

It's a nice story. Erin is relatable, positive and fun, with a fabulous sense of humour. It's easy to see why Harry likes her.

A month after that opening, Harry was looking at the headline on the front page of *The Daily Telegraph* on Friday, 17 November 2023. He smiled and shrugged his shoulders.

It was all about the NSW Premier, Chris Minns, taking on the responsibility for the NSW housing crisis.

"Nobody has ever looked at the big picture," Harry says.

"In the past 60 years I've built nearly 80,000 apartments, but I could have built a whole lot more had someone had the foresight to take future needs into consideration.

"The housing situation didn't just creep up on us. I've been banging on about it for 60 years. It's a long time to play catchup!"

Harry still welcomed the news that the Premier meant to make it his job to solve the state housing crisis and had put planning bosses on notice to deliver. He intended to also name and shame councils that dragged their heels on planning approvals, stating, "The culture has to change."

"I totally agree," Harry says. "The culture has needed to change for a very long time.

"I used to be hammered by the government, councils and media because I had a different vision. You were never going to solve the housing crisis on the outskirts of Sydney with cottages alone. There's always been a practical need to go vertical. The rest of the world was way ahead of us on that."

In November 2023, the average take-home salary was $70,000. Of course, there are people who make a lot less and people who make a lot more. The median apartment price in New South Wales at the time was $820,000. Even if you have the 10 per cent deposit of $82,000, with a mortgage of $738,000, the repayments are still beyond your means at around $4,000 a month when your take-home salary is $4,615 a month. This doesn't include stamp duty, strata fees, electricity, gas or internet services.

So, unless the average Aussie buys with a parent, partner or peer, which comes with its own set of complications, they will never be a homeowner.

When the interest rates were at an all-time low, the average Australian was able to buy. Many did so with the promise that a rise in interest rates would be on hold until the end of 2024, if it happened at all. The Reserve Bank's cash rate then increased 13 times in 15 months, hitting a 12-year high of 4.35 per cent in March 2024. The board of the bank had indicated in 2021 that interest rates were not expected to increase for "at least three years". The leap started more than two years before it was expected.

"The government should be pushing people into homes, not pushing them out of them by increasing rates so dramatically in such a short period of time," Harry says.

"If the government had listened way before now, we wouldn't be in this position where we have no supply.

"You can only fight so hard when you're facing a brick wall. I really hope Minns does as he has promised.

"I am very happy to help him," he says.

Rhonda & Harry dancing at his 80th birthday party.

Travelling in China.

Wherever Harry goes, the sheets will follow.

Ken McDonald and Harry.

With friends Chris & Judith Crawley.

Harry, Will Steinberg, Yossi Eshed going for their weekly Sunday walk and coffee.

Watching the Australian Open finals.

Playing billiards at home.

Harry with Wests Tigers players Robbie Farah & Chris Lawrence.

Harry with former Wests Tigers players Benny Elias & Steve Roach.

Harry with longtime friend, Scots alumnus Pat Corrigan.

Harry with house manager and friend, Elizabeth Cunningham.

NINETEEN

HARRY AT HIS BEST

Many who have crossed paths with Harry would be surprised to learn about his terrific sense of humour. They wouldn't even be able to imagine it because they haven't had the opportunity to see him in that light. To them, he is tough, determined, steely-eyed, intimidating and all business. When good-humoured and relaxed Harry turns up, he is someone everyone should meet at least once. Those there on Friday, 22 March 2024, did just that. At 91, and as Harry would say, "in my prime", he had everyone up on their feet cheering and clapping.

Harry had been invited to speak at the Ray White Surfers Paradise Group's annual Business Meets Sport lunch, held in support of the Surfers Paradise Surf Lifesaving Club. The chairman of Ray White Surfers Paradise Group, Andrew Bell, had been asking Harry to speak for years. This time, he said yes. There were nearly 900 people at the lunch – the biggest turnout ever – and most were there to hear Harry speak.

That in no way diminishes the other speakers. All sporting heroes, they are exactly the legends Harry admires, and he listened to their every word. First was the greatest Australian cyclist of all time, Anna Meares. She made Olympic history in Rio in 2016 by being the first and only Australian athlete from any sport to have ever won individual medals at four consecutive Olympic Games. During her 15-year career as an elite athlete, Anna collected 18 gold medals, 16 silver medals and 10 bronze medals at the Olympics, World and Commonwealth Games.

There were other amazing athletes who spoke on the day, with standouts being Ali Day, who had won the Gold Coast Sports Person of the Year and the Queensland ironman championship, and Lucy Derbyshire, the state's ironwoman champion. Harry loves a winner, and they were all winners to him. After listening to them speak, he donated $100,000 to the lifesaving club. To him, no club was more deserving.

Harry, while enjoying lunch before he was due to speak, smiled broadly as a young man came up to his table, introduced himself and called Harry 'his hero'. Others queued up to do the same. One of the organisers tried to stem the flow, but Harry insisted he was fine. He wasn't just fine; he was in his element.

Harry is a corporate giant, one of the most successful businesspeople in the world, yet he has never taken himself too seriously. On this particular day, he was in one of his favourite places in the world, with Rhonda by his side, some of his team in the room, and he was heading into a weekend at Surfers. He was at his most relaxed.

When Harry took his seat for the interview with Andrew Bell, he was also at his good-humoured best. Harry, a great storyteller, is quick-witted and can easily make others laugh. His overall body language and facial expressions convey his feelings and add to the humour.

Harry remained quiet while Andrew went over his early life, just nodding his head occasionally in agreement. Andrew then asked Harry his first question, in relation to his early milk run and taxi businesses.

"Were they successful?" Andrew asked.

Harry looked out to the audience and gave a two-word answer: "Of course". Everybody laughed because Harry looked at Andrew as if to say, *What sort of question is that?* It should have been a given that any business Harry touched would be a success. The tone was set.

Andrew asked Harry of those early days, "What inspired both you and your mate to build apartments?"

It wasn't the first time Harry had been asked these questions, but every time the answer has been different. The context is the same, but you can always take something new from it when you hear it from Harry.

On this day, his story was powerful in its simplicity. It was so obvious, in fact, how did so many others miss it?

"Well, I was born in China, and in China we all lived in apartments," Harry started.

Remember that Harry left China when he was 14 to come to school in Australia, so those formative years had a huge influence on the direction his life took.

"In the 1960s when I looked at Bondi, I didn't see any apartments," he continued. "I was so lucky that people were against apartments, and for every person who was against, there were 10 who wanted them, and they weren't available.

"Ever since I started, there has always been demand. Sydney for me, at that time, was very good because we had many different areas that were zoned for apartments. When I started to build, I naturally knew how to make money out of it.

"I knew how to supply the building. That I knew. So, I got a foreman. The foreman is always the bricklayer, never the carpenter. So, I told him you're no longer just a bricklayer, you're also the foreman.

"Very good. Then I decided to do another two or three blocks, but one bricklayer cannot be everywhere. I thought the sub-contractors had a brain for business, so I told the sub-contractor that you are now the builder too, so we had a group of little builders, and I was very successful."

In less than 200 words, everyone understood how Harry had the formula to his success: build and keep building. The demand was always there.

"Finally, came the decision that to succeed I had to provide the finance," Harry said. "People here on the Gold Coast had no money." The audience laughed.

"Thank God they have a lot more now!" More laughing.

"So anyway, I give them the money and tell them, 'It's yours'. So,

I charge them some interest, maybe a little more interest," he said with a chuckle. More laughing.

"I wasn't making my money on the interest; I was making my money on the bricks because many people didn't own bricks. So that's why it was very successful.

"We started very small. I was smaller than the others who started in my time. But then I passed them, but I thought we were underpriced in my mind. Where else in the world do you have such a beach, such a climate, and I love the people of Surfers, they're very friendly, very friendly."

Andrew Bell chipped in and said, "Especially the real estate agents." Everyone laughed.

Harry totally ignored Andrew's comment and said, "So anyway ..." and everyone laughed again and clapped. "And Rhonda, my wife, loves it here," Harry said, looking at Rhonda on the Meriton table.

"She has fun here. I've been building here for a long time – I arrived here in 1980. You must give consistent work to help the people. The worst thing you can do is start the job and stop the job. The workers want stability.

"All my people get along together, which is interesting. For me, people must always get on. Our people," Harry says as he turns to the Meriton table, "get on very well."

Harry went on to explain that even when we had the pandemic, everybody at Meriton still turned up to work. Nobody asked not to work.

"Thank you all for being a part of it," Harry said, again looking at the Meriton table.

"Your friends are prime ministers, Reserve Bank governors, but your two real pet loves are councils and the unions," Andrew said, and the audience laughed. Everybody knows they are Harry's two pet hates!

"How did you deal with these roadblocks?" Andrew asked.

"I would win every time," Harry replied. "When they say I'm right, I ask them why they don't do it my way. They say, 'You're right, Harry, but if I do it your way, I'll lose my seat.' It took me a long time to convince them that not everyone wanted to buy cottages … until I did convince them. I'm no longer the enemy, but I'm still no friend," he said.

"I hope also to beat inflation. I don't just look at bricks and plans; I also look at banks. I'm very angry with the banks because they give no money to builders. They have to find a way to do it. They have to force the government to find a way to work with them. They need to give money to the builders. A builder without money is nonsense. So, I set myself many different tasks, and I talk to people, and they agree with me. We will succeed because this is the best country, the best place and we will win," he said as the audience clapped.

"Recently, you gave the Gold Coast City Council the thumbs up. Best council to work with. Are you going to do more work here on the Gold Coast?" Andrew asked.

"I'm already building a lot. I cannot be too aggressive with purchasing," Harry replied. "The unions many years ago were very bad in Sydney. Really bad, not like here. Here they are gentlemen. There, they were rough guys. My workforce was very loyal. The unions could never beat us; in fact, we beat them every time, again and again. Their workers didn't like their policies, but they liked my policies, so I asked the unions why they had their policies.

"We want unions who think like we do. In the early days they never came here, they went to Brisbane and Melbourne. There was nothing on the Gold Coast. The councils? Whatever they want, and if it doesn't make sense, we try to change it. We do what the customer wants. The customer is always king."

Andrew then asked Harry how he had singlehandedly built 80,000 apartments and provided homes for people who wouldn't otherwise have been able to afford a home.

"A lot of it had to do with my workers," Harry said. "At my 90th birthday my main guests were the people who worked for me. There were prime ministers there as well, but the majority were my workers. These are the people I spend my time with. These are my friends," he said.

"Harry, you clearly have a love affair with the Gold Coast and now you're focused on Surfers Paradise. Why the love affair?" Andrew asked.

"Well, I want to add as much life as I possibly can to Surfers," Harry replied.

Andrew said he had a site Harry might be interested in. Harry glared at him, and everybody laughed. Harry didn't say a word.

Andrew moved on. "You love being in the centre where the action is. How much taller can the buildings get and what is the answer to our housing crisis?"

"We don't want the buildings to get any taller in Surfers and, in relation to the housing crisis, negative gearing is rubbish. The big problem for us is the bureaucrats," he said.

"What's the difference between $1 million and $24 billion?" Andrew asked.

"It is the same," Harry replied. "I've already told you who my friends are, and they're the ones who work for me. The money has made no difference. People ask, 'Where's Harry's boat? Where's Harry's aeroplane? What does he spend his money on?' I tell them that I only have time to spend money on the business. My business is my pleasure, so there you are."

"So, what inspires you now?" Andrew asked.

"My sheets are a big deal for me," Harry said. "That is how I get ideas. You have to read them and understand them. Things change all the time, so you change with them. So, I like the process. I also like to walk with my friends on the weekend, and I play word games with my wife, see, my family. I am very happy."

"What great pieces of advice can you give about running a business today?" Andrew asked.

"You must always work in an industry that is successful," Harry said. "Next, you must work with people who get on with each other. You can't have ones that fight all the time.

"Then you must find out what you're good at. Nobody knows. You can get a degree but that doesn't mean you can do something well.

"I think also you must be happy. At 91 I am still working, and I'm very happy. This is very important."

"What about life lessons?" Andrew asked.

"During COVID, my staff were all happy to come to the office. I didn't ask them, they just came. That is very good to have that relationship.

"This is a very big company, and I hope they succeed and continue to run the business. You must have a business where people are happy and they're doing something that has a future."

"What do you think is the best way to summarise Harry Triguboff and the life that you have?" Andrew asked.

"You summarised it for me!" Harry laughed. "So, I tried my best, I did my best, and my people are my partners," he said as he smiled at the Meriton table.

"Of course, my wife is my everything." He looked to Rhonda, and she smiled. "She gave me her life, and I gave her my life. That goes without saying."

At the end of the lunch, Harry found it impossible to get away. Everybody wanted to talk to him as he headed for the door. They all talked about how engaging he was and how simple he had made his very complex life seem.

Ali Day was a bit tentative about approaching Harry, but Charbel Rabie – Harry's head of construction – encouraged him and pushed him in Harry's direction. Charbel and Ali went to school together.

"Thank you so much for your generous donation, Harry," Ali said.

"You're the champion," Harry said.

"You're amazing," Ali replied. Then, they fell into a nice rhythm and had a chat. Harry was always going to make time for the champion.

Harry patted Ali on the arm before he left. That is Harry's great gift – he makes everyone feel important, even the ones who already are, like Ali Day.

Harry at His Best

After a huge day and with Rhonda trying to encourage Harry to go home, he hesitated momentarily before telling his driver to take him to his building site. His day was not done. Lunch had been fun but there was still business to attend to. Thirty minutes later he was being lifted in a bucket at the end of a crane so that he, Rhonda and Charbel could purvey his beachfront Iconica project in a way only Harry could do.

As it turned out, many people had travelled from Sydney for the day to hear Harry speak. At the taxi rank, everyone was talking about how fabulous he was.

"They say he doesn't even have a computer on his desk and that he has never sent an email in his life," one commented.

"Yep, they say he only communicates on the phone or face to face. They say he speaks to more people in one day than most of us would speak to in a month," another said.

"Who here still wants to be working when they're 91?" another asked.

One piped up, "If it means being that brilliant at that age and still having a room of 1,000 people hanging on my every word, then I choose Harry's methodology."

At the airport later, people waiting to board the flight back to Sydney still talked about Harry. One passenger said to their friend, as they put their bag in the overhead locker, "How remarkable to love what you do so much that you never felt like you worked a day in your life – and you're still doing it after 60 years."

Later, as the flight descended into Sydney, and there was the click of laptops being closed throughout the cabin, Harry, still in Surfers, would have finished a nice meal with Rhonda, poured himself a wine and would be either relaxing into the football or donning his glasses to do a bit of light Friday night reading. *The sheets* would have arrived. He could pore over them on the weekend, but just a quick look for now … he just couldn't help himself.

He keeps adding pages to *the sheets*. After a decade of sticking mainly to the Gold Coast in Queensland, Harry has closed the deal on what he believes is 'the best site in Brisbane'.

It's in Alice Street, overlooking the beautiful Botanic Gardens, and Harry is planning two towers, each rising more than 80 storeys.

The $130 million deal was struck after all 107 apartment owners had agreed to sell. Some had lived there for more than 40 years.

"Everything in my life has been about reaching new heights," Harry says.

"I will never stop. I'm High-Rise Harry and I will go the distance doing what I love."

A packed Star Gold Coast Event Centre for the Ray White Surfers Paradise Group's annual Business Meets Sport lunch, 2024.

Andrew Bell interviewing Harry.

EPILOGUE

It is almost noon on a beautiful Sunday morning in August, 2024. There is not a cloud in the sky. Pagewood Green's Central Park is the hive of activity. There are a couple of families setting up for a picnic. Obviously, it's a birthday party. There are balloons and a cake, and Dad's ready to hit the barbeque. There are a few young kids trying to dunk hoops on the basketball court. When they do shoot the ball, they are surprisingly accurate.

There are other children giggling with delight as they play on the jungle gym, watched over by Mum and Dad sipping freshly brewed coffee from the café across the road. There is a little boy learning to ride his bike and a couple of girls doing yoga. There is an older couple sitting on a bench enjoying the sun, and many of the people walking their dogs nod and smile in recognition.

As some return to one of the many apartment buildings on the fringe of the park, others are exiting those same buildings. A pilot in Qantas uniform jumps into a cab to take the quick 10-minute trip to Sydney Airport. Two teenagers with surfboards are clearly heading to a nearby beach. A little girl calls out to a friend in the park to say she is going next door to the cinema to see a movie. Another woman, shopping bags folded under her arm, is clearly headed to do her grocery shopping at the Coles supermarket, a minute down the road in Meriton's retail precinct.

What people called Harry's 'pipedream' is a stunning reality of community living, and a picture Harry could clearly see in his head.

Now, after 60 years, Meriton is the only way some people have ever lived. Like the generations of sub-contractors who have worked for

Epilogue

Harry, you now have generations who have been loyal to the Meriton brand. One couple who originally bought their first apartment in one of Harry's buildings in Potts Point 30 years ago, moved to a larger Meriton apartment at Mascot, had their children, and today live at Pagewood Green. Their son has bought there, and his grandparents live there as well.

"It has never been surprising to me that people would eventually see apartment living as the preferred option," Harry says.

"It's Sunday. Everyone is out enjoying themselves rather than mowing their patch. The lawnmower, may it rest in peace!" He smiles.

"Our three-bedroom and four-bedroom apartments are a big drawcard for families."

A Chinese-born buyer, with permanent residency in Australia, recently bought 165 apartments across Meriton buildings in Zetland, Mascot, Lidcombe and Pagewood. He then tipped all of them into Meriton's rental pool.

He did it with demand in mind, and he knew his investments would be looked after.

"Smart man," Harry says. "But whether you buy one apartment or 165, you still have the same experience. We are top of our game for a reason. I won't accept anything less."

Harry says that in all Meriton buildings, the Chinese now have strong competition from the locals.

"The tide has definitely turned," Harry says. "It took 60 years to get here but it was worth the wait.

"This is the new way of living. Aussies have found a greater Australian dream.

"We're untouchable now. There is no way of ever going back."

With his methodology perfected in communities like Pagewood Green and others across the eastern seaboard, Harry's now signature Meriton lifestyle befits every generation.

"Families, if they choose, can stay together in one community," Harry says.

"Outside the community, there is not a thing you could want for that is not here in Pagewood. It is close to everything. The best beaches, the best schools, the best parklands, the airport, the best hospitals, major shopping centres and just 15 minutes from the CBD.

"That's not puffery, that's fact. These community developments offer the very best way to live."

And Harry will stick to his guns, honed and perfected over 60 years.

"As long as I remain as healthy as I am, I will remain at Meriton for as long as I am able. Aside from Rhonda, it is the great love of my life.

"I also know that I must look to the future, and that is why I recently named my grandson, Daniel Hendler, as my successor.

"Daniel has spent over 10 years working with me directly, so he best understands how I do business. He is now the deputy managing director of Meriton, and the most important thing is that he understands *the sheets*.

"Although they are far more comprehensive today, since day one they have been the heart and lifeline of Meriton."

As detailed earlier in the book, Ella and Ariel also have very prominent positions at Meriton, but it is Daniel who has been across every area of the business.

"I am very proud of my two girls," Harry says of Orna and Sharon. They have very much led their own successful lives, and although they have not been heavily involved in my business, they have given me grandchildren who do want to be involved with Meriton.

"If I've been jealous of anything in my life, it is that Rupert Murdoch had his offspring in his business, Frank Lowy had his boys in his business, Kerry Packer had James in his business – and that list goes on.

"I didn't have that blood in my business.

"Thanks to my girls giving me four beautiful grandchildren, three of whom are working in the business, now I do."

With the 2024 Summer Olympics now over in Paris, and Australia once again doing us proud, Meriton had won their own gold. Named Developer of the Year at the UDIA NSW & Urban Property Group

Epilogue

2024 Awards of Excellence, Harry was there to accept the award.

"I have accepted many awards over the years and each one is an honour," Harry said.

"It is recognition of the difference we make, and that in turn makes me very proud of everything we have achieved, sometimes in the most extreme of circumstances and sometimes against all odds.

"There is no 'I' in awards. I share our success with everyone who is part of my Meriton family."

But this leader does maketh Meriton. He is the mastermind behind building nearly 80,000 apartments, and they are the proven *units* of his success. Harry is the ultimate high achiever, in every sense of those words.

Another High-Rise Harry? Highly unlikely!

CINDY MARTIN

I have known Harry for over 25 years. We first met when I was working in the media as a property editor.

Our relationship started off on rocky ground. Harry had been treated unfairly by the media and on first meeting him, I took the brunt of others' actions. These days Harry has a fantastic relationship with the media.

Back then, very few journalists went to see Harry, let alone his buildings, before writing atrocities about his projects. He was going to take full advantage of having a reporter from "your lot" sitting in front of him. I didn't get a single word in for about 10 minutes before asking him, "Considering your feelings on the subject, asking you to take me to World Tower to have a look around is probably going to be a hard no?"

Surprisingly, he laughed. "Come on," he said as he handed me a brand new yellow Meriton hard hat. "Let's go!" Seize the moment.

So off we went, right there and then. He spent the next hour showing me around. The lift stopped 10 levels from the top of the building so Harry sprinted up the 10 flights of stairs to reach the top. He was in his mid-60s; I was in my mid-30s. I was the only one that had to catch my breath when we reached the top.

From that day on, we became great friends, and, to this day, Harry is the most extraordinary person I know. Over the years I

Cindy & Harry.

have heard all the stories, and being scribe to his life has been an honour. Told only the way Harry wanted to tell his story, he sees his life as simple and straightforward. The reality, more likely complex and considered, but it comes from the heart of a man who truly loves what he does: "Every minute has been fun. I've had a very happy life and I continue to have the very best life. The massive success is just icing on the cake."

Completed 1995 | The Crest, 15-21 Breaker St.